Women, Politics, Media
Uneasy Relations in
Comparative Perspective

Political Communication
David L. Paletz, Editor

Women, Politics, Media
Uneasy Relations in Comparative Perspective

Karen Ross
Coventry University

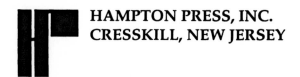

HAMPTON PRESS, INC.
CRESSKILL, NEW JERSEY

Library of Congress Cataloging-in-Publication Data

Ross, Karen, 1957-
    Women, politics, media : uneasy relations in comparative perspective
       p. cm. -- (The Hampton Press communication series. Political
    communication)
    Includes bibliographical references and index.
    ISBN 1-57273-397-7 -- ISBN 1-57273-398-5
     1. Women in politics--Great Britain. 2. Women politicans--Great Britain.
3. Mass media and women--Great Britain. 4. Mass media--Political aspects--
Great Britain. 5. Women in mass media. I. Title. II. Series

HQ1236.5G7 R67 2002
320'.082'0941--dc21

                                              2001051999

Hampton Press, Inc.
23 Broadway
Cresskill, NJ 07626

For Josie, Lizzie, Robyn and Chris—you can do anything

Contents

Acknowledgments

This book has been a long time coming, traced back to at least the early 1990s when I really began to seriously what I now think about to be uneasy relations between women, politics and media. I would therefore like to acknowledge my great respect for *all* those women around the world who have battled to achieve their rightful place at the tables of executive and legislative power and especially to those excellent women who gave up their time to talk to me about their experiences with candour and grace—a sincere and heartfelt thank you. And to my colleagues, some of whom I am pleased to also call friends, especially Celia Brackenridge, Carolyn Byerly, Sarah Hill, Virginia Nightengale, Shelley Sagauro and Diana Woodward, with whom I have shared ah-ha moments of insight and who have provoked clarity when sometimes I saw only chaos. Feminist scholarship is sometimes hard to pursue, but the endurance of friendships and support makes such an endeavour at least possible. I would also like to thank those women who, at different points in my career so far, have pushed me to achieve and provided support for me to do so, including Jennifer Tann, Annabelle Sreberny and Elaine Cutting. There are others, too numerous to mention, all of whom in their own ways have encouraged—students, colleagues, friends—and to all, again, thank you. And of course to my editor, David Paletz, and my publisher, Barbara Bernstein, for keeping faith with the project. Almost lastly, to my sister Elizabeth and the rest of my extended family—a thank you for your unconditional support and unfailing enthusiasm. Lastly, to Barry, for never letting his eyes glaze over during endless discussions of drafts, for doing double kitchen and dog-walking duty, for endless supplies of tea, but mostly for endless love.

1

Introduction

> We all know that women have to do everything a little better than
> men. Women cannot afford to make [a] faux pas . . . that is quite
> clear. We're all so very, very tolerant when men make mistakes, but
> I don't know of any society that is tolerant when women make mis-
> takes . . . there's a tendency to say . . . "well, she's a woman." You
> never say, "well, he's a man, it's natural that he makes a mistake."
> You do not say a thing. You only accept it. (Vigdis Finnbogadóttir,
> President of Iceland, cited in Liswood, 1995, p. 69)

The year is 1994. The leader of the British Labour Party, John Smith, in
whom many of us had high hopes, has died suddenly, leaving a gaping
hole in the fabric of reason and much uncertainty over the direction of
the Labour Party in an important (European) election year. In a matter of
days, three serious hats are in the ring—Tony Blair, Gordon Brown and
Margaret Beckett. From the very beginning, Beckett is cast in the role of
outsider by the media, as representing the old-guard "leftie" tendency,
as being too old, too emotional, too . . . female? She doesn't win. Fast-
forward to 1995. After several years of active membership of my local
Constituency Labour Party, I receive the suggestion that I stand as a
local councilor, which will be good practice for when I get to appear on
the Labour list to campaign for a Parliamentary seat. I think about it. I
am a 38-year-old university lecturer, enthusiastic, dynamic, committed
to the socialist project, an experienced campaigner, and a good speaker.

1

I am an ideal candidate. Except . . . except that I have very short hair, and I wear black jeans, and I have several piercings in my ears, and I wear workboots and prescription spectacles. What will the media make of me, ask my party colleagues? Could I wear a dress for the photoshoot? Could I bring my husband along to show that I'm "normal"? Another candidate and I have our photos taken at party headquarters for our campaign leaflets. He is a lay preacher, balding, conservatively dressed, shirt and tie. I am none of those things. I wear a black T-shirt and show my best half-profile to the camera, making visible my one earring and my AIDS ribbon. "Peter" looks at me with disgust: I am the new face of old labour, and I will surely pull the party down with my talk of women's sections, equal opportunities, and an inclusive welfare state. I win; Peter doesn't. The local press want to know what my husband thinks about my triumph and if he'll mind my coming home late after committee meetings? They have no interest in my views on the threatened closure of a local infants' school or plans to build a hospital incinerator in the middle of a residential area. One of the guys counts the holes in my ears.

Thus began my real interest in exploring the relationship between women, politics, and the media and, over the past six years, I have been engaged in researching various aspects of this complex set of relations, focusing on both consumption and production, on women as audiences for news, and on women as producers and targets of news. Crucially, I wanted to explore whether my own anecdotal experience of the media as a woman politician, albeit one with a local rather than national habitus, was similar to that of other women; to find out what was going on beneath the surface of the media-politics nexus when the politician in question was a woman; to better understand the subtle and more overt processes which come into play when women, politics, and media collide. In the early years, I concentrated my efforts on the British scene, undertaking a content analysis of the Labour leadership elections in 1994 (Ross, 1995a), investigating the extent to which gender and women's issues were more generally a part of the agenda in the 1994 European Elections, interviewing women MPs about their media experiences and strategies[1] (Ross & Sreberny, 1997, 2000), talking to women consumers of news about their attitudes towards and use of news media (Ross 1995c), and monitoring the gender dimension to the news media's

---

[1] I carried out the substantive interviews with British women MPs in 1995 and conducted follow-up interviews in 2000. The 1995 interviews were carried out while I was a researcher at the Centre for Mass Communication Research, University of Leicester, under the Directorship of Professor Annabelle Sreberny, and I am indebted to her for all the support she gave me during my time there, including during this preliminary phase of the project.

coverage of the 1997 general election (Ross 1998b). I then turned my attention to other women in other places and sought to explore the experiences of women politicians in other anglophone countries, focusing on Australia and South Africa, in an attempt to identify any common experiential threads of their relations with the news media and the strategies they employ to encourage the "right" kind of media exposure.

Extending the scope of my interest beyond Britain[2] seemed to be the logical next step in better understanding the ways in which women experience elite politics and in determining whether the routine practices of British journalists in marginalising and trivializing women were situation-specific or global phenomena. The choice of Australia and South Africa as additional research sites was the consequence of both deliberate decision making and serendipity. Originally, I chose Australia as my British comparitor because its political system is broadly similar to that of Britain—although the upper and lower house in Australia is not directly comparable to the House of Commons and the House of Lords in the UK, the constitutional arrangements are similar, and the media of both nations are linked, inextricably, by the global hand of Rupert Murdoch. Having then carried out two sets of interviews where women's experiences were remarkably similar, I then decided to introduce a third comparitor in order to explore other characteristics, such as ethnicity, since none of the women I had interviewed in Britain or Australia belonged to minority ethnic communities. I was interested in finding out whether women in different political contexts had the same experiences; that is, was their gender the dominant aspect of their political selves which their respective national media focused upon? I chose South Africa since it represented a very different political context for women politicians because of the apartheid legacy, it was a predominantly anglophone country in terms of its elite structures, and the constitutional arrangements, as a Commonwealth country, were similar to those of Britain and Australia. I was also clear that I wanted to explore the experiences of women whose voices are seldom heard outside of their own countries.

Much of the work on women politicians and media has a strongly American orientation since many of the communication scholars working in this broad area are American-based. While that work is, in and of itself interesting and important, I wanted to expand our knowledge of the women-politics-media relation beyond the relatively con-

[2]As with the British study in 1995, I wrote to all the women Parliamentarians in the Australian and South Africa Parliaments and interviewed all those women who agreed to take part in the study; the subsequent political skew is a result of who decided to opt in to the research rather than any deliberate stratification on my part.

fined and particular context of North America in order to provide alternative perspectives which would or would not be similar to those well-documented American experiences. In the event, as the chapters in the book demonstrate, the experiences of women politicians across different continents is remarkably similar. The frustrations which Australian women report over lobby journalists' lack of interest in their policy positions is mirrored by the anecdotes related by British women. The irritations which South African women display over their colleagues' disrespect towards them as serious politicians is echoed by numerous studies of American congresswomen who experience the same thing. The exasperation of British women over the media's lack of interest in women's issues and the likely implications for voter turnout is echoed by South Africa's Joint Standing Committee on the Quality of Life and Improving the Status of Women, which has undertaken gender audits of successive budgets and legislation, and yet millions of women and children are still subject to discrimination and unfair practices. It becomes irresistible to suggest that there are global phenomena at play which are organised around the twin pillars of patriarchy and capitalism, where politics and media function to repel or at least limit the incursions of women into their domains.

This book, then, has as its principal ambition to explore the ways in which women, politics, and media impact each on the others, to tease out the various relations which women have to politics and news-making. If the point of studying news media is to understand the impact and import of their messages, then the contexts of both consumption and production are important: if content analyses provide us with discourses to deconstruct, so too do the testimonies of political actors themselves. The text draws on both primary and secondary data, and thus attempts to bring together both the extant literature in the field and new, unpublished empirical work with women Parliamentarians. In organizing the book in this way, I hope to provide an accessible text which brings together the diverse literatures which are evolving on the uneasy relations which women have with politics and news media.

The first chapter following this introduction considers women's relationship to the political process, both informally and in elite politics, and looks at the way in which gender and politics have been theorized. It moves on to consider the ways in which women's representation in elite politics has been operationalised, including a consideration of affirmative action strategies and the responses to such initiatives. Chapter 3 considers the experiences of women politicians in Parliamentary contexts, drawing heavily on the interview data to develop an analysis of the ways in which women are circumscribed by the traditional (male) Parliamentary structures. While all the women interviewed for this study were members of their respective elected Parliaments and Congresses, some subsequently lost their seats or stood down at the next general election. It looks at the manner in which women have begun to change the way in which the business of politics is actually done, from changing the style, discourse, and policy agenda, to making the very fabric of Parliaments shift and accommodate women's demands for a saner, more collegial working environment, as well as one which includes and welcomes all people. Chapter 4 begins to map out the way in which politics and politicians are routinely portrayed by the news media, moving from generalities to the specific example of women politicians. As in the previous chapter, the thematics explored here are drawn from the interviews with women politicians and comprise their general views on themes relating to women and news media as well as their own personal experiences. Chapter 5 considers the ways in which women politicians engage with journalists, the strategies they have developed, and the cautions raised in trying to have a more proactive engagement with news practitioners. Chapter 6 considers the way in which elections are covered in the media, again moving from general points to specific ones relating to women. This chapter weaves together the narratives of women interviewed for this book together with secondary data, mostly American-oriented, which is more content-driven. As well as looking at content studies, it also explores the ways in which voters respond to media discourses around elections and campaigns, arguing that the way in which women politicians are framed by the media can have an impact on their chances of success. However, this point is not overstated, since there is also evidence that women candidates are viewed particularly positively by women voters. The concluding chapter draws together the threads of the previous arguments, setting out some of the reasons why representation matters. Women politicians are caught in an awkward double bind: they need the oxygen of publicity offered by the media in order to be noticed—"so my constituents can see me earning my salary"—but fear media intrusion into the private aspects of their lives.

This book has a strong research base and the "insider" insights—provided by women Parliamentarians across three continents—into the political process in general and the media's relationship to politics in particular, are of especial interest to political communication theorists interested in the gender dynamic. As a political communication researcher who is also a feminist and an activist, I believe that I bring my own layer of complexity to the process, and I have therefore included in Appendix 1 an abridged version of one of my fieldwork diaries, written during the last set of interviews in South Africa in 1999. While the points made and the problems encountered (and solutions found) in that setting were particular to that country, in many ways the issues raised were pertinent to all three case study sites. We seldom get to know about the trials and tribulations of conducting real research with real women, and I hope that this research note will make its own contribution to our understanding of what is often a significant divide between the theory and practice of doing real-world research.

At the time of writing (Fall 2000), voters in Britain are already being exposed to subtle forms of politicking in readiness for the likely general election in 2001; voters in the United States have already had months of extended campaign coverage and are poised to elect a new President. This book does not present a very rosy view of the relations which women have with politics and the media. The routine ways in which women are represented by the media, and the potential impact on democracy that these specifically gendered forms of portrayal have is mostly negative. However, there are sufficient positive gains and new policy agendas which have resulted from women's more proactive involvement in the democratic process to give us hope for the future. But we still do well to heed the warning of the suffragette Millicent Fawcett because, even now, we are still a very long way from achieving equality between women and men in a number of fundamental ways, including formal political representation:

> For those of us who have been working for the vote all our lives, it is an historic occasion . . . but we must not imagine that our work is over. Our cause is a long way from full success. (Millicent Garrett Fawcett, 1928, on women achieving the vote, cited in Stephenson, 1998, p. 141)

2

Women and Politics: *Herstory*

Up until 1992, women did not wear trousers in the House unless they were being held over to vote on Fridays. Now it is very common to see some of us in trouser suits which are much more practical. But it just wasn't done for women to wear trousers. I remember one hot summer people were complaining about what was appropriate dress and the (male) Speaker said that appropriate dress was a three-piece suit and in hot weather it was acceptable for the waistcoat to be removed provided that a shirt and tie were still worn. Well, what were we supposed to wear? He'd completely forgotten that women are here. (Dawn Primarolo, Labour, UK)[1]

INTRODUCTION

The demand for greater rights for women, including political rights, has been at the forefront of many women's agendas for 300 years, with campaigning treatises by women such as Mary Wollstonecraft and Abigail Adams. Women's location in and relationship to the democratic process has been one of continuous marginalisation and heroic endeavor, from the struggles to achieve full emancipation for women, to more contem-

---

[1]All the verbatim quotes are taken from the interview transcripts, and cited using the format: name, political party, country.

porary efforts to secure women's representation in Parliament. Most historians trace the provenance of the movement to enfranchise women to the period in which significant campaigns to abolish slavery began to take a real hold in the 1830s and 1840s (Finnegan, 1999). Those campaigns provided a vibrant language in which to promote political reform as well as a focus for collective action, and in the United States enabled women across that nation, irrespective of class, to discuss the development of their political status (DuBois, 1978). Arguably, the first credited demand for women's enfranchisement took place at the now-famous Seneca Falls convention of 1848, where Elizabeth Cady Stanton and other women leaders met to debate the status of women in America at that time. They laid out their demands for the achievement of democratic rights and the ratification of the Nineteenth Amendment to the Constitution of the United States, which formalized women's political enfranchisement as voters and as candidates (Walkosz & Kenski, 1995). Speaking within the context of the *American Declaration of Independence*, Stanton and her supporters insisted that

> We hold those truths to be self-evident: that all men and women are created equal that among these are life, liberty and the pursuit of happiness; that to secure these rights governments are instituted, deriving their just powers from the consent of the governed. (Flexner, 1975, cited in Finnegan, 1999, p. 4)

These were fine words and sentiments, but unfortunately, as many scholars have subsequently commented, the inherent conservatism of many of the early suffragists meant that campaigns promoting the emancipation of women were often in conflict with each other because different factions adopted competing perspectives on the suffrage of disenfranchised male groups (such as African Americans) and had widely varying positions on the issue of race more generally. So high were the suffrage stakes during the late 19th century that DuBois (1978) argues that even a radical suffragist and campaigner for human rights such as Elizabeth Cady Stanton found herself espousing an elitist and racist agenda which attempted to justify the proposition that middle-class white women deserved the vote more than black men and members of migrant communities more generally. Arguably, the most successful campaign strategies undertaken by suffragists to get their messages across were those which made an explicit link between consumption and politics, arguing, for example, that a "responsible" approach to consumption was a demonstration of good judgement: a wise shopper is a wise voter, and suffragists learned quickly about good marketing, using every opportunity and mode to present themselves as well and as professionally as they could: "They mastered modern means of advertising, publicity, mass production, commercial entertainment, commercial design, retailing and publishing. They put up billboards and colorful posters; they created artful window displays; they wore sandwich boards, badges, pins . . ." (Finnegan, 1999, p. 11). Thus, by being in the vanguard of political actors who recognized the power of image management and the potential of mass culture, and who utilized the modes and methods of commercial enterprise, suffragists, "contributed to the commercialized political sphere that now dominates American culture" (Finnegan, 1999, p. 12).

In Britain, concerted campaign efforts to promote women's suffrage were mobilized a little later, and the first wave of women's suffrage occurred after women over 30 years of age were granted the right to vote in 1918. In the decade following this historic "allowance," working class women flocked to join the Labour Party and the Co-operative movement. Within four years, 100,000 women had joined women's sections in the Labour Party and a further 35,000 women joined the Women's Co-operative Guild (Graves, 1994). The mass incorporation of women into party political structures gives a comprehensive lie to the traditional notion of women's so-called antipathy to involvement in political activity, and many women genuinely believed that their presence, enthusiasm, and commitment to equality could be expressed and pursued through formal political channels. Millicent Fawcett (after whom the contemporary campaign group, the Fawcett Society, was named) spoke passionately about the impact that women in politics could have on furthering the cause of equality, arguing that the entrenched style of male-oriented politics could be replaced by "something greater and more uplifting for the whole of humanity" (Fawcett, 1918, p. 104). Yet, despite women's involvement in party structures in increasing numbers, few were elected onto executive committees or as conference delegates, effectively excluding women from the decision-making apparatus. During the 20 years between the two world wars, only nine women were elected as members of Britain's Parliament.

This inability of women to penetrate the decision-making echelons of male-dominated politics was reflected elsewhere in the world where women's suffrage had been achieved at a similar time, but where the potential to flex their political muscles was stubbornly circumvented. For example, in New Zealand, where women were enfranchised for Parliamentary elections in 1893 and eligible for election to the House of Representatives in 1919, it took until 1933 for a woman (Elizabeth McCombs) to actually achieve the status of Parliamentary Member (McLeay, 1993). In Australia, on the other hand, women were achieving a little more success in their political ambitions. Having been given the vote in 1902, Edith Cowan (National Party) became the first woman to be elected to a legislative assembly (the Parliament of Western Australia) in 1921 (Millar, 1993), although it wasn't until 1943 that women were elected to the federal Parliament, when Dorothy Tangey (Australian Labour Party) and Dame Enid Lyons (United Australia Party) came to the Senate and the House of Representatives, respectively. Although *history* books appear to suggest that women's involvement in formal political structures was so minimal as to require no commentary, women *were* influencing policy-making in subtle ways (cf. Vallance, 1979). For example, Graves argues that in Britain women's membership in both the Labour Party and the Co-operative Movement forced gender onto the political agenda and provoked enduring debates between women members and the exclusively male leadership over policy concerns and power differentials, while simultaneously, conflict arose between labour women and middle-class feminists where the focus was on class and political differentiation and goal achievement. ". . . By challenging both the patriarchal party and organized feminists, labour women helped define the agendas and set the parameters of interwar working-class politics" (Graves, 1994, p. 2). To take account of the emerging push towards equality, particularly in the political arena, the Labour Party revised its Manifesto to include a section entitled "The Complete Emancipation of Women" which promised women an equal franchise and equal pay (Labour Party, 1918).

Women have always been involved in grass-roots politics, particularly at the level of local government, as councilors, agents, and campaigners, and the sociopolitical concerns which occupy women in the early 21st century have an extremely lengthy provenance. The fundamental agenda on which today's Fawcett Society campaigns—pensions, childcare, equal pay, poverty—are remarkably similar to the goals espoused by many women in the 1920s:

> After 1925, the "new feminist" agenda was almost indistinguishable from that of labour women. It included family allowances, birth control, nursery schools and the prevention of maternal mortality. At the same time, labour women and the new feminists joined equal rights feminists in supporting married women's right to work and equal pay. (Graves, 1994, p. 118)

The concerns of those early suffragettes—for a more inclusive policy agenda and for equitable and just representation of women in elite politics—are echoed still by women today. Part of the problem of rendering both visible and important women's concerns has been the way in which notions of citizenship have masqueraded as gender inclusive, obscuring the very real differences between women and men's experiences of society and democracy and their relative importance in and to that democracy:

> The theory and practice of democratic liberalism are much criticized at present on the grounds that they exclude women from full citizenship. They do this in two ways: by denying women the full complement of rights and privileges accorded to men, and, more insidiously, by taking for granted a conception of citizenship which excludes all that is traditionally female. (James, 1992, p. 48)

GENDER AND POLITICAL THEORY

Liberal democracy has been eschewed for its definition of citizen as actor in the public (masculine) world with its implicit (and excluding) positioning of women in the realm of the private. Numerous feminists have sought to pursue an emancipatory politics located broadly in Habermas' "public sphere" model, which argues that the exclusive notion of conventional political participation—which takes place in traditional, narrow, political environs—should be modified to accommodate activities which occur in other discursive spaces such as the social and cultural realms (Habermas, 1989). The significant point of feminist departure from Habermas' public discourse scenario, however, is in rejecting his gender-blind analysis of the public-private split. (See, for example, Fraser, 1989; Benhabib, 1992). Habermas consigns "women's" concerns (home, family, patriarchy, domestic violence, sexual relations) to the realm of the private so that proper "masculine" interests are left to constitute the *real* substance of public sphere discourse. The construction of the public/private dichotomy is employed as a convenient and apparently neutral tool which continues to marginalise women:

> What the women's movement and feminist theorists in the last two decades have shown is that traditional modes of drawing this distinction [between the public and private sphere] have been part of a discourse of domination which legitimizes women's oppression and exploitation in the private realm. (Benhabib, 1992, p. 110)

But what do we mean when we talk about women and men, society and democracy, politics and communication? Are we talking about ourselves? About men and women we know? Or about some kind of archetype? When we talk about politics, society, "them" and "us," do we comprehend a gender-free social context? Much of the work on political economy has concentrated on menspeak: women's voices have been strangely absent. While early political theorists attempted to justify their misogyny with elaborate arguments, privileging the mighty public/male sphere over the lowly private/female one, later commentators took women's invisibility so much for granted that it scarcely merited acknowledgement (Phillips, 1991). It is a perfect irony that the feminists' battle-cry—that the personal is political—has been taken so to heart by the media that the fourth estate is now often incapable of distinguishing between public, private and political, reporting on the intricacies of a politician's sex life on the same page—and with the same gravitas—as a terrorist bombing, giving each a grotesque equivalence.

As women have become more confident in their analyses of a faulty democracy and the urgent requirement to overhaul a political system which continues to exclude half the population, so feminist discourse on gender and politics has developed a number of perspectives and thematics as the paradox of women's crucial involvement in, but marginalised position to, formal politics has become more glaringly in need of exploration. While women have historically been excluded from politics where "politics" is taken to mean the formal politics of Parliament and government, they/we have at the same time been irrevocably inscribed into policy/politics if it is taken to mean a struggle for power and resources (Squires, 1999). The ways in which feminist political theorists and critics have thus framed their thinking about women and politics has, interestingly, often followed a tripartite developmental model of gender politics which more or less mirrors the fundamental approaches of feminist theory more generally, that is, "liberal" (incorporating women into the existing system), "radical" (women in opposition to status quo) and "poststructural" (reframing society). So, for example, Di Stefano (1990) has a three-part schema she describes as "rationalist," "anti-rationalist" and "post-rationalist" where the first position has women subsumed into a so-called neutral humanity, the second frame has women tied into an orthodox femininity with no transformative potential and the third rendition has women and men mixed together in a soup of differences. Squires (1999) suggests that the three principal ways of thinking about the subject is via a typology which figures "inclusion," "reversal" and "displacement." Inclusionists aim to include women in existing political fora as expressive of an equality politics, reversalists aim to recast politics so as to take more account of the specificity of gender and espouse a difference politics, while those promoting a displacement approach aim to fracture the polarity of the other two positions, instead pursuing a politics of open diversity. Deconstructing those three positions rather pithily, Ferguson (1993) observes that in the first instance, women's exclusion is tackled, in the second scenario men are the problem, and in the third frame, the socially gendered world is itself put under the spotlight. The potential loss of the sexed self is quite a troublesome concept for a number of theorists; for example, Baudrillard (1992) laments precisely this loss of gender specificity, complaining that we now operate in a void in which nothing is either masculine or feminine, a state of affairs whose cause he lays at the door of sexual liberation (cited in Segal, 1999, p. 66). In counterpoint, it is perhaps precisely the differences between women and men which are important to highlight and celebrate, and attempts to smooth out the gendered contours of masculinity and femininity could very well have the effect of making women conform to men's values since it has always been men's interests and characteristics which have masqueraded as a universal humanity. While it is legitimate to suggest the notion of a universal citizenship, implying that we are all citizens now, the corollary is that we must also all be the same, we must ignore those aspects which make us different. Instead of leading to a genuine common interest, this apparent homogeneity could secure the dominance of privileged groups (men) who nod pretence to universality:

> In a society where some groups are privileged while others are oppressed, insisting that as citizens persons should leave behind their particular affiliations and experiences to adopt a general point of view serves only to reinforce that privilege; for the perspectives and interests of the privileged will tend to dominate this unified public, marginalising or silencing those of other groups. (Young, 1989, p. 257)

But perhaps the distinctions between men and women have been rather too strictly delineated and a future progressive democratic project could draw on aspects of both? While it certainly seems worthwhile to draw attention to the value of so-called feminine traits, such as compassion and care, in pursuing an egalitarian and liberal agenda, it is not also necessary to valorize those traits by denigrating their "opposites," allegedly masculine characteristics, such as rationality and logic. To do so is surely to slide into an unhelpful Orwellian four-legs good, two-legs bad dichotomy where feminine values are uncritically privileged over their masculine counters. The insistence on using dichotomous sets such as public-private, rational-emotional to exemplify the masculine-feminine divide is forever to seek differences rather than similarities, continuously to set up conflicts rather than find resolutions. This is not to argue that inequalities do not exist, they clearly do, but rather to suggest that there are more similarities between, say, liberal and feminist perspectives on citizenship, than the rhetoric sometimes allows. As James (1992) points out, if traditional notions of citizenship are predicated upon the male subject, then the nature of politics must change, and this will be more easily wrought by seeking collaboration rather than conflict. Despite the differences in perspective, though, there does seem to be a tentative consensus that traditional political thinking has offered a normative "man" masquerading as a universal human which has effectively excluded women from political debate. Given that "citizen" is irrevocably en-gendered, the demands of feminism should perhaps now be articulated through appeals for equality which incorporate diversity (Eisenstein, 1989). Arguing for a society in which sexual difference is no longer constantly invoked as the determinant of differential treatment is not the same as arguing for the abolition of gender distinctions.

If most feminist political theorists see their principal work now, in the 21st century, as being the reconceptualisation of the very meaning of "politics" (Squires, 1999), then perhaps we should see that as a development of earlier interest in the assimilation/opposition binary rather than a denial of the value of those discourses. If we see feminist theorizing as essentially a process of iteration and synthesis, then we can feel secure in our own contemporary endeavors without having to reject out of hand what has gone before. As Whitworth (1994) argues, "Combining the best of each theory will help us to move from an examination of women to an analysis of gender in world politics" (p. 83).

If the potency of gender as a means of social division is acknowledged and problematised, it is also clear that the feminist enterprise can no longer be developed with an incorporated notion of an essential female subject who has a fixed identity and shares precisely the same concerns with all other women. The rejection of traditional feminism by many black women has made explicit the (albeit unconscious) cultural assumptions embedded in conventional feminist movements which assumed whiteness as the unproblematic and unquestioned given. (See, for example, hooks, 1991; Ware, 1992; Bhavnani & Phoenix, 1994.) The development of a universal sisterhood to replace man as norm is seen as a Eurocentric and middle-class pretence which glosses over the very real differences in both ideology and power within and between women, and in particular, within and between women from the developing and developed worlds. Thus, care must be taken to develop an inclusive gender politics which, at the very least, acknowledges manifest and implicit differences between women along the traditional faultlines of ethnicity, race, disability, religion, class, sexuality, and age. The abandonment of the essential female subject which, in its going, enables a celebration of difference, does not necessarily mean that women cannot mobilize action around characteristics and interests which we share and on which we want to campaign together (Bryman, 1992).

At a very basic level, women share experiences of inequality in a variety of contexts and a common discursive marginality. As "black" is to "white," the social construction of "woman" is only comprehended in her relation to "man," the extent to which she differs from the masculine norm, the extent to which she is the same. To invoke a specifically woman-centered discourse in the political arena can therefore be a useful political tactic, not so much essentialising as empowering (Braidotti, 1991). "Distinctively feminist theory begins from the recognition that individuals are feminine and masculine, that individuality is not a unitary abstraction but an embodied and sexually differentiated expression of the unity of humankind" (Pateman & Gross, 1986, p. 9). But in any case, if we expand our definition of politics to include the rehabilitation of the unfashionable slogan of the personal/political, where issues of power and control are inextricably linked to notions of gender and politics, then we can begin to reframe gender politics as constitutive of the larger structure of patriarchy and subordination. "The more extensive power-based conception of the political both emerges from, and makes possible, the feminist challenges to the orthodoxy of politics" (Squires 1999, p. 9).

FORMS OF POLITICAL ENGAGEMENT

For many women, questions of democracy have always been wider in scope than simply getting more women into Parliament. They have also been about addressing more fundamental issues such as the meaning of politics, insisting that the personal is political is public. Although women have been making small, incremental inroads into the hitherto exclusively male preserve of Parliament, there has been a much more marked tendency for women to operate outside formal political frameworks, working instead as community activists, in schools, with tenants' associations, and in other kinds of specifically *local* action groups (Pelling, 1954; McKibbon, 1974). Such actions have often had an overtly "peace" or "green" political agenda, for example, the years-long protest camp at the weapons bases at Greenham Common in the United Kingdom or at Puget Sound in the United States (Mies & Shiva, 1993) or "roads" protesters rigging up tree-houses to stop forests being decimated in favor of highways, or campaigns to "reclaim the night" or pro-choice demonstrations and student sit-ins. And, of course, the blossoming of any number of feminist journals and bookshops over the past few decades attests to the concrete nature of women's political activity and engagement: the politics of housework, as cipher for the larger issues of women-men relations, reframe those "private" negotiations as political acts (Narayan,

1997). The reluctance to operate within explicit "state" arenas can be seen as having its base in a refusal to collude with the existing capitalist and patriarchal forms which such incorporation would require. Instead, many women have sought to develop a political practice which has run counter to the conventional system, thereby allowing state institutions to retain their masculinist and excluding orientation (Pringle & Watson, 1992). The sadness, in some ways, is that many women do not recognize their acts as political, seeing them more as "community" which again makes the call for a recasting of what politics actually means, more pressing. If women are seen as being disinterested in politics—a recent British government poll reported that only 7 per cent of women claimed to be "very interested in politics" (cited in Squires, 1999, p. 196)—then this is surely because they do not perceive their acts as parent governors, local councilors, or one-day marchers as political since the routine perception of politics is the formal politics of Parliament.

It could be argued that the relative lack of involvement, traditionally, of women in the formal political process—that is, as elected members—has meant that the "practice" of politics has been a mainly male pursuit and the "content" of politics has been similarly gendered— big "P" politics has always seemed to be about "big" issues like war, defense, and the economy, and less about what could be described as "real" politics which are about the felt experiences of the *outcomes* of policy, such as decent pensions, affordable childcare, and efficient transport. When women politicians are asked, some say that they *do* have a different political agenda, that having more women in Parliament will (and does) make a difference to what is done in the name of politics (Ross & Sreberny-Mohammadi, 1997). But when "ordinary" women are asked if the "official" political agenda accords with their own priority list of political and social action, they believe that a rather large credibility gap exists between the two (Ross, 1995a). When "ordinary" women are asked what they want, politically, they appear to want very different things from those which appear to be the key issues on formal political agendas (Vallely, 1996). We already know the mechanisms by which men's interests are powerfully represented and served in liberal democracy, but how are women enabled to pursue their own agendas, their own concerns, their own interests, in all their rainbow shades? The questions for contemporary political analysis are not simply about the power or rationality of "the State" but also about understanding its constituent parts; not simply about identifying how the state encourages patriarchal family relations, but also about understanding the specificities of local and regional arrangements, identifying the historical and cultural contexts which have produced such a hostile environment for women.

ISSUES OF REPRESENTATION

Liberal democracy has made great claims for the relationship between democracy and representation, democracy and universal suffrage, but regards the sex of political representatives as irrelevant. The campaign for women's voting rights has been inextricably linked to the right for women to be elected to political office, but success on the former has been followed by scant progress on the latter. While Britain's cross-party 300 Group and the socialist Emily's List (originated in the United States but now with branches in both Britain and Australia) both campaign to promote more women into Parliament, the special skills and perspectives which women bring to political life are scarcely articulated: rationales rarely get beyond a crude discussion of numbers. The prerequisites for political involvement, for example, military service, property ownership, and "the capacity of rationality," have often been such that they easily excluded women (Squires, 1999, p. 195). With such rules in force, the political participation of women was hard won and was achieved at different rates across the globe and always allied to the franchise was the right for women to stand for political office. In Britain, for example, since 1918 (when women over the age of 30 won the vote, followed by women over 21 in 1928), it has been possible for women to stand for election, but they have nonetheless failed to become elected members in significant numbers, not because they lost at the ballot box, but more usually because they were not selected in the first place by their respective parties. Throughout the history of global politics, the election of women to regional and national Parliaments has been lamentably poor. At the new millennium, after fierce campaigns to achieve a greater proportion of women as elected members during the 1980s and 1990s, there are now fewer women Parliamentarians than even 10 years ago. How can we be going backwards? Fox (1997) argues that there are fundamental challenges facing women who attempt to achieve political office, and these are often associated with sex-role stereotyping—normative assumptions about the "place" of women in society—which make it more difficult for women to compete as effectively as men. Crucially, women have to spend a lot of campaign time presenting themselves as "serious politicians" even before they consider how best to make clear their policy positions. For men, this is not an issue which they need to confront.

Broadly, there are four fundamental justifications for expanding the role of women in the democratic process: first, democratic justice; second, maximization of resources; third, to represent the special interests of women; and fourth, as role models (Phillips, 1998). Squires (1999) provides a useful way to consider the fundamental question at the core of campaigns to improve the proportion of women politicians—why does gender matter? She argues that included in this one big question are four smaller ones: when claiming to be a representative what is one representing, how does one represent, where does one represent, and what is the purpose of representation? There are, clearly, any number of "answers" to these questions, often in either-or couplets, for example, possessing the same characteristics of those one represents or symbolizing the identity or qualities of a group of individuals, and one's belief in any of them will be determined by one's ideological position, one's experience, one's gender and all those other aspects of "personal and past" which influence "present and future." While appeals to justice and efficiency are relatively unproblematic, there remain conceptual and political antagonisms towards ideas such as whether one woman can actually "speak for" her sisters with whom she might have nothing in common apart from her sex, whether there are such special issues as "women's" issues, and whether gender makes a difference in deciding to pursue specific (and different) political aims. Many feminists strongly contest the existence of "women's issues," for example, and their disputations are not dissimilar (although they are usually made for different reasons) to those who would oppose the entire feminist project (Lovenduski, 1996). For example, many Liberal/Conservative women whom I interviewed for this book also rejected the idea of women having "special" issues, but this general disdain was bound up in a wider agenda of refusing to recognize the salience of gender in any area of life, be it personal, professional, or political. The ideological positioning which is embodied by this kind of argument has been identified by numerous studies (Simms, 1985; Sawer & Simms, 1992) and even Labor women are largely reluctant to be drawn into supporting an overtly feminist agenda (Ross & Sreberny-Mohammadi, 1997).

But crucially, in the context of representative politics, how can politicians (women or men) "know" what women's interests are unless women themselves articulate a sense of those interests? Sapiro (1998) argues that political systems are unlikely to advocate for previously silent groups unless those groups know what their campaign agenda is and make those demands known to those who can do something about them. In Britain, the setting up of the Women's Unit in 1997 was a deliberate strategy by the Labour administration to institute a structure which would genuinely try to explore what women wanted from government and which would mainstream the "gender question" across all government departments, so as to raise the gender consciousness of politicians and civil servants alike. Interestingly, their slogan—Better for Women, Better for All—could be seen as a pre-emptive strike against calls of special pleading, aiming to make the point that policies which work in women's favor inevitably benefit everyone. But concrete action emerging from the activities of the Women's Unit, including their widespread consultation with "ordinary" women and their final report (Cabinet Office, 1999) have yet to make an impact on real women's real lives.

If there are fundamental questions to ask about the reality of so-called "women's issues"—although I would argue whether women's "concerns" are actually identifiably different to those of men (see Women's Communication Centre, 1996)—there are also awkwardnesses around the idea of "role model" with arguments for and against such an outcome taking the form of dependence versus independence. On the one hand, proponents argue that role models are important as indicators of success and encouragement to achieve, while on the other hand, they are viewed as patronizing and unhelpful, implying that women do not have the confidence to try things for themselves. Of course, as we know, if we waited for "the market" to equalize the representation of women in parliaments and congresses around the world, we would be well into the middle of the 21st century for most Western democratic systems— excluding the Scandinavian countries which have a considerably better track record than elsewhere in the developed world—and probably a century more for less enlightened political systems. Most women who have aspirations to become elected members can't wait that long, nor can many of the rest of us.

AFFIRMATIVE ACTIONS AND CHALLENGING BEHAVIOR

For many women who aspire to become elite politicians, the difficulties begin early in their ambitions, in simply having the confidence to put themselves forward. While there are now a number of campaign groups which give support to women in those early stages, including funds for campaign activities, such as Emily's List (a Labor organization which operates in the United States, Australia and the United Kingdom) and the 300 Group (a British-based, cross-party group), the crucial hurdle is being selected to stand by constituency parties themselves. Grassroots parties at local and regional levels are typically dominated by men who have traditionally selected candidates who fit their own perceptions of suitability and "where a dominant male culture still prevails regardless of fundamental political ideology" (Reynolds, 1995, p. 130). While public antipathy has been the overt reason given by political parties to avoid putting women up for selection, almost every study which has looked at the credibility of this assumption has found it unquestionably false (Darcy & Schramm, 1977; Hunter & Denton, 1984; Welch & Studlar, 1986).

The ways in which political actors initially become Parliamentarians generally work against women because they often lack the kinds of "experience" which selectors look for in candidates, often including long-serving union activity or experience as a local or regional councilor (Yishai, 1997). It was precisely to support and give confidence to women to fight for selection that pressure groups like Emily's List were formed, and they function to mentor and train women to hone the political skills and develop the presentation skills which are so important in winning at selection panels. The name "Emily" is an acronym which stands for "Early Money Is Like Yeast," by which it is clear that a fundamental problem for women seeking endorsement is not their lack of political abilities, but rather their incapacity to raise campaign funds. As a subscription-based organization, Emily relies on donations which are then routed through to women aspirants, and such support networks are important aspects of women's campaign strategy since the hurdles they will have to conquer are considerable. Carmen Lawrence (Labor, Australia and co-founder of Emily's List Australia) is very pleased with the way in which candidates supported by Emily's List Australia are beginning to come through to election:

> In Queensland, the most recent elections [1998], we supported 13 candidates, nine of whom are in and four of those are new members, which is terrific. It's been a combination of financial support which is worth a couple of thousand dollars to each of the candidates . . . plus the support which we give by sending more experienced women Parliamentarians to assist them with their campaigns.

One of the reasons that the 1992 American election year was dubbed "The Year of the Woman" was because a record number of women stood as candidates, and part of that push was a consequence of the Anita Hill-Clarence Thomas hearings and subsequent verdict. The newsreels showing the all-male committee cross-examining Hill highlighted perfectly the absence of women in Congress and also brought back into focus the perennial problems of sexual harassment and equal pay (Witt, Paget & Matthews, 1994; Walkosz & Kenski, 1995). Outrage at the outcome among professional and other elite women resulted in a huge increase in funding for political support campaigns for women (Wilcox, 1994); notably Emily's List (USA) saw an exponential increase in donations over the 2-year period of 1990-1992, from $973,124 to $4,257,404 (Nelson, 1994). Although talking specifically about the Australian context nearly a decade ago, McAlllister's (1992) comments retain considerable resonance with political parties in other places and at other times, including now, at the start of the 21st century: "The hurdles for women to gain election to legislative positions in Australia are mainly those that take place within 'the secret garden of politics'—within party selectorates, hierarchies . . . [which] tolerate the continuing advantages of incumbency for men" (p. 225).

The Scandinavian countries are almost always promoted as countries which have very positive approaches towards women's political representation, both in terms of consulting with "ordinary" women and thus hearing their political perspectives, but also in terms of the proportion of their elected political representatives. From the early 1960s, women were highly effective campaigners for the cause of women's representation, where efficient organizing led political parties themselves to take the issue seriously. Norway is now one of the world's leaders in women's elite political representation, although there is still considerable debate about the relative importance of different factors in this success story—"electoral system, social movement organizations, party nomination procedures, district magnitude and political culture" (Matland & Studlar, 1996, p. 716). But whatever the mix of reasons, the outcome is very clear: politics in Norway can be seen to be genuinely representative of women and men, at least in the proportions of their women and men political representatives, and this reality is very far removed from the situation in most Western democratic legislatures.

But in the 1980s and 1990s, political parties began to realize that women politicians were not the voter turn-off that they had always believed, and in Britain, after yet another election defeat in 1987, the Labour Party's own internal study revealed the level of women's antipathy towards the party, largely because of its image as male-oriented and male-dominated. For Labour, this recognition was particularly hard since their own research also showed that many women supported key Labour values but didn't see the party as actually articulating those policy stances and therefore didn't vote the party in (Short, 1996). Two years later, at a party conference in 1989, a resolution was passed with overwhelming support, committing the party to the introduction of a quota of 40 per cent for elections at every level and to achieve 50 per cent representation of women in the Parliamentary Labour Party within 10 years (or three elections). However, despite support for these principles, there has subsequently been considerable resistance to their active implementation, and it wasn't until the 1993 annual conference that the formal introduction of quotas for women candidates was endorsed, but with considerably scaled-down ambitions. The formulation which was eventually carried stipulated that all-women shortlists would be used in half the winnable seats and half the "safe" seats where MPs were retiring, but such was the level of resistance within the membership that even this more modest effort was ultimately defeated (as discussed below).

The two major parties both realize now, because of polling, that if they've got a marginal seat, a confident woman is more likely to win than a man, that's the reality. Providing the abilities and the quality of the candidates are matched, the woman is likely to have that edge of credibility with the electorate. (Dee Margetts, Green Party, Australia)

Elsewhere, other parties in other countries were also beginning to develop formal mechanisms to ensure the candidacy of women politicians as they, too, realized that women were electoral assets rather than liabilities. During their national conference in 1994, the Australian Labor Party introduced their own rule on quotas, which included the stipulation that,

> ... Pre-selections for public office positions at state and federal level shall incorporate affirmative action. The intention of this is to produce an outcome where 35 per cent of public office positions held by Labor or a majority of seats needed for government, whichever is the greater, will be filled by women ... by the year 2002. Each state and territory branch must ensure that its rules are in line with this objective ... (cited in Reynolds, 1995, p. 130)

It has tended to be Labour parties in different national contexts which have made formal incursions into the awkward territory of fracturing patriarchal party traditions, but even Conservative- and Liberal-oriented parties have more recently begun to espouse the desirability of enabling a wider pool of talent to be considered for selection. If orthodox contagion theory (Duverger, 1954) is correct, then as one party begins to promote women as viable political actors, then the other parties will feel pressured into following suit. This *should* happen because, by nominating women as candidates, smaller parties or those in opposition are implying that women do not alienate the electorate, and thus the larger parties might feel they, too, need to follow that example or else risk losing votes by being perceived as more reactionary (Matland & Studlar, 1996). In Keswick, Pockley, and Guillaume's (1999) exhortation to their own British Conservative Party leaders to select more women as candidates, they explicitly point to Labour's winning strategy and to the fact that women voters support women candidates. But the grounds of that argument are about winning elections, they are not about equity and justice. In the Fawcett Society's (1997) survey of women MPs immediately after the 1997 general election in Britain, while the great majority of Labour MPs thought that getting more women into Parliament was "very important," Conservative MPs were more likely to say that it was "not" or "not at all important."

But even before the Conservative defeat in the 1997 elections, political agents within the party were already unhappy about the lack of women being considered as candidates and one laments the rejection of good women for poor men: "You'd think they'd beg for women after the sex scandals, instead of choosing middle-aged family men who drop their trousers the first chance they get" (cited in Nadelson, 1996, p. 26) British Conservative women have begun to campaign within their party to make the case for better representation of women in the party; by late 2000, fewer than 10 per cent of their MPs were women, and a mere 16 out of 73 candidates selected to fight the 2001 general election were women, mostly allocated to unwinnable seats. In a well-argued report, three high-profile women in the party make the controversial suggestion that quotas are the key way forward, consciously acknowledging that such a mechanism is highly unpopular among many members, but insisting that without them, or a significant attitudinal change, the Conservatives may become a spent force (Keswick et al., 1999). After the 2001 British General Election, the Conservatives had 14 women MPs, the same number as in 1997.

Coupled with any quota system must be robust support structures for women, and another Conservative woman in Britain has also been exhorting her party to consider the problem of women's representation by suggesting that good women must be encouraged to stand as candidates, that they must be supported and trained, and that selection panels in constituencies also need training to overturn potentially discriminatory attitudes (Buxton, 2000). Parties of the center and the right have historically been chary of institutionalizing any kind of quota system, preferring instead to operate on a laissez-faire approach which promotes the cause but stops short of insisting on its implementation in any formal way. In the face of all the evidence to the contrary—men will not easily cede power to women—it is sad that so many women politicians continue to suggest that although there should be more women representatives, this should (and will, apparently) occur because of a sense of justice. The acceptance that we currently have an iniquitous system across the globe has no corresponding suggestion for change other than encouraging a more equitable distribution:

I understand that perhaps for a period of time at least, one will have to have a push for more women because it might not come naturally. So one would push for women's representation, although you don't push for a quota. You would just keep on alerting the people so they will remember also to give women a chance. And that could be a natural process. (Sheila Camerer, New National Party, South Africa)

   In the Scottish Parliamentary and Welsh Assembly elections in 1999, while Labour operated a formal "twinning" strategy, whereby party lists had to have equal numbers of women and men, none of the other parties initiated any affirmative action strategies, although Plaid Cymru did promote an equal opportunities agenda during the application form process. In the event, Labour and the Liberal Democrats returned similar numbers of women and men to the Welsh Assembly, while the Conservatives have no women and Plaid Cymru has 6 women and 11 men. In the Scottish Parliament, Labour again returned the same number of women as men (28: 28), the Liberal Democrats returned 2 women (out of 17), the Conservatives returned 3 women (out of 15) and the Scottish National Party returned 15 women and 20 men. Not only did the twinning strategy have the effect of enhancing women's likelihood of success at the ballot box, but the broader equal opportunities agenda in operation also meant that, unlike the Westminster MPs, the newly elected MSPs have much in common in terms of their career paths, so that "one could hypothesize that the Labour MSPs are more likely to behave in a cohesive manner than their Westminster counterparts" (Cavanagh, McGarvey, & Shephard, 2000, p. 18).

   Nonetheless, in an exit-study conducted immediately after the Scottish and Welsh elections, the majority of women candidates recognized that their parties need to continue to use specific affirmative action strategies to ensure that women continue to have the opportunity to stand as candidates, let alone win at the ballot box (Fawcett Society, 1999). However, genuine support for encouraging greater participation by women, even by Labor parties, has always been a little half-hearted, largely because the "solution" to under-representation—quotas and all-women shortlists—has always been seen as inherently unfair. In the Fawcett Society's (1997) exit-survey of women MPs, there was strong agreement with the statement that the reason why there are so few women in Parliament is because "women are not given the opportunity by parties' selection committees" (p. 8). The "merit" argument is inevitably invoked in the face of demands for and rules on quotas, usually accompanied by a solid refusal to engage with the obverse of the merit argument—that is, on the balance of probability, how likely is it that the 80 per cent of British elected politicians who are men achieved their success on the basis of merit? While it is true that some women (mostly Conservative and Liberal supporters) also rehearse the merit argument in their rejection of quotas, it is largely a male response and Dale Spender's (1994) observation is well made: "[Men] can't (or won't) see that their definitions of merit, qualifications and experience are nothing more than rules they have made up to protect their own positions" (p. 8). Margaret Reynolds (1995), commenting on when she was still a

Senator for Queensland, asks the inevitable question and follows up
with a heartfelt response:

> When it is suggested that women take a share of power, sections of
> the community doubt their ability to do so. But when was merit ever
> used to pre-select candidates for political office? Is there an open
> advertisement listing the qualifications and experience necessary?
> Are structured job interview procedures adopted? Are panels of
> interviewers independently appointed to select the best person for
> the vacancy? Politicians' positions are determined by their ability to
> win support from a narrow section of a political party or trade
> union, by their knowledge and experience within that structure and
> by their ability to attract the numbers in pre-selection ballots. Merit's
> in the eye of the beholder and, traditionally, Australian mateship has
> perpetuated the assumption that men will be more likely to have the
> appropriate mix of qualities necessary for Parliamentary life. (p. 131)

It was precisely on the basis of unfair practice that the British
Labour Party's resolution on all-women shortlists was deemed unlawful
under the Sex Discrimination Act (1975) when two disgruntled party
members (Peter Jepson and Robert Dyas-Elliott) took the Party to an
industrial tribunal in late 1995 because they wished to stand in constituencies which had been "forced" to have all-woman shortlists rather
than an open list. It is extremely telling that the Labour Party almost
immediately capitulated to the tribunal's ruling, which deemed the resolution unlawful, not even attempting to mount a challenge or appeal.
The gloss put on the defeat by the Party was that it had only intended
the all-women shortlist system to operate for one election (in 1997), as a
short, sharp, shock to the system which would, at one go, redress the
historical problem of women's under-representation in the
Parliamentary Labour Party. Interestingly, although the all-women
shortlist strategy was found to be illegal, many constituencies who had
used the strategy to select their candidates stated that they did not wish
to go through another selection process with an open list because they
believed that they had selected the best candidate anyway. Yet, there
was considerable relief among many members and constituencies that
the strategy had failed, particularly in those areas which were already
annoyed at being forced to adopt London-based candidates in preference to ones of their own choosing. "This is just a metropolitan idea that
nobody in the local constituencies wants. Many of the women being put
forward are so bloody out of touch" (Anonymous political agent cited in
Malone & Byrne, 1995, p. 10).
   What is chastening to realize from the British Labour Party's flirtation with all-women shortlists in the Westminster elections is its

instantaneous acceptance of guilt that the strategy was "illegal": when faced with its first minor challenge, the commitment to the principle of equality showed itself to be lukewarm, to say the least. Part of the Party's reluctance to fully embrace affirmative action strategies lies, arguably, in concerns about the Party's more reactionary membership and how they have already and might again react to the imposition of any kind of system which upsets the status quo and which appears to give women an advantage. Similarly, despite the Australian Labor Party's conference resolution in 1994 to achieve 35 per cent female representation by the year 2002, the ALP has managed to return even fewer women Parliamentarians over the past two general elections (Nelson, 1998), largely because of the selection process. Judi Moylan, Australia's Minister for Women, and Carmen Lawrence know the answer to why women fail to be selected as candidates:

> The major impediments are men, pure and simple! They control too many processes through which members must go in order to eventually be preselected. (Moylan, cited in Nelson, 1998, p. 13)

> Existing political figures look for representatives who are exactly like themselves . . . women do not share [the] culture of blokey mateship . . . they do not share that implicit understanding of what it is to be a mate. (Lawrence, cited in Nelson, 1998, p. 133)

So, regardless of resolutions and good intentions at party conferences, the rank-and-file members of political parties wield considerable power in the selection of candidates, and without concrete strategies which insist on giving women the opportunities to stand, it is clear that progress will not be made quickly. The success of women in the Scottish Parliamentary and the Welsh Assembly elections in 1999 was significant, but it was won at some considerable cost to the women themselves and to the parties in Scotland and Wales, even though "twinning" is only about equal representation—not quotas—and could therefore be seen as absolutely fair to both women and men. But it was *not* seen in that way. Comments from women who fought in those elections tell a story of considerable struggle and personal attacks which has everything to do with internal party politics and very little to do with the election itself: "We fought a rather hard and nasty campaign on the twinning issue—it was very, very hard, I mean, I've lost quite a few friends from other areas over twinning." "We constantly had men saying that twinning wouldn't happen, that the Executive wouldn't back it. They seized every last speck of hope that it wouldn't happen." "I received two anonymous poison-pen letters . . . someone cut out bits of newspaper and sent them to me." "I met one member of the public who said he wouldn't vote for me because I was a woman. He was perfectly nice about it, but he said he hated Margaret Thatcher." "I just think they had their own ideas of who should be the candidate, the sort of favored son. I know I wouldn't be here if twinning hadn't happened."

It is, perhaps, a consequence of the bitterness provoked by the "twinning" strategy which effectively squashed any possible use of something similar in the British general election in 2001.[1] This is in stark contrast to the enduring commitment to enhancing women's participation in Scandinavian democracies, which continue to operate a quota system, and to that of some of the newer political systems, such as that of South Africa, where a 30 per cent quota for women in the party was introduced in 1994 by the African National Congress. As with the examples in Scotland and Wales, women nearly always do better when some kind of list system is in operation coupled with overt affirmative actions which together produce a more balanced party ticket (Matland, 1998, p. 112).

> PR electoral systems are often seen as more friendly to the election of women than plurality-majority systems. In essence, parties are able to use the lists to promote the advancement of women politicians and allow the space for voters to elect women candidates without limiting their ability to vote with a mind on other concerns. (Matland & Taylor, 1997, p. 204)

However, such outcomes are not always the case if specific actions such as quotas are not also brought into play. As Ballington (1998) points out, other countries with PR structures similar to that of South Africa, such as Israel, have very low levels of participation by women in elite politics, and Norris (1997) makes the key point that the first democratically held elections to take place in Eastern and Central Europe saw significant falls in female participation as a consequence of the removal of party quotas. Political parties need to be careful about what mechanisms they choose when attempting to enhance women's role in elite politics since, as in the case of all-women shortlists, the reactionary forces that reside in many constituencies, which remain bastions of male dominance, leave parties open to legal challenge when "reverse discrimination" can be "proved." Even list systems, as in South Africa, are open to abuse in terms of who gets to be nominated to them; strategic canvassing for particular individuals means that women can often be marginalised when the votes are cast. As Ntombazana Botha (ANC, South Africa) suggests,

---

[1]It should be noted, however, that in the 2001 British general election, only two fewer women were returned to Westminster (118) than in 1997, again indicating that women candidates were just as attrative to the electorate as men.

men will often canvass for themselves and other men, but women tend to be a little too reserved to be good at self-promotion:

> They [the list members] get nominated by branches, they get voted in, at the provincial level, but I'm going to be very very frank . . . along the way in that process, people get manipulated. They get manipulated into nominating people, by certain other people, and mainly it's our male counterparts that do that, who go around canvassing and misleading people. I'm not saying women don't do that, I'm not sure, but I know of men who do that. And sometimes I feel that process is also flawed.

The closing decade of the twentieth century demonstrated, in very real ways, the limits of electoral tolerance for bad government, for male politicians who seem incapable of keeping their trousers zipped or their hands out of the till or their wallets closed to corruption. Their breathtaking arrogance, those Ministers and Presidents, to lie to both the House and the polity and expect to evade punishment by their repetitive insistence of having done nothing wrong is testament both to the contempt with which they hold the public they serve but also that with which they treat the business of governance and the role of politicians in the world. But with journalists keen to expose every small instance of inconsistent policy stance, bad taste, embarrassing personal practice or behaviour or indiscretion, let alone criminal acts such as bribery or corruption, we surely need to ask questions about many of our politicians' overarching fitness for purpose, especially if they do not have the wit to understand their vulnerability to exposure by the upstanding fourth estate.

That women politicians are scarcely ever featured in these exposés—and this is not just because they rarely achieve high visibility—is something which is becoming increasingly apparent to the electorate at large, and women politicians are certainly not the electoral liability which was once suggested. In Britain, for example, the former Minister for Social Security, The Rt. Hon. Harriet Harman, initiated a campaign in early 2000 to alert the Labour Government to the fact that recent polling showed women's serious dissatisfaction with the treatment of women MPs and questioned their demonstrable lack of promotion to Cabinet positions with real authority, especially to the politically and economically important portfolios (Jonathan Carr-Brown, *Independent on Sunday*, p. 6). In the same article, an anonymous "party source" was credited as saying that, "Women [supporters] tell us they are still going to vote in the next election but their loyalty will only be secured if we move away from a male-dominated leadership" (p. 6).

In the newly formed Parliament in Scotland and National Assembly in Wales, the high proportion of women elected as members (37 per cent in Scotland and 40 per cent in Wales) was due, to a very large extent, to the fact that, in both Scotland and Wales, a system of twinning constituencies was adopted which forced Labour constituencies to select two candidates, a woman and a man (Fawcett Society, 1999). So, it is possible to increase women's representation but not without positive action strategies, but why are these so bad? Does anyone seriously believe that the reason why so few women manage to become politicians is because they are less competent than men? Or less politically interested? Or less idealistic? Or even less ambitious? So, if men get into Parliament for reasons other than merit—which is demonstrably the case, even discounting the miserable misjudgements referred to above—then how can a rejection of strategies to redress the gender imbalance (positive actions, quotas, twinning, and so on) be made on the grounds of unfair practice? What is "fair" about an existing practice which clearly works against women? If two wrongs don't make a right, they can certainly go towards making the situation more right than wrong.

Part of the resistance to even the *idea* of more women in Parliament is rooted, I would suggest, in a fear of change and a fear of women organising to meet their own agendas, but it is possible to square the circle of inequality which nonetheless produces a win-win situation, with power-sharing being a realistic outcome for everyone. More women in Parliament would enable some of the old orthodoxies which favoured a very few men to be replaced by strategies which support and encourage everyone. The pink ribbon in the Members' Cloakroom in Britain's House of Commons—for men to hang up their swords—is an anachronism in a modern Parliament, and the existence of the now-infamous rifle range but no crèche in that place betrays the determinedly macho atmosphere which exists, to the detriment of all those women and men who are outside the inner circle, out of choice or exclusion. It is arguably male paranoia and fear which lie at the root of most anti-women propaganda (see, for example, Faludi, 1991; Figes, 1994), sentiments which incorporate all the old orthodoxies of male chauvinism dressed up in new clothes. As previously thought "certainties" about women's roles and men's roles are increasingly brought into question, the privileged position of white, middle-class men is being challenged, and they fear they might be found wanting. Part of this uncertain and changing landscape manifests as an acute anxiety, that once they achieve power, women will do to men what men have done to women down the ages, but more skillfully and with more devastating results. They will take no prisoners. Politics has become the new zero sum game and men its new casualties:

There is a conundrum. People say yes, we want more women to be
involved but think that automatically less power for men and therefore people constantly look for ways in which to involve women
more while at the same time not giving them any more power.
(Dawn Primarolo, Labour, UK)

3

Practical Politics and the Gender Turn

There are a lot of women who are leading forces in their party groups on male cancer and I say to them, look, give it to the boys and what's interesting is that the boys are beginning to take it on and that's actually quite a shift . . . to take responsibility for their own health and . . . playing a leading a role in these kinds of intimate issues and not leaving it to the women to do the messy bits. I'm quite happy to do breasts, I'm quite happy to do wombs, I'm quite happy to do cervixes, but the guys should do the balls. (Fiona McTaggart, Labour, UK)

INTRODUCTION

Although there is little research evidence, in Britain at least, for suggesting that women and men politicians do pursue a different politics—largely because it is only recently that there have been sufficient numbers of women MPs to even ask the question—several American studies report that salient differences in approach and priorities *do* exist which fracture along gendered lines. (See, for example, Thomas, 1991; Boles, 1991; Blankenship & Robson, 1995; Schumaker & Burns, 1998.) Thomas' (1991) study, for example, found that women prioritize legislation which concerns women, family, and children, whereas men prioritize laws affecting business and the economy. Importantly, women are likely to be more vigorous in pursuing policies when they have critical voting mass. Boles (1991) selected a number of so-called "women's issues" to examine and found that, when considering issues such as day care, domestic violence, sexual assault, displaced homemakers, children's library services, and childbirth, women were more likely to deem them important legislative issues than were male colleagues. Some women Parliamentarians whom I interviewed believe that their involvement in their local communities, as workers, mothers, and partners, brings a perspective to their politics which is more rooted in local rather than national issues, and thus they are more likely to think about the impact of policy on actual communities than in more abstract terms:

> One of the things I do is bring it back to grassroots level, so that even if I'm talking about . . . regional development, I actually illustrate my answers with real examples. (Fran Bailey, Liberal, Australia)

> I don't think we would have got to the twenty-first century without a crèche in this place, without nationally assisted nursery provision, without adequate childcare policies, with discriminatory pension schemes. I just don't think that if women had been properly represented in all areas of decision-making, that our society would be like it is today. (Angela Eagle, Labour, UK)

> We're more aware of what is needed in the community, and we're more aware of what people's expectations are of us. (Elizabeth Grace, Liberal, Australia)

Looking at the speeches of Congresswomen between 1990 and 1994, Blankenship and Robson (1995) argue that they detected "feminine" political discourses which they characterize as including basing political judgements on concrete, lived experience; valuing inclusivity; conceptualizing public office as "getting things done" and empowering others; approaching policy formation holistically; and moving women's issues to the top of the agenda. Schumaker and Burns' (1998) study of policy priorities in the city council of Lawrence, Kansas, found that priorities were markedly different between women and men on 20 issues, where men favored laws on economic development and women placed neighborhood preservation and social welfare higher on the priority scale. These studies all suggest that women and men politicians view social and economic issues *differently*, not perhaps as being specifically "women's issues" as opposed to "men's issues" but at least *prioritizing* issues differentially, and that the recruitment of more women into positions of political authority could potentially have a far-reaching impact on the socioeconomic agenda (Fox, 1997).

Years ago, we had a woman called Betty Solomon[1] and when she came into power, she just said that women had a totally different view of legislation and the legislation that they become involved in becomes softer legislation. And this is perfectly true. For example when we were looking at the maintenance laws, it was being done by the Justice Committee. They brought the Welfare Committee in and the women looked at it from a totally different point of view. The male lawyers looked at the legalistic methodology, and the welfare and justice women looked at the practicality of implementing it and the effect it would have on the women and the children. We look at things from a totally different point of view. (Val Viljoen, ANC, South Africa)

Some work on gendered political priorities for women politicians suggests that they are more concerned with and will push forward policies which directly affect the lives of women and children (Barrett, 1995; Center for the American Woman and Politics, 1995; Horton, 1999), especially legislation which relates to women's reproductive rights (Berkman & O'Connor, 1993; Thomas, 1994). And if politicians view the policy agenda in gender-specific terms, the electorate seems to as well; for example, in a series of elector studies carried out between 1984 and 1992 in New Zealand, men consistently prioritized "the economy" while women consistently scored "unemployment" as being the most pressing problem in the country. However, despite these very clear and consistent policy biases, Levine and Roberts go on to argue that gender on its own does not have sufficient predictive value in terms of actual voting preferences. But then one also has to take into account two things: first, that words and behaviour are often very different, among politicians as with the rest of us; and second, that it is easy to say positive and generous things when in opposition, but the reality of being in the ruling party is often a rude political awakening for many politicians and what seemed possible from one side of the benches can be a little more difficult to pursue from the other. The hopes that many of us have for our women politicians seem so much more significant when they are dashed because of our own investment in their achievement and what they could mean for social transformation, than when our political opponents or male colleagues unfailingly manage to deliver our worst fears. In Britain, Segal (2000) amongst others suggests that the high expectations that many "ordinary" women had of an incoming (1997) Labour government which had more than 20 per cent women MPs elected, have been comprehensively unfulfilled in the first few years of that administration, with scarcely any discernible difference in the tenor of legislation which

---

[1]Bertha Solomon was one of the pioneers for the women's vote in the late 1920s and 1930s and was an MP from 1938-1958 for the United Party.

continues to penalize households which do not conform to the mythical contours of the "nuclear family." Even women MPs themselves recognize that women do have higher expectations of them to deliver for women than they have of their male colleagues, but even then, there seems to be a lack of commitment. Fiona Mactaggart (2000) (Labour, UK) argues vigorously to defend Labour women's impact on legislative change, but then gives a rather odd example as evidence, relating to the media's interest in MPs who vote against their party line:

> And then a habit developed in the papers to judge political effectiveness by propensity to vote against the government. This followed the revolt by some Labour backbencheers on plans to reduce the lone parent benefit premium. It is an issue about which many Labour women members are concerned, many spoke directly to ministers asking them to amend the policy, 10 signed an early day motion, but only seven of the 47 who voted against the measure were women. (p. 4)

Mactaggart goes on to argue that women tend not to believe that voting against their government is effective unless one can be sure of being on the winning side, but there is a certain circularity to this argument. What cannot be easily understood, other than for reasons of cynical political expediency, is why only 7 of the 101 Labour women MPs chose to vote against a proposal which would adversely affect the financial provisions of millions of lone parents, most of whom are mothers; even the men managed a better turnout. In some ways, their reluctance to stand up for vulnerable women backfired on them in terms of the media's immediate approbation of their actions (or rather, *in*action), and demonstrates, perhaps, a certain lack of judgement about cause and effect as far as the voters' memories are concerned. One small act of rebellion which would probably have caused only mild (and temporary) embarrassment for the government could have paid dividends at the ballot box and, equally, could now presage the opposite. But then, there *have* been quiet workings behind the scenes and Mactaggart's Labour colleague Yvette Cooper insists that women have had a significant impact on improving the lives of women, but they are too modest or uninteresting for the media to trumpet their victories:

> Don't underestimate the impact of having so many women on overall government policy, particularly the '98 budget which benefited women five times more than men, or the work that went into designing the Working Family Tax Credit so that it helps women or the amount of family friendly polices in the Fairness at Work Bill which could have been all about boys' stuff. (cited in Perkins, 1999, p. 6)

But what people will remember is cutting benefits, not improving women's position, and it is that legacy which could prove lethal for women in the 2001 election. How, ordinary women ask, is it possible to square the circle of espousing feminist values (see Fawcett Society, 1997) and then vote to cut benefits from lone parents, most of whom are women? When The Rt. Hon. Harriet Harman, as Britain's Minister of State for Social Security stood up in the House of Commons and defended her own government's bill which would make the process of claiming child benefits considerably more difficult for lone parents, that event was widely viewed not only as the apotheosis of Harman's own credibility—she had, only months before as an opposition spokesperson pledged that Labour would never target lone parents in this way—but as a damning indictment of the failure of Labour women MPs to commit themselves, politically and morally, to defend the interests of those most vulnerable in society. But perhaps it is we, the onlookers of "ordinary" women, who are out of order? Perhaps it is the projection of our expectations onto a group of politicians for whom our shared gender was never the real agenda which is completely misplaced? If, as I have argued elsewhere (Ross & Sreberny, 2000), the distinctiveness and alleged inherent differences between women's and men's politics, or women's and men's values is often overplayed—Margaret Thatcher and Nelson Mandela seem appropriate exemplars of the potential to operate against the orthodoxies of gendered behaviour, although Thatcher was also a devoted mother and grandmother and Mandela was a freedom fighter—then there is no reason, really, to believe that women and men, as political actors, will campaign for different things solely on the basis of their different biologies. Their policy agendas *may* be different, but biological determinism may not necessarily be the defining feature of such differences. Rather, a desire to succeed in their chosen career may be a far more powerful element in their everyday thinking and behaviour than solidarity with others of their sex. As Coote (1999) points out, "the current advice to aspiring female politicians is, 'don't use the F-word': if you want to get on, don't mention feminism" (p. 10). Conforming to organizational norms of obeisance and flattery as a professional fast-track strategy in the political arena enjoys a long history, and why should the women who have finally managed to storm the barricade of male privilege in the political domain be expected to behave any differently or feel that they can do so without penalty? Looking at the potential for strong women in Britain's Labour Party to move into positions of authority, Langdon (1999) is pessimistic that they will actually be able to exercise their right to be heard, let alone make policy suggestions which run counter to the narrow and increasingly punitive agenda of New Labour:

> The Prime Minister does like his Ministers to be competent . . . but
> more important even than capability is compliance . . . Most ambi-
> tious young Labour MPs have recognized the significance of this if
> they wish to pursue a meaningful career in the Government, as is
> only too evident in the sycophancy so brazenly demonstrated by
> those who seek promotion [and the] independent-minded women in
> the lower and middle ranks of this administration may soon find
> that they are facing a dilemma in their careers if they exhibit any
> facility for stubbornly asserting their own view of significant politi-
> cal issues. (p. 17)

As Langdon pointed out, 30 months into New Labour's administration—although there were then, in December 1999, more women at
Westminster and more women ministers in office than at any previous
time in history—no women were actually in charge of a major department of State. While women comprised 25 per cent of the Labour
Cabinet and *did* occupy important-sounding positions—Chief Whip,
Leader of the House, Leader of the Lords, Cabinet Coordinator—these
roles have no real substance or power but are merely the political equiv-
alents of good housekeeping: "the Prime Minister has, in effect, told the
girls to get on with the dusting" (Langdon, 1999, p. 17). It should be said
that Langdon's analysis is not absolutely correct inasmuch as, at the time
that she wrote her damning polemic, Clare Short was doing sterling service as Minister of State for International Development. After the 2001
British General Election, which Labor again won, the "reshuffled"
Cabinet included seven women which, while being an increase of two
on the previous Cabinet's women members, nonetheless excluded
women from the key portfolios of domestic policy (Home Office), foreign policy, defence, employment or finance. Instead, women are now
Ministers for Trade and Industry (Patricia Hewitt), Culture and Media
(Tessa Jowell), Environment and Food (Margaret Beckett), Education
(Estelle Morris), Scotland (Helen Liddell) and International
Development (Clare Short). In addition, Hilary Armstrong has become
Chief Whip. This is absolutely *not* to deny the importance of either these
roles or the fact that women occupy them, but rather to indicate that
women are still struggling to achieve senior policial positions which
have serious political decision-making responsibilities attached to them.

Even in Australia's Parliament, which has seen quite a creditable
inclusion of women ministers over the past two decades, given their relatively small numbers overall, there still appears to be a belief that
women can't be responsible for key ministries such as finance, defense,
internal, and foreign affairs:

> Portfolios in which women have most often been appointed are
> those responsible for the status of women and family/community
> services. Appointments in this group occur at about twice the rate of
> the second group of portfolios, which includes consumer affairs,
> local government and environment, followed by education, the arts
> and ethnic affairs. (Reynolds, 1995, p. 109)

As early as 1987, Bob Hawke, then Australian Prime Minister, made a
public commitment to bringing a minimum of three women into his
Ministry, and in July of that year, Rt. Hon. Susan Ryan, Rt. Hon.
Margaret Reynolds and Rt. Hon. Ros Kelly were duly installed, although
Ryan (who was the only one of the three to be brought into the Cabinet)
retired at the end of that year and Kelly was brought into the Cabinet in
1990, leaving two years without any women in the Cabinet at all. Paul
Keating then followed Hawke's lead in ensuring that women did
achieve high political office, although as Reynolds (1995) points out,
only one woman at a time has ever been a member of the Australian
Cabinet, a not inconsiderable responsibility and, probably, burden.
Across many Parliamentary contexts, women do find it extraordinarily
difficult to achieve and sustain Ministerial office. Yishai (1997) points
out, for example, that in 1992, Israel saw two women Ministers in the
Knesset, but before the following election in 1996, they had not only
both stood down, but had resigned from political life altogether. One of
them, Ora Namir, was quoted in a national newspaper at the time as
saying, "For both of us [she and Shulamit Aloni]—men have decided
that we shall discontinue our political activity" (Namir, cited in *Ma'ariv*,
17.5.1996).

Quotas for British Labor Party Ministers have been in place
since at least 1989 when the then leader, Neil Kinnock, introduced the
ruling that MPs must cast three votes for women in order to "protect"
the existing Cabinet, and the numbers were increased from 15 to 18. This
quota was raised to four in 1993, which provoked a backlash among
men who were accused of systematically distributing their votes so that
only three women could actually achieve a place (Cole & Howe, 1994).
There is a slightly better picture in the United States, with women holding less stereotypical portfolios, such as Attorney General (Janet Reno),
Labor (Alexis Herman), and Foreign Affairs (Madeleine Albright), and
in South Africa's new government under Thabo Mbeki, 8 out of 29
Ministers are women who are working with such diverse departments
as communications, public works, health, agriculture, and land affairs
and housing (Ballington, 1999). But more generally, the promotion of
women into pseudo-important positions such as Leader of the House
scores two significant hits for a Government which has only ever been
half-hearted in its *genuine* desire to encourage women into politics. It

demonstrates both how "well" Government is doing—look how many we've got!—while at the same time ensuring absolutely no threat to the status quo because these senior positions are without any real power. That four of the five women in question—Rt. Hon. Margaret Beckett, Rt. Hon. Mo Mowlam, Rt. Hon. Clare Short, and Ann Taylor—are all temperamentally, philosophically and politically "old" Labour and have had to take on the mantle of "New Labour" in order to survive, provides a salutary lesson to other wannabe politicians, including male aspirants. This is that, in order to thrive in Blair's government (and probably *any* government), it is necessary to espouse (if not necessarily hold) political convictions which match those of the Leader *himself*. Will those women who came into government with such high hopes of making a difference find their ways blocked if, having bided their time and palpably *not* done those very things which women voters thought they were electing them precisely *to* do, they, too, find themselves shunted into the political sidelines, doing the dusting with the Leader of the House? In mid-2000, the most popular female Minister, Mo Mowlam announced that she would be standing down at the next election (in 2001) because of a wish to pursue a second career outside Parliamentary politics (the *Guardian*, 5.9 2000). The "real" reason being suggested by political pundits was her dismay at being sidelined as "chief nanny" after her spectacularly good stewardship of the volatile Northern Ireland portfolio, which saw her broker the Good Friday Agreement. Why was she relieved of that office when she was performing so well?

But change can be achieved by women who achieve political power. When Scotland had its first national election in 1999, one consequence of the Labour Party's strategy of "twinning" was that 37 per cent of the Members of the Scottish Parliament (MSPs) are now women and, unlike their Westminster counterparts, were immediately given serious portfolios rather than the usual gender-flavored ones. The Ministers for Health (Susan Deacon), Transport (Sarah Boyack) and Social Inclusion (Wendy Alexander) were making their mark as soon as they took up their offices (Riddoch, 1999). In Health, Deacon launched a £250,000 project to stop smoking amongst young, socially disadvantaged women, backed a pilot project to give young women free bulk supplies of the morning-after pill and, in so doing, laid down a direct challenge to the radical pro-life organization—Precious Life—not to mention the Catholic Church—with the setting up of more family planning clinics. In Transport, Boyack has proposed road tolls to fund improved public transport in a nation which has the lowest rate of women car drivers in Britain. These are initiatives which would probably not have been proposed by men and it is ironic that the women MSPs who were immediately dubbed "Donald's Dollies" (after the Scottish Minister, Donald

Dewar), parroting the "Blair's Babes" label which the media gave to the incoming Westminster MPs in 1997, are anything but toy politicians.

There is also a recognition on the part of women politicians themselves that they are actively seeking out support on key gender issues from their male colleagues and, moreover, that men are much more likely to at least pay attention to policy affecting women than they have been in the past (Conway, Steuernagel, & Ahern, 1997). So, it is not just gender which predisposes a politician to support woman- or family-friendly policies; something else is also going on: some other sets of variables or issues need to be factored into the analysis to enable its complexities to be discovered. Some researchers, for example, have identified two very different "types" of gender-based policies, one which strives for equality—for example, equal pension rights for women and men—and another which challenges the role of women in society—for example, making childcare affordable and thus enabling more women to work outside the home (Gelb & Palley, 1987). With these two types drawn out—role-equity and role-change—Gelb and Palley argue that legislation supporting "equity" legislation is more likely to succeed, whereas that supporting "change" is more likely to fail. This suggests that supporting the orthodoxy that there exists a simple socialist-conservative basis for voting choices on legislation affecting women no longer has sufficient explanatory conviction. While women Parliamentarians do tend to be more liberal in their legislative support than male colleagues (but then elected women politicians are much more likely to be Democrats than Republicans anyway, so that's hardly a surprise), recent work by both Gelb and Palley (1987) and Horton (1999) provides compelling evidence to suggest that there is a powerful gender, as well as party, effect in play when voting decisions are made which have women at their core. Importantly, what seems to be at stake is the extent to which legislation attempts to equalize the material conditions of women and men (equal rights) which tends to find general favor as a broadly liberal "good," or which attempt to enable women as a group to take control of their own lives (role change), which is seen as more controversial.

EN-GENDERING STYLE POLITICS

Some commentators suggest that women politicians have a fundamentally and inherently different political style from male colleagues, that women bring a higher standard of moral behaviour, are more honest, less manipulative, and less combative in their approach (see, for example, Woods, 1992). Such views construct women's politics as being biologically determined by insisting that women are "naturally" more prin-

cipled than men, with more integrity and more propensity to concilia-
tion and compromise. While such a view is seductive in its touching
faith in the intrinsic "goodness" of women—what other position is possible when thinking of mother, babies, and apple pie?—its corollary is
that women are just too nice to get involved in the dirty business of big
boys' politics. When Carmen Lawrence (Labor, Australia) was facing
intense media (and political) scrutiny over alleged misinformation, she
commented that she didn't mind being called to account, but she object-
ed to the fact that different standards were expected of her:

> I remember at one stage during the worst of the Royal Commission
> saying, "look, I'd be happy to be judged by the same standards that
> male politicians are, I just don't want you to move the goal posts"
> and that was seen as special pleading. I don't think women are more
> virtuous or more likely to make wonderful politicians, but it's a mat-
> ter of justice.

In some ways, ceding a special (i.e., higher) morality to women is to
make a generalization which can become hard to defend, but the more
modest claim for a set of experiences which are gender-specific and lead
to a different perspective is a more tenable position which can be seen to
be rooted in an experiential rather than biological model of decision
making based on gender rather than sex. While the principles of equity
and justice should be sufficient to argue the case for increasing the representation of women as elected members in national politics, women
also bring different perspectives and can bring a different leadership
style to the political process:

> I don't know if I've become more sensitive or whether it's got worse,
> but I sit there [in the Chamber] sometimes and I feel cringing embar-
> rassment to be there, I really know how the public feels. And yet,
> there are lots of perfectly good people who get trapped in it because
> they go in and everyone shouts and then you get some clever dick
> laughing. It's horrible and that feeling is widespread round the
> country. Women say to me how mindless it is, that if children
> behaved like that, we'd tell them off, they just despise it. (Clare
> Short, Labour, UK)

As Callaghan (1991) observes, the life experiences of many
women can "provide the material content or the experiential data which
some women will interpret in ways that may predispose their moral
decisions to differ from those of some males" (p. 67). While there are so
many contingencies in Callaghan's fuller analysis as to make it almost
meaningless, there is a very real issue at stake in terms of identifying

individual action and experience while considering them also in the context of a differently gendered consciousness. The debate about a gendered morality is fierce and ongoing, with commentators usually taking up one of the two bi-polar positions (gender-neutral or gender-specific) with many others positioned somewhere along the continuum. The work of scholars such as Carol Gilligan (1981) stands at one end, espousing a theory of irrevocable gender difference which is rooted in biology but also maintained by socialization. From this view, women are more interested in the importance of relationships and use a personal moral view to inform decision making, while men are seen to operate in wholly rational and logical ways where the personal dimension is absent and where moral and ethical behaviour is informed by a more abstract reasoning process. This theoretical position leans heavily on psychoanalysis, with its emphasis on biological determinism which compels women to remain circumscribed by their own biological and apparently natural imperatives. This position has been heavily criticized by scholars who insist that women too can use the rational-logical model in decision making and that homogenizing all women's experiences is not only to deny a sense of autonomous will but also conflates and thus renders invisible all those other *differences* among women which determine specific perspectives, behaviours, and actions. As one of the veteran campaigners for women's representation in Australian politics, Joan Kirner (Premier of Western Australia, 1990-1992), suggests, strength in politics must be related to commitment and determination in decision making, and not simply be about who can shout the loudest on the floor of the Chamber (cited in Reynolds, 1995, p. 120).

There are surely far too many examples of women behaving badly, who are *not* interested in nurturing and caring for others, to allow absolute credence to a theory which frames women as eternal earth mothers. While women the world over *do* take the major responsibility for care provision, especially of children and older dependents, where women have the choice to, say, *not* become mothers, they are increasingly taking up that choice, using a rational-logical framework to inform that decision. "Notions of nurturing femininity are always at least partially at odds with themselves, as women seek their own freedom and authority . . ." (Segal, 2000, p. 13). This is not to say that women and men do not bring different experiences and perspectives to their choices and reasoning, but rather that women do not always privilege the maintenance of their relationships with others (an intrinsic sense of interconnectedness) over their own selfish desires, are not also capable of bringing justice and principle to their intuitive moral behaviour, cannot be both rational and emotional.

As postmodernism drives us towards rejecting a totaling essen-
tialism in other areas of social and cultural life—we are all unique amalgams of our diverse histories and experiences—it seems a strange contradiction that, at the same time, the political arena demands that
women and men are determined by their differentiated biology and
work in different ways because of their sex rather than as a result of
their politics. While women and men *are* different, biologically and in
other ways, their different approaches, priorities, beliefs, and value systems have as much to do with their different experiences as women and
men in the world as they have to do with their genes. Women's
approaches to politics, their distinctive forms of campaign address, their
choices of presentational style and content are more likely to be driven
by a pragmatic understanding of the political climate and what will
work for them, than by any spuriously "feminine" traits such as honesty
or integrity. Women who choose to enter the political fray have *already*
challenged normative assumptions about what women's role in society
is. They can be just as aggressive as many of their male colleagues and
can enjoy the adversarial style of political discourse, at least that performed in the theatre of Parliament, the Chamber, and will use their
position as women to attack female adversaries in ways which would
perhaps be seen as sexist if operated by men. Their male colleagues are
often surprised and discomfited by these assertive and confident displays by women, not only giving as good as they get, but deliberately
using the small advantages they have to good effect.

> We can have a swipe at another female or toss in an interjection or
> make a comment the blokes couldn't because it would be regarded
> as sexist. I've had occasions when they've [male colleagues] said to
> me, "you're a hard bitch" . . . but if you go in thinking that it's not
> gladiatorial in there, then you had better get out fast. (Sue West,
> Labor, Australia)

> Without being too idealistic about it, I think women have a different
> politics which is more inclusive. But more women wouldn't neces-
> sarily mean less shouting. I like shouting at the Tories across the
> Chamber. I don't buy all that earth mother stuff, why can't we all be
> nice and cooperate with each other. (Angela Eagle, Labour, UK)

In any case, as Carmen Lawrence (Labor, Australia) points out, women
can't afford to show any weaknesses: "You can't afford to appear uncertain or tentative or equivocate in any way which is, to an extent, difficult
for some women, given our upbringing and the sort of social context in
which women are often asked to behave." For her and other women,
adopting a confident persona which is assertive is a prerequisite for

achieving credibility among Parliamentary peers and, in the end, can become a more authentic part of oneself; but, it is always hard to operate against the grain of one's preferred modus operandi. Yet, some women feel very uncomfortable when women use aggressive tactics with each other, believing that such confrontations simply play into men's hands, who then sit back and watch the spectacle. There are, of course, double standards at work here since such behaviour between men is both completely acceptable and encouraged as the cut and thrust of ordinary political discourse, but for some women, this is merely to get caught up in the conventions of the male-ordered macho environment (which intimidates as many men as women) rather than change the context:

> I have seen harsher, crueler comments coming from women in Parliament . . . today, a woman kept interjecting when I was speaking, kept commenting all the time on my appearance, "oh, look what she's wearing today" and "your hair is even blonder today," it was weird. I would never do that to her, and I can see the men thinking, "cool, a cat fight, we'll let the women go for it." (Natasha Stott Despoja, Australian Democrats)

But women need to convince a traditional polity that they are competent as politicians *despite* their gender, not *because* of it. In the 1993 General Social Survey in America, 26 per cent of respondents agreed with the statement, "Most men are better suited emotionally for politics than are most women" (Davies & Smith, 1993). Given that the margin for political success is somewhat smaller than 25 per cent, it is clear that women in politics face a considerable battle for initial acceptance because of their gender, irrespective of their political colors. Of course, women do find themselves in an irrevocably awkward place, criticized if they are too aggressive and patronized if they are too mild:

> Despite the political machismo demonstrated on a regular basis by men in power around the world, strong women are regarded as traitors to their sex, while women adopting a quieter low-key approach are seen as not tough enough for the harsh world of politics. Determined women who continue to advocate their point of view are often described by some male colleagues as "over-emotional," "hysterical," "loose cannons" or "trouble-makers." At a recent state cabinet meeting, a woman minister was described by colleagues as going "right over the edge," yet she had merely defended her portfolio responsibility from being totally undermined by economic rationalists. A comparable defence by many of her male colleagues is normally recognised as a sign of strength and earns the respect of colleagues. (Reynolds, 1995, p. 120)

There was a strong view among women from both parties that when (and all were very positive that this time *would* come) there are significantly more women in Parliament, the way in which business is conducted will be different. Most women believe that women and men have different working styles and that a more women-friendly approach to the political process would actually benefit both women and men.

> The House of Commons is an aggressive, Hooray Henry silly place a lot of the time. It's not like that all the time but it's got a lot of silly characteristics and they won't completely disappear because it's a confrontational set-up. Women are just as capable of being passionate and angry about the things they believe in. I think that men in the House of Commons are grown up versions of boys who throw bits of hamburger at each other, it's about male bonding behaviour, the way that men go on when they're all together alone. There will still be conflict and passion but I think the agenda will broaden. Some of the sniggering when you say "cervical cancer" will go. (Clare Short, Labour, UK)

> I think we would bring a better balance into decision-making and the attitude of the House generally. Men and women are equal but we're not the same. We go about things in a different way. I'm the only woman chairman [sic] of a select committee and I conduct my committee meetings in a totally different way than my male colleagues. (Marion Roe MP, Cons, UK)

> I remember when the Finance Minister stood up and said that he couldn't change the tax laws which discriminated against women because we couldn't afford it. Well, within six months that had all changed because there was such an outcry amongst us women. (Sheila Camerer, New National Party, South Africa)

While many women recognize that some of the traditional institutions of Parliamentary politics would take a long time to whither away, the more consensual style of managing and chairing debates and committees will bring about profound changes to the way in which decisions are made. In predominantly two-party Parliamentary systems, the adversarial slant to politics is unavoidable, but most real work is done outside the Chamber, and it is in committees where more women are making a significant difference in the way in which the business of politics is done. In Kirkpatrick's (1974) study of American State Parliamentarians, she found that, contrary to the traditional view of politicians towards their profession as akin to a gladiatorial contest, with a strong emphasis on winners and losers, women legislators tended to have a much more task-based approach to their work and to the practice of politics more generally. She argues that the more common sporting or war analogies were almost entirely absent in women's versions of their lives as legislators and their hopes for what they could achieve. "There is almost nothing of the 'game' model of politics with its teams, alliances, strategies, victories and losses" (Kirkpatrick, 1974, p. 143). Instead, women stressed the problem-solving nature of politics and articulated a common goal of working for progress, fundamentally espousing a view of government which is avowedly public spirited and pledged to pursue the common good. "Government for most, is one instrument among others through which good citizen can seek to improve the quality of their life" (Kirkpatrick, 1974, p. 144). Similarly, the former prime minister of the Netherlands Antilles, Maria Liberia-Peters, points to a desire for consensus as a specific attribute that some women politicians bring to the practice of politics:

> I would not like to generalize, right, but leadership styles, the difference in leadership styles between women and men is . . . that as a woman I would prefer the consensus type of leadership. Why? Because, again . . . it is so that you get the best results when you convince the other partner, why we have to meet each other . . . and you also stimulate them to be more creative, also, in adding their little grain . . . of sand to the finding of the solution. (cited in Liswood, 1995, pp. 80-81)

WOMEN IN A MAN'S MAD WORLD

While all the women interviewed for this study have made a conscious decision to pursue a career in elite politics with at least some knowledge of what that would entail, many were nonetheless unprepared for the culture shock which awaited them when they first entered Parliament. For those who have been there for more than one term, many are still frustrated with the way in which some of their male colleagues continue to disrespect them, with the continuing battles to get additional facilities, with the uphill challenges they face when pointing out the myriad ways in which life in Parliament is physically difficult for women—but does not need to be. Women are more than "happy" to be targeted as individual members of an opposing side, as fair game in the war of attrition which is regularly carried out on the floors of debating chambers around the world, but they object to the use of their sex as the primary weapon of assault.

The issue of unwritten dress codes was something which many women commented on, both in terms of normative expectations and policies (only men are politicians), censure over particular forms of women's dress and challenges to the "rules." There was a strong sense that women could rarely get it right, damned for being too colorful (politics as frivolous fashion statement), damned for being too conservative (you all wear the same uniform, how are you different?), and damned if they wore the same outfit twice in one week.

> Women can't win: if they dress in sober attire, they're criticized for being boring, if they're dressed in something loud, then they're calling attention to themselves and their sexuality—we have to liberate the men before we can liberate ourselves. (Lyn Allison, Labor, Australia)

> There's a lot of things that have to be adapted. Some are very simple, like the first invitation from the Prime Minister had "dress" on it—cocktail dress. And my husband said he's never worn a cocktail dress in his life! (Elizabeth Grace, Liberal, Australia)

Women new to Parliament talked about the pressure to conform and found themselves consciously making themselves over in order to better fit in, although as time has worn on and they have found their feet, they have felt emboldened to revert back to their more "natural" state:

> I started wearing more conservative clothes and I started not dying my hair, which I've done for years . . . fortunately that phase has passed. Once I dealt with that pressure of conforming and said, "hang on, I'm surviving, I'm still politically relevant within my own party and community." . . . and I haven't compromised myself too far, it's OK to be myself. (Kate Lundy, Labor, Australia)

> Basically, the testosterone level is palpable and it required a change in me. . . . I am not an aggressive person, but it required a change in demeanour . . . it required a much more aggressive approach which you learn to live with [but] I don't think many women are particularly comfortable with it. (Sue Mackay, Labor, Australia)

The sartorial presentation of self is important, and this was recognized instantly, not only as a way of signaling obeisance (conformists) but also its opposite (radicals), and women have acknowledged that it was often much easier to make a statement in opposition, especially in a minority party, than in government. But women are challenging the rules by, for example, expanding the range of acceptable modes of dress, often by simply wearing trousers or earrings or high heels or short skirts and seeing the reaction. Talking up women's impact on democracy in terms of extending our understanding of who can be an elected politician or the characteristics of a serious Parliamentarian through their conscious clothing decisions might sound ridiculous, but it is significant. Jane Public likes to see her own sex reflected back to her from the Parliamentary benches: she has become accustomed to women in senior positions in other parts of her life, why not politics? For Joe Public, the changing picture might not be so attractive, but he, too, is benefiting from a more inclusive politics which speaks in the register of real people's lives.

> I don't think many Australians relate to middle-aged, middle-class men in suits who have lifestyles and experiences that most of us never dreamt of, so that is already a mismatch. (Natasha Stott Despoja, Australian Democrats)

While some women may well find the media's constant request for comments on the number of women's toilets in Parliamentary complexes irritating (see McDougall, 1998b), there are very real problems in the culture of elite politics which continues to perpetuate the myth that only men are and can be Parliamentarians. Notwithstanding the acknowledgement that many fathers do take their child-caring responsibilities seriously, it is mostly women who undertake the primary care of children, and many women, not just mothers, suggested that a day care centre would be a positive first move to providing a more welcoming environment for parent politicians:

> We could have a child care centre in this building. We could have a place where families could come in and be welcomed and could spend time together and our children could feel free. I walked out in the corridor yesterday and saw a baby crawling down the corridor. I don't know whose the toddler was, but I must say it gave the place a human feel for a moment. (Jeannie Ferris, Liberal, Australia)

While this is not a solution for everyone, especially for politicians whose homes can be thousands of miles away from the seat of government, childcare facilities could enable families to visit and allow politicians to spend time with their partners and children during the long periods when Parliament is sitting. And the point is that it is precisely the little things that make the difference. There are lavatories in the South African Parliament which still have a hand-written sign on them saying "Ladies," several years after the first democratic elections saw an exponential increase in the number of women Parliamentarians. Gertrude Fester (ANC, South Africa) suggests that the new Parliamentary buildings do have designated lavatories for women, but they are located at the furthest end of corridors and the more numerous men's lavatories are "five times the size and they need a quarter of the space." Such practices comprise small but crucial signifiers of the way in which women's presence in Parliamentary life is "accommodated." Val Viljoen (ANC, South Africa) points to the seemingly trite issue of seating in the Chamber, where the original design only envisaged men:

> I am not particularly short but if I sit so my back is supported, my feet don't quite touch the floor! A lot of us take books in to put our feet on and perhaps it is something we should campaign about, but you have to choose which issue to concentrate on.

Fiona Mactaggart (Labour, UK) makes a similar point about the stone floors in the House of Commons:

> It might seem trivial but since I've become an MP, I wear rubber-soled shoes all the time because this place makes your feet hurt instantly, but women are supposed to [look feminine and] wear heeled shoes with thin leather soles and I'm not bloody going to because they make my feet hurt too much.

Such things *are* important because they materially affect the way in which women (and many men) are enabled to do their job by working in (un)comfortable surroundings; they signal the considerable ideological work yet to be done which will enable these practical issues to get resolved because of their impact on efficiency, not as grudging accommodations to the whining of women Parliamentarians who should be grateful just to be there.

Women recognize that their sex often precludes them from joining in the kinds of activities that men feel comfortable doing, so that if not directly excluded from the "boys club," they opt out of it themselves. This argument is very much about not being able to "fit in" with the dominant norms of the (albeit informal) Parliamentary culture, and it carries with it an acceptance of the difficulty of trying to penetrate this male world rather than strategising how to make that world more inclusive:

> If you're not a boy, and you don't like to drink beer or scotch, and are not particularly interested in talking about the share market or the footie, then there are going to be times when you're not "in" because you're just not of the same culture. (Amanda Vanstone, Liberal, Australia)

Women also acknowledge the conscious and explicit efforts to marginalise their work by male colleagues who are often confident enough in their own security and belief in a shared (misogynistic) view to make overt their prejudices towards women Members. "I'm very familiar with that facial expression which says, 'a woman speaking, I don't need to listen'" (Kathy Sullivan, Liberal, Australia). This happens both within and between parties, where women are often seen as soft targets for particularly crass forms of barracking. However, women are mostly (but not always) reluctant to retaliate in similar terms, unwilling to resort to personal attack and invective but rather choose to keep focused on the policy issue at hand.

> There's very much this tribal mentality among the men, to the point where when I was fortunate enough to become chairman [sic] of a committee at one stage—quite by accident as the men had tried to fix the numbers—one of the men leapt to his feet and said, "Oh god, we've ended up with a blasted woman." (De-Anne Kelly, National Party, Australia)

> As I've got under the Government's skin, they've increased their attacks on me and they can get very nasty. They call me a witch, they yell at me, you know, "where's your broomstick?," the language is horrific. (Jenny Macklin, Labor, Australia)

> Whatever I talked about, I was a woman you know, and they'd twist it. It wasn't an opinion that would count. It's the way they treat the women in their lives, you know, like the tea lady. (Kathy Sullivan, Liberal, Australia)

> Sometimes the men on committees think they have done you a huge favour just by letting you be there . . . and they also think that if they flirt with you, they've done you a big favour, a compliment, and sometimes if you open your mouth and speak they attack you, all at once. (Dee Margetts, Green Party, Australia)

Margaret Reynolds (Labor, Australia) describes vividly the frustration of trying to retain one's own sense of propriety in discussions with male colleagues in an avowedly aggressive debating context, and she notes her realization that, whatever tactic she used, she could still be undermined. For her, neither aggression nor hysteria came naturally, so that her only means of survival was to be true to herself and hope, often fruitlessly, that quiet reason would prevail:

> I used to come into my office after some fairly horrendous Cabinet sessions and say to my staff, "do you think it would help if I thumped the table, if I lost my temper, screamed fucking this and fucking that to whoever cared to listen?" and they'd say, "no

Margaret, it wouldn't work for you, just keep your information, your knowledge of the subject and just keep going calmly." But there were times when I used to think, you know, this is ridiculous, I'm one of the few reasonable people at the table, and I still lose. But I knew that if I burst into tears or kicked or screamed and shouted, I'd still lose, so I had no option but to play it straight.

Women, by their sex alone, are already outside the dominant (male) norms of Parliament, and they believe that they are often judged against a male paradigm of how a Parliamentarian *should* behave and conduct himself, and they don't match up and are thus open to criticism. "I think that the way men perceive us is still as an aberration" (Kate Lundy, Labor, Australia). Often, the crucial "test" is how one performs in the theatre of Parliament, which is the Chamber: "Basically, the formula is about your aggressive behaviour in the House" (Judi Moylan, Liberal, Australia). Women simply don't measure up against that marker as far as their male colleagues are concerned. For younger women, they are doubly marginalised by their gender and their youth. The woman currently credited with being the youngest ever Australian senator, Natasha Stott Despoja (Australian Democrats) has a fund of stories and anecdotes of the routinised putdowns she has experienced from men in the few years she has been in Parliament:

Every day, there's some comment, like "your skirt is too short" or "isn't it past your bedtime?" or "be more polite to your elders," or people treat me like their daughter—well intentioned but patronising or just constant references to age, "you are too young," "you'll grow out of it," "what would you know, you haven't lived in the real world" and they add up to a point where it wears you down, it demeans you, it is *designed* to irritate you but it gets to you.

I'm finding being a young woman much more of an issue than being a woman per se. It identifies itself in the dismissive attitudes of older colleagues who believe it is inconceivable that I have sufficient experience to have a view. (Marise Payne, Liberal, Australia)

Melanie Voerwoerd (ANC, South Africa) says that women with even a small bit of power are constantly denigrated by male colleagues by the articulation of a lewd discourse of, say, about how they have slept their way to the top. This seems to be a defense mechanism to rationalize why they themselves haven't managed to achieve quite the same success. It is clearly unthinkable that women could attain positions of authority merely on their ability to do the job. By reducing women to their base sexuality, their threat is diminished and tamed:

Every woman that I know who is quite powerful in Parliament is always rumored by all my male colleagues to be having at least three or four affairs at the same time. How they would be getting time to do that is quite extraordinary and for the women I know, it is absolute bullshit. Where there are strong women in opposition, they say either that she needs some sex or alternatively that she is sleeping with all her male colleagues. I have had stories about me that have reached my ears, up to a point where it was quite laughable. I think there is something . . . about that moment when women become strong, almost a threat, not even as a conscious thing, that men bring women back to being sexual beings. (Val Viljoen, ANC, South Africa)

Although the great majority of women I interviewed for this study had stories to tell about their own (negative) experiences of male colleagues, there were a small handful of women who completely rejected any suggestion that they had been treated badly by male colleagues, claiming that they had been treated merely differently. Those women tended to be unable to conceptualize the validity or possibility of women's experiences which were different from their own, in some cases suggesting that claims of gender discrimination were both party-specific and exaggerated. The argument here seems to be that women come into politics as a conscious decision, and once there, they should not complain about unfair treatment: it's a hard world and they had better toughen up:

It's not [discrimination] in our own party, but it looks like it is the case in the ANC because they are the people who make all this noise about it . . . I mean they really go to ridiculous lengths about it . . . after all, God did make us male and female and one must know how to handle it . . . because you cannot run away from your biological destiny. (Tersia King, New National Party, South Africa)

Interestingly, while women are frustrated with the way in which they have had to battle to achieve even small gains for themselves in their working environment, there remain quirky anomalies about facilities. For example, unlike in Australia and Britain, the South African Parliament does have a well-used crèche and men will take their children into committees with them quite unselfconsciously.

I have been amazed at the responsibility that a lot of the men here take for their children. You have a lot with partners who are either here or in the provincial legislature. It is not unusual for us to have an ANC study group and for one of the male MPs to arrive with a baby or child on his knee and have the child crayoning or whatever, while the meeting is in progress. (Val Viljoen, ANC, South Africa)

On the other hand, the Australian and British Parliaments have facilities such as gyms which are open to all, whereas when a new gym was recently built within the South African Parliamentary complex, the only entrance was through the men's urinals.[2] While it is tempting to compare the progress of different Parliaments to each other in terms of embracing women, the different cultural contexts which exist in different places mean that it is always difficult, if not inappropriate, to try to give meaning to those differences. The point is that in all three study sites, women continue to campaign to improve both their own lot as Parliamentarians and the lot of women more generally, with varying degrees of success. What matters, arguably, is that they see such campaigns as worthwhile for themselves and for the women who come after them.

While no one expects that the job of a politician should be easy, the environment in which Parliamentarians work is not conducive to the development of balanced women and men who are able to combine work with some kind of personal life, and the impact can be devastating. Melanie Voerwoerd (ANC, South Africa) reports that, in the first year of the first democratically elected Parliament in the country, there were approximately 30 divorces, "all of them women MPs. It was extraordinary." And women in politics are experiencing the same kinds of backlash as women are facing in society more generally. While high-profile women such as Harriet Harman (Labour, UK) are trying to force their own parties to acknowledge that ordinary women want more women to represent them in Parliament, there appears to be the opposing view that women have already had more than their fair share of accommodations to their unreasonable demands:

> Many people simply don't see the importance of the debate [on women's unequal position], and its categorised as, "oh, there they go, those Beijingers" and "what do you want now? You've already got the Gender Commission, the Office of the Status of Women, the Human Rights Commission, what more do you want?" (Suzanne Vos, IFP, South Africa)

In other words, "Don't push your luck because we might withdraw the few concessions we have already made." Even in the South African Parliament, where nearly thirty per cent of all Parliamentarians are women, "the leadership is 99 per cent male" (Suzanne Vos, IFP, South Africa).

The ways in which women cope with the awkward and often difficult aspects of Parliamentary life are many and various. Some

---

[2]A second entrance has since been built to enable women to access the facilities by an alternative route.

women who are already assertive appear simply to exaggerate those so-called masculine traits, so that they function (and are often perceived) as honorary men. This was especially true of a politician such as Margaret Thatcher, but other women, such as Golda Meir were also described as pseudo-men, the latter most famously termed as the only man in the cabinet at the time of her Premiership (Yishai, 1997). While Margaret Thatcher was one of the most high-profile women politicians of the 1980s, analyses which map her ascent and time in office rarely avoid an allusion to her gender, as in the journalist Hugo Young's assessment of the task she had before her when she took over as Prime Minister in 1979. "She possessed no trace of the effortless superiority of the Balliol men, Macmillan and Heath, who went before her. For her, each step up the ladder was a struggle against the odds posed by her gender and her lack of fraternity with her male colleagues" (cited in Critchley, 1994, p. 167). But what is implicit in Young's positive endorsement of "Balliol" is more than simply an attention to gender, it is also about class and Thatcher's provenance as a grocer's daughter was variously highlighted and effaced, dependent on the circumstances and the point she (and others) wished to make.

For many women, the support of other women colleagues, either semi-formally through friendships and mentoring programmes or formally through mechanisms such as the women's caucus (usually Labor-oriented networks), has been invaluable in keeping them grounded and able to survive, especially in their first months, in the male-ordered world of Parliamentary politics. Outside Labour networks, cross-party or other kinds of party-oriented women's networks have no tradition of success, largely because Liberal and Conservative Members are often few in number and rarely believe that their shared gender is much of a reason to work with other women unless they have similar political ideas and want to fight a common cause:

> We have a women's caucus and we have to assert ourselves to retain the legitimacy of the caucus here . . . but we're tight with each other and we're all good friends . . . and those networks are as close and solid as ever. And there's a strong personal rapport amongst us as well. (Kate Lundy, Labor, Australia)

But as Gertrude Fester (ANC, South Africa) points out, it is sometimes hard to prioritize gender issues when so many other things are equally important, especially in the South African context, which continues to overcome its bloodied history of apartheid. In such circumstances, talking about gender in the context of Parliamentary processes becomes almost an indulgence when women have such heavy workloads anyway:

> Because of the demands of one's portfolio committees, the [ANC]
> women's caucus has met only once in seven months. And even then,
> it was in the tail-end of the [mainstream] ANC caucus, which meant
> that it was over lunchtime and we didn't have much time because
> we sit again at 2 pm, so we really had, shall I say minimal time—not
> quality time at all—people were rushing, people going in and out,
> and the issue we were addressing was a very important issue in
> terms of strategy—in terms of elections—and we actually couldn't
> really address it. To be very honest with you I'm trying to sort it out
> myself. I'm trying to understand whether it's a time problem or
> whether it's that people are just gender-blind.

But, with the ANC's commitment to its one-third quota rule for
women throughout its structure, including candidates, many women
coming into Parliament with little formal political experience have had a
hard time coping with their new roles and responsibilities, and it is precisely such structures as the women's caucus which could offer support
to those women. However, the follow-through to supporting
Parliamentary women in South Africa's new democratic society is taking
time to become established, not always helped by some women's suggestion that a women's caucus has as its primary intent the denigration
of men. Tersia King (New National Party, South Africa) argues that,
although she did go to the women's caucus[3] when it was first set up, she
didn't return a second time as she felt that she didn't want, "to gang up
against the men, I think that's wrong, one must become part of the system and although it is difficult for women, I think that I have made it
easier for those who've come after me." While King may be right in that
women in nontraditional domains do become role models for others, it
is arguable whether her desire to become "one of the boys" and "part of
the system" is, in fact, a good model to emulate since it stresses incorporation into the status quo rather than challenging the basic tenets of that
existing system to make it, if not more women-friendly, then at least
more human.

The lack of time given to discussing gender issues by
Parliamentarians also spills over into the after-hours culture, where it is
easy to privilege domestic demands over those which seem to have a
more selfish aspect but which are important for forming relationships
and developing support networks. It does not help that most meeting
places within Parliamentary complexes which are open in the evenings
are smoke-filled bars which many women find offensive. But the after-
hours socialization is important, but hard to justify for women who have
families or other kinds of responsibility:

---

[3]The Joint Standing Committee for Improving the Quality of Life and Status of
Women.

I think the one weakness of women is the camaraderie that we don't have amongst ourselves. There are several pubs around Parliament here, and I normally leave at 6 or 7 o'clock, but some nights I go down to the pub and most of the time I am the only woman there and you listen to the conversations that some of the men have, they talk about what happened today, either jokingly or seriously, sharing of ideas. . . . I don't think they realize that they are empowering one another just by discussing things. You don't see that happening with women. (Patricia de Lille, PAC, South Africa)

Val Viljoen (ANC, South Africa) rehearses a familiar argument in her insistence that it is important that women Parliamentarians meet regularly to review progress in pursuing a women-friendly agenda both within Parliament but also more widely, to support women in society, but the enemy of such good intentions is time. Speaking specifically on the ANC women's caucus, she says:

I have been to the odd meeting to keep in touch, but it is not nearly as effective as it should be. It is our fault. It is always a time issue, trying to find the time to have a meeting which suits people. There are a few strong women in the caucus and they do a marvelous job, but we don't really support it as much as we should. Everyone agrees with it and we are all thoroughly behind it but we just don't put this into action.

Perhaps part of the problem of women's caucuses is how they are viewed by men, who tend to be suspicious of them; they fear what might be taking place amongst these women whose shared gender excludes their male colleagues from their cozy embrace. In the case of South Africa, the fact that the ANC women's caucus is tagged on to the end of the mainstream caucus meeting suggests something more deliberate than simple oversight:

Well, I can say that it's something that maybe was not thoroughly thought about, you know, not to have a slot for the women's caucus and maybe like many other issues, it's like, "ach, you know, what are they talking about? They're only gossiping or they just want to put us men down." (Koko Mokgolong, ANC, South Africa)

For many South African women, although gender is firmly on the agenda and the Gender Commission regularly carries out gender audits of the budget and other legislation, much of the policy rhetoric remains precisely that, with severe problems in actual implementation being recognized by almost everyone. It is not that there is a lack of will to make change happen, but rather that, having agreed that this or that legislation is discriminatory, or having drafted new legislation which has passed through to law, the actual implementation of the law in communities is very difficult. Sometimes women feel that they continue to beat out the same rhythm but still no one dances:

> You often wonder the extent to which you become boring to yourself, let alone to anybody else, just by repeating the same things again and again. . . . In politics, we are not just dealing with policy, we are dealing with policy that has to be implemented and it is not that it can't be implemented, but the people who have to implement it are in very many respects totally unreconstructed. So you could put forward legislation here, you know that it is eminently feasible and realistic, but to get something done about it means that the people who are doing it have to understand those things as well. (Janet Love, ANC, South Africa)

What is at issue here is the dissonance between making and implementing policy, between government or parties deciding on how things should be done but then not managing to win the hearts and minds of people on the ground, be it in parties or in local government, who can easily subvert such policy decisions by finding any number of ways to stall progress.

GENDER IMPACT ASSESSMENT: STYLE AND SUBSTANCE

Despite some of the issues and problems described above, however, most women are positive about the way in which their presence, in increasing numbers, is materially changing the political environment and atmosphere in which they work, challenging the orthodoxies which took for granted that only men could be Parliamentarians. Tersia King (New National Party, South Africa) was a member of the South African government in its predemocratic mode and remembers being one of the first women to take up her seat in government and the unpreparedness of the political structure for the inclusion of women Parliamentarians. For her, challenging the system just by her presence signaled a sea-change in attitudes, but she nonetheless played by men's rules to become "accepted," a strategy which was probably safest in the circumstances at the time:

> I remember the first time we arrived here, we were taken around the building and this Whip of ours said, when we got to the snake pit, of

course we didn't know what it was because the doors were closed—
he said "this is the snake pit. It's members only. We will invite the
ladies from time to time" and I said "now what ladies are you talking about?" and he said "well er er . . . " and then he realized he'd
made a mistake, so he said "well, the new lady members" and I said
"well, what is this place?" and someone said "it's the bar, the members bar." I said "well as members aren't we allowed to go in on our
own, do we have to be invited?" and of course he didn't know how
to handle this at all so he said "no, of course you can go." So I actually tried it. I gathered together all of my courage and walked through
those doors and I didn't know what was going to happen on the
inside, I didn't even know what it looked like on the inside, and got
a fantastic welcome from the men . . . because I dared to do that.

We had a seminar for new senators and I asked about dress codes—
there isn't a written code—and I asked him [the deputy clerk of the
senate] about trousers and he said, "oh no," quoting an example of a
female senator who'd been made to feel very uncomfortable. So I
made myself a pant suit and I thought I would wear it on the second
week. So I did. And some other female senators noticed and they
walked across to see, and not a word was spoken, so we started a
revolution and codes have changed. (Dee Margetts, Green Party,
Australia)

Often, it has been the small triumphs which have made most
difference, in the same way that it is often the small irritations that cause
the most damage because of the slow accretion of so many tiny but
debilitating discriminations and discourtesies:

The moment we came into government, smoking just stopped.
Apparently before you smoked in committee meetings, everywhere
was smoking. It didn't occur to us that you would be able to smoke
in committees, so we just threw the ash trays out and there was
never anything written down. It was almost overnight that it became
accepted that you didn't smoke in committee meetings. That was
really the women in the committees that pushed that out. It wasn't a
decision, it was almost a mutual consensus. (Val Viljoen, ANC,
South Africa)

Elsewhere, it has been women's campaigning, together with some male
colleagues, which have resulted in, for example, reductions in the number of late-night sittings. There are clear historical precedents for a culture which thought it "normal" to be taking votes on key policy areas at
midnight. When politicians were always men who had women to "service" them in a variety of ways, who would spend their afternoons
drinking in bars and have dinner in-house, there was little hardship in

spending a few hours after port in the Chamber, secure in the knowledge that any family they had would be looked after by their wife and other domestic staff. For contemporary women and some men who want to spend time with their families, the life of a politician is difficult and new rules on late-night sittings begin to make it possible to have a "normal" life for part of the week, at least, and to work and meet with constituents whose interests they are supposed to be representing in Parliament.

It is interesting to note that the newly formed (1999) Scottish Parliament has sitting hours which reflect a more "normal" professional schedule which enables women and men with family commitments to be able to enjoy a private life which is not endlessly compromised by late night sittings and long-distance travel. While such "family friendly" policies are often seen as responses to women's demands to "have it all," the benefits to *men* with families are often obscured in the rush to cite women as needing special dispensations. Patricia de Lille (PAC, South Africa) reports that changing the sitting times to enable women (and men) to have a more normal family life was a priority on first arriving in Parliament, and she argues that, although men were hostile to the suggestion at first, they soon saw the advantages to their own lives. The principal reasons for resistance can be seen in terms of "punishing" women for their audacity to seek Parliamentary office—when they should really stay at home and look after children—and that once there, they had to adapt to the existing structure rather than to change that structure to make it more welcoming to *all* members with families. Having a strong voice in the form of the Speaker of the House was also significant in women's securing change:

> We had to look at the time of the sittings of Parliament so that it enabled women to see to their children. Before we used to meet late at night, so we changed that although the men complained and said you can't have it both ways. But I think they also enjoyed the earlier times because it gave them more time to go and sit in the bar and the pubs! And we were fortunate to have a Speaker who is a very outspoken women, Frene Ginwala, who has also contributed a lot to change all of this. (Patricia de Lille, PAC, South Africa)

> Having more sensible hours is good because it means we get a reasonable night's sleep. We could make it easier. We could have a ladies' members room where you could sit instead of sitting in a smokey room if you don't smoke; we could have a few more loos. When I came here there were hardly any because it was built for men. I think it's the small things which would make a difference. (Elizabeth Peacock MP, Conservative, UK)

More women also make male politicians more circumspect when they get up to speak on policies which affect women's lives. Lynne Jones points out that the existence of a significant number of women MPs has already meant that men "feel less able to stand up and pontificate about issues which affect women when there are a load of women sitting on the benches" (Lynne Jones, Labour, UK).

> I feel that when you have a combination of men and women as you have here, it creates a very different dynamic, very lively, no longer the hallowed tombs where the men in suits walk around . . . it is more in touch with life . . . (Gill Marcus, ANC, South Africa)

For many women, the driving force in their ambitions to get involved in elite politics has been their disgust with the way in which women's lives are circumscribed as much by their elected (male) representatives as they are by other forms of male dominance. A desire to be on the inside making change rather than on the outside being ignored has pushed many women to seek election to Parliament. Cheryl Kernot (Labor, Australia) recalls looking down on a debate in the Chamber as one of many events which consolidated her commitment to stand:

> I looked down on an abortion debate and men were deciding my reproductive fate in Queensland and I was just astonished and appalled at how these things could happen—this was in the seventies—that I just never forgot . . . I don't like the agenda that's set and I'm sick and tired of the way women are always responding to the agenda and we're not in there to argue about what should be on the agenda and that really keeps driving me because I think it's so wrong.

> Because of the higher proportion of women in the Parliamentary Labour Party already, the culture has changed. A few years ago it would have been quite impossible to get perhaps 30 members of the PLP to table questions on women's issues, childcare and so on and that has changed completely. There is a far greater acceptance, so just having those numbers actually does make a difference. (Judith Church, Labour, UK)

The shifts which women have brought about have not just been about encouraging more awareness about women and gender more generally, but they are also about giving "permission" to men to allow them to be less macho and possibly to be more themselves. Contributing to a debate in the Chamber on fertility clinics, Fiona Mactaggart (Labour, UK) spoke about her own experiences of undergoing treatment. A short while after, a male Conservative colleague approached her and said that he thought she'd been brave in exposing herself in that way. Mactaggart says, in her self-effacing way, that she wasn't really brave but perhaps she had given *him* the courage to tackle something risky for himself. It is such an irony that women spend time reflecting on how they might have helped their male colleagues, when those same colleagues are probably *not* thinking about how they might make their practice more gender-inclusive.

Yet, the impact of women in Parliament has been much more than simply changing internal systems, important though these are, nor simply about making their male colleagues more conscious, if not yet influencing their attitudes towards gender equality. Crucially, their presence is materially affecting the lives of real women as they challenge policy and put forward the questions which have never before been asked. Sheila Camerer (New National Party, South Africa) recalls a specific incident where government was forced to rescind an earlier decision because of the force of the women's voices which rose against it. Part of that show of strength has been underpinned and nurtured by the Joint Standing Committee on Improving the Quality of Life and Status of Women, where women from every political party fought for the establishment of that committee for three years, and are still fighting to get it more formally recognized and supported:

> One incident was when the Finance Minister, three months into a new government, stood up in Parliament and he was one our side at that point in the government of national unity. He tried to say that he couldn't change the tax laws which discriminated against married women because we couldn't afford it! Well, within three months this had been changed because there was an outcry. I actually tackled him on it and six months later the law was changed. So that kind of thing doesn't wash anymore. It is always a struggle to get these things done but there has been great improvement. The whole framework has changed.

When Fiona Mactaggart (Labour, UK) was compiling a report to document the changes which British women MPs had wrought in their first 1000 days in Parliament (the 1997-2001 term), she recalls asking a colleague, who was a member of the defense select committee, what contribution she felt she'd made to effecting change. The colleague in question left the room abruptly, and when she returned she looked relieved. When Mactaggart asked what had happened, her colleague said that she thought that some positive things *had* come out of women's involvement, but she had no knowledge of the former regime, so she had checked things out with the Clerk. "So I went and talked to him and I asked him if it was different now, and he said, god, of *course* it's different. This used to be the committee for boys with toys and now it focuses on service families' lives and personnel issues and so on—it's completely transformed."

> I think women just bring the added perspective into politics, you know, what it actually means for women's lives, in fact, it just normalizes the perspective, I should say because everything is seen from a man's perspective, you know, writing a book and thanks to the wife who did the typing. (Gertrude Fester, ANC, South Africa)

Where women have been promoted into Ministerial positions, particularly in South Africa (but also elsewhere) where many women are members of the ruling party, their different perspectives and experiences are materially affecting the lives of women in ways which may have happened anyway, in the dismantling of discriminatory legislation, but where the involvement of women in senior positions has effected a more speedy progress of key policy in the areas of gender discrimination and other unfair practices against women and children. For many, the fact that women have tended to have backgrounds in community development or otherwise worked in communities as teachers, doctors, and other community-based environments rather than politics before they come to Parliament, gives them unique insights into how legislation affects real communities. Indeed, some women have made a deliberate decision to take on "tough" portfolios in order to have a voice in an otherwise male-ordered domain:

> In Welfare, you have a young minister who is a women, and very aware of those aspects of legislation. Certainly, in that context, women have made the whole thing more humane, more family orientated, and because the majority of them have been in communities, not sat somewhere going from councilor to MP, they have been part of the community and have lived the reality of South Africa. This is where their kind of inputs come from. (Inka Mars, IFP, South Africa)

> A lot of the things that the Deputy Minister for Justice—a woman—has been doing is access of women to courts, maintenance issues, things that directly affect women in a much stronger way, rape and how it is dealt with in the courts. Those are issues precisely because she is a very conscious woman, that you find her able to go and support and act in relation to women's rights. (Gill Marcus, ANC, South Africa)

Women, then, are making a difference in shifting the policy agenda but, as we have seen from some of the actions (and, more importantly, nonactions) of women Parliamentarians, gender alone will not bring about change in policy—changes which will actually have a material impact on the lives of women and families. Perhaps gender isn't even part of the equation and what is required are more politicians who genuinely believe in redressing old iniquities. That such people are *likely* to be women seems common sense, but that is not necessarily so. For many of the Labor women I interviewed who continue to support feminist ideals, their goal (as with Emily's List) is not simply to get more Labor women elected, but to get women elected who actually believe in the feminist principles of inclusivity and women- and family-friendly polices. For many women voters, their disappointment in the lack of women-centered policies to emerge from governments with significant numbers of women politicians, is palpable:

> There were a lot of disappointed people who saw a lot of the coalition women completely disregard women's issues, although they had got themselves elected on that ticket. Net more women in Parliament doesn't mean net better deal for women. And it's really tough to say that . . . but we want more progressive women in Parliament and we want more progressive policies for women, *more* than we want more women. (Kate Lundy, Labor, Australia)

4

Framed: Women, Politics, and News Discourse

Of course I have a view about what the media think women politicians are like, what they ought to be like. If you do something different, you're a problem, but then if you fit in with the stereotypes you're a problem. I think that generally the media have a problem dealing with women. They either treat us like men or as lightweight. They have a long way to go before they treat us as people with views who happen to be female and are happy being female. (Hilary Armstrong, Labour, UK)

INTRODUCTION

The mass media are often described, especially by their own members, as constituting a "fourth estate," an independent and impartial public sphere through which the polity gain insight and information about local, national, and international affairs and where, through the diligent ministrations of the corps of journalists, the government of the day (and any other appropriate target) is held to account. Clearly, such scrupulous accountability requires complete independence from the "targets" of the media's interest, especially from government, as John Thadeus Delane, editor of *The Times* (1841-1877), argued more than 150 years ago:

> To perform its duties with entire independence and consequently
> with the utmost public advantage, the press can enter into no close
> or binding allegiance with the statesmen of the day, nor can it sur-
> render its permanent interests to the convenience or ephemeral
> power of any government. (cited in Baistow, 1985, p. i)

But the media's rhetoric in this regard is seen increasingly as more aspi-
rational than real. The alleged independence of much of the media has
been questioned for quite some time now (see, for example, Tunstall,
1977; Baistow, 1985; Jones, 1996; Franklin, 1997; Negrine, 1998) and it is
important to acknowledge that, despite the famously independent
nature of the media which the industry claims for itself, few people really believe the homily. On the contrary, I would argue that the relationship between politics and the media is a mutually dependent one, both
politically and economically, each tied to the umbilicus of the other to
keep its lifeblood of credibility/visibility (politicians) and stories/sales
(news industries) pumping. The media, and television in particular, is
increasingly the *real* public space in which politics occurs and through
which citizens comprehend the political process (Lewis, 1991; Franklin,
1997; Wheeler, 1997; Negrine, 1998).

The form of the relationship between politics and the media has
changed significantly over the past few decades as the deference with
which politicians have traditionally been treated has gradually given
way to a much more critical engagement. In Britain and elsewhere, satir-
ical political comedies such as *Yes Minister* have been humorous but
sharp in their analyses of politicians, their lifestyles, and their values
(Watts, 1997), and this kind of challenging pose to politicians' authority
is carried over into serious political reportage. Thus, many political journalists now assume an interrogatory stance towards political actors, acting as interlocutor for "the people" in their attempt to hold politicians to
public account. Arguably, it was the advent of television which first signaled a change in the way in which politics began to be comprehended
by polities, not least because the small screen offered publics the opportunity to assess the merits of political candidates almost in real-time, and
suddenly "looks" mattered. The bringing in of cameras into parliaments
was the second significant shift in communicating politics and,
arguably, has contributed to growing public cynicism in all those countries where cameras report the debates in Chamber, making manifest the
"bear-pit" style of political discourse and the rows of mostly empty
seats. The fact that most publics are only given a slice of parliamentary
life, which usually comprises highlights from Prime Minister's
Questions, which is by far the most gladiatorial and combative aspect of
modern government/opposition interchanges, gives them/us a rather
distorted view of the practice of politics:

The problem with the electronic media is, you know, it's only 10 seconds which is of course, going to come out of Question Time, because it's the only colour and movement of the day. The rest is the "normal" process of making laws, committees and there are a lot of positive things that go on but you wouldn't put it on the telly at night because it's as boring as anything. (Jenny Macklin, Labor, Australia)

Commenting on the televised debates between Stevenson and Eisenhower, Jamieson (1996) argues that, "for the first time, baldness became an issue of concern in a presidential campaign," since the angled shots of the two contenders reading their speeches meant that their balding pates were in prime view (cited in Watts, 1997, p. 10). The harsh lens of television's cruel honesty makes second-raters of nearly all of us and some of our past presidents, prime ministers, and assorted politicians may well have missed their place in history if they had had to compete for power in the glare of television's lights (Rees, 1992).

Analyses which aim to identify the various mechanisms with which the media cover particular groups, events, or activities are usually structured around core theories of media effects, and this study is no different. The theses of interest to me in this work are those of agenda-setting and priming, both of which have important implications and outcomes for the portrayal of women and politics, and both of which are elaborated upon later. Briefly though, the media's agenda-setting tendencies operate to make visible some (and therefore *not* others) policies and issues which then, because of their repetitive coverage by the media, come to be *seen* as the crucial issues of the day by the public, regardless of their actual importance for government (see below for a fuller discussion and see also McCombs & Shaw, 1972; McCombs, 1981; Iyengar & Kinder, 1987):

They are extremely selectively informed. When I hear the press rabbiting against censorship, the press are the censors, the press and the media are the censors. They decide what we'll know, what bits of the news will be shown, what bits of the news will be hyped, what will be tucked away on page 10 and what will not be reported at all. (Ann Widdecombe, Cons, UK)

As both the politician and the journalist pay lip service to the fiction of their independence from each other, an excellent contemporary lesson in making explicit what we have, of course, always known about the discrete use of the media to achieve political ends was the spectacle of media mogul Silvio Berlusconi using his own channels to promote his candidacy as Italy's President and, more astonishingly, winning. In a strange playing out of Orwell's apocalyptic "Big Brother," Berlusconi was accused of hijacking Italy's political system through annexing the media to his own ends. Throughout his 8-month reign as Premier, Berlusconi never felt it necessary to relinquish his media empire, apparently oblivious to the conflict of interest that exercised so many of his critics in Italy and elsewhere (Wheeler, 1996). However, when Berlusconi again stood and again won, in 2001, he agreed that he would scale down his media interests. Interestingly and in total contrast, when Greg Dyke was preparing to take over as Director-General of the BBC in 1999, he quickly sold off his controlling interests in global media networks, astutely wrong-footing any potential detractors who would cry "conflict of interest".

As is by now obvious and almost trite to say, the media do not operate in an ideological vacuum and, instead, are influenced by news routines, opinion polls, elite media priorities, and, of course, a fundamentally commercial imperative, looking to a variety of sources for inspiration and stories. "Sources, particularly those in government, are the lifeblood of news" (Perloff, 1998, p. 223). And, of course, there is also the issue of elite media influences within the industry itself, so that often newspapers, especially in the United States, will look to the most prestigious among their number, for example, the *New York Times*, to cover a particular story before they themselves regard it as newsworthy, a phenomena which Perloff (1998) calls "intermedia agenda-setting" (p. 226). Kate Lundy (Labor, Australia) graphically describes the importance of opinion leaders working in the press gallery and the way in which networks of relationships operate to produce a shared "understanding" of the politics of the day, shaped only by the views of one or two of the "usual suspects" from both the media and the political sides:

> Structurally, the press gallery is under-resourced so what tends to happen is a story emerges and it's like bush fire, it flows through the gallery. So automatically, the opinion leaders in the gallery are sought and they determine the flow of the headlines or the gist of the story, not jut the story, but the direction the story's going in. It's highly competitive . . . you have five or so major papers and they all measure themselves against each other. So if you miss as story, you're in deep shit. So in that environment, you start to see the significance of the leading political editors in setting the flavour and flow . . . and their relationship with the respective Minister or Shadow Minister is absolutely key.

Cook (1998) suggests that the media are more than just agenda-setters; rather, they constitute an intrinsic part of the apparatus of government and are themselves political actors, albeit of a nonelected and "intermediary" variety. In this model, news is regarded as a "co-production" between news media and government because journalists operate as key participants in decision and policy making. News media as an institution operate as a central political force in government, both by way of the intimate relationship which exists between politics and media—each feeding off the other—but also because of the latter's influence on the electorate. The way in which the journalistic conventions for news work means that the reporting and representation of politics is less about producing stories and events which are true or even useful, and more about creating a plausible background against which information is provided within a complex system of relations among politicians, publics, and the press. The news thus comprises a regular negotiation between various stakeholders and actors who occupy differing places within the information "ecosystem" (Bennett, 1996a): politicians seeking to persuade, journalists seeking to challenge but also to market their product, and audiences who need to believe the news they receive is credible.

> As political actors and media have grown dependent on each other, politics has become not only a persuasive but a performance art in which considerations of style, presentation and marketing are equal to, if not greater in importance than, content and substance. (McNair, 1995, p. 189)

But, of course, both journalists and politicians are mutually involved in setting the policy agenda and importantly, neither can be effective on their own. And it is not only the effects that each of these institutions have on each other which continue to make the news media important actors on the political stage, but the power which is ascribed to its members by other stakeholders who constantly try and improve their media and public relations strategies and presence. While the public expect "official" politicians to attempt to persuade them/us, the firm hand of the journalist on the agenda-setting tiller is obscured by her or his insistence on neutrality and impartiality, an artifice which Tuchman (1972) has aptly described as objectivity as strategic ritual. However, as Cook (1998) explains,

> . . . by applying standards of objectivity, importance and interest and judging stories by how well they fit the "production values" of the news . . . the news media are political because the choices they end up making do not equally favor all political actors, processes and messages. Far from holding up a mirror to external political actions, the news media are directly involved in instigating them. (Cook, 1998, p. 165)

The dangers in the news media wielding such power are at least two-fold. The most obvious is the tension between traditional journalistic practices and routines which have very specific criteria for newsworthiness—for example, colour, drama, immediacy—and the complexity of social policies/politics which have pasts, presents and futures which are antithetical to the "News nów!" imperative. The second, equally important, problem is accountability, or rather the news media's lack thereof. While journalists may cite their audiences as those to whom they are principally accountable, as Cook (1998) points out, their own influence on the political agenda would suggest that their accountability needs to be both more transparent and more honest. The way in which the media's power over their audiences has been conceptualized has shifted considerably over the seventy or so years in which we have had a mass media to observe. Early theories of the 1930s-1950s posited a pervasive, propagandist, and sinister role for media on the public, while later theories in the 1960s and 1970s contended the precise opposite—that is, that the mass media have very "limited effects." More contemporary theories identify highly complex sets of relations between different media and different consumers, but in the end, they put up so many conditionals as to make any actual effect only measurable at the micro-analytical level of the individual reader, listener, or viewer. For example, "This study argues that agenda-setting studies . . . document that some kind of public learning does result from some media content under some kinds of conditions" (Shaw & Martin, 1992, p. 903).

And, as most studies suggest that television is a more influential medium than print media, often because voters use television more than newspapers as their primary source of political information, television comes to be seen as more significant in volume terms. Yet, Bartels and Wilson (1996) argue that, when analyzed, an elite newspaper such as the *New York Times* shows much stronger agenda-setting proclivities than television shows like *ABC News*. In their study of media coverage of a series of events—Bosnia, Medicare, NAFTA, and Whitewater—they suggest that although the media tended to broadly follow the government line in their coverage of those activities, the *New York Times* led political activities even more than it followed them, and this was especially the case with reports on NAFTA and Whitewater. The reluctance to go against the government line on issues of war (as opposed to "only" issues of national security) has been noted by other scholars investigating the intricacies of the press-politics relationship (see Glasgow University Media Group, 1985). Another principal finding from Bartels and Wilson's (1996) study was the accommodating reaction of local media to these national events, largely taking their lead from that of the political spokespeople and the national media. The tendency to cover national events in superficial detail while concentrating most of their coverage on activities of local and/or regional concern is a crucial part of what makes local newspapers attractive as an additional source of information, that is, as a supplement to the other mainstream sources of news information where the detail is of more personal and immediate interest (see Franklin & Murphy, 1998).

For my purposes, the media's agenda-setting proclivities function to privilege men and male concerns, and women politicians struggle hard to attract the oxygen of publicity for their policy stances—with two principal exceptions: when they are fielded specifically by their parties to act as spokespeople for particular issues, often those which are either allegedly woman- or family-oriented or where a female mouthpiece is used cynically to convey a faux integrity, and when women say or do something outrageous, especially briefing against their own side. The mechanism of priming is equally problematic for women since the theory proposes (with some highly persuasive research findings to corroborate it) that the media choose to focus on particular character traits and value positions which, allegedly, stand as the criteria against which political candidates should be measured and judged (Iyengar & Kinder, 1987, 1991). In the case of women politicians, the media's expectations (and therefore, the ways in which they direct their audiences) make them doubly damned; on the one hand, journalists focus on their sartorial style, the extent of their femininity (or lack of it) and their domestic arrangements, while on the other hand, they complain that they are not leadership material because they are too feminine. (See Chap. 6 for an elaborated discussion of the media's role in framing women candidates.) Walkosz and Kenski (1995) suggest that the media's coverage of the very first female member of Congress, Jeannette Rankin (Montana), provided the blueprint for coverage which continues today, where "the press focused on what she looked like and wore not what she stood for or accomplished" (p. 10).

THE CHANGING FACE OF POLITICAL NEWS

It is unarguable that the news media do not merely *report* the important events of the day, they decide what *are* the important events of the day—they construct the agenda, if not telling us what to think, then at least telling us what to think *about,* and the circulation of meaning is not ideologically neutral, but rather carries with it certain assumptions and certain perspectives which frame (in every sense of the word) the news agenda in particular ways. Women politicians themselves are very clear that the way in which politics is reported has changed over time, and certainly not for the better in their almost unanimous view. In general, women from all three case study sites were very negative about how the news media choose to portray politics, the political process, and politicians more generally, with a broad consensus among women from all political colours that the media has become depressingly tabloid, that the cult of the personality interviewer has taken over from straightforward reporting on what is actually said in Parliament, that political speeches and policy positions are constantly filtered through a journalistic lens which seems intent on "dumbing down" to the lowest common denominated soundbite, and that part of the reason for all the above is a general lowering of academic standards in journalism courses and a need to get reports filed as quickly (and therefore necessarily superficially) as possible:

> I think the danger [with the media] is twofold. The first is sheer triviality and the second is hype. It is very hard to get going a sensible long-term debate about anything. Unless you can get a good headline, it is very difficult to get a debate going. The second kind of triviality is that I think interviewers insult listeners' and viewers' concentration. I think they are quite capable of concentrating on a three-minute response whereas in fact what you get is that the interviewer will interrupt after the first half-minute. The media's idea of a good discussion is one Labour person there saying the Tories are rubbish, one Tory person there saying Labour is rubbish but not actually a discussion of the issue. But hype is even worse than triviality. I find my own comments are very frequently hyped into something which is utterly unrecognisable. (Ann Widdecombe, Cons, UK)

> The push of technology, speeding up, allowing expectations of speedier news, has been pushed back onto journalists to provide news in a much shorter timeframe and that has dreadful limitations. And when you couple that with a need for ratings and readership, it really means that the reporting of politics has become a ratings game and entertainment, rather than substance. (Amanda Vanstone, Liberal, Australia)

For most of the women I interviewed, there was considerable agreement on the "dumbing down" of the media's focus on politics, moving from a position which reported what was said by whom in Parliament towards a brief interpretation of Parliamentary politics and a much greater interest in the sex lives of politicians. The investigative journalism track seems almost completely preoccupied with the disclosure of scandal, always with the apparent "public interest" in mind as a convenient explanation for such probing analyses. In the Fawcett Society's (1997) exit survey of British women MPs immediately after the

1997 general election, more than a third (37 per cent) of women respondents reported being targets of media intrusion. In particular, women say that while they do not believe that politicians should not be called to account for misconduct, the miscreants are few and far between and are rarely women:

> I am very concerned with the intrusive manner that media people treat politicians and I feel that it is putting off a lot of people who would otherwise like to give public service. (Dame Angela Rumbold, Cons, UK)

> We are now accused by the press which is then repeated by the general public as if it is gospel, that we're all into sleaze, that we're all greedy, that we're all making thousands of pounds on the side doing this, that, and the other. It is outrageous. And we're all being accused, that every MP is into some sort of corrupt practice and that is going to undermine our democratic system and it is totally irresponsible and I all I can say is that I would love to have the opportunity to do an exposé the other way round, to actually have a look at who these people are, who write this stuff, who are producing this stuff, it's sheer hypocrisy. (Marion Roe, Cons, UK)

Many comments by politicians focused on the conflict between the media's agenda and that of politicians, with the predominant view being that the media generally win and that the media are always trying to "expose" politicians in some way, usually for being economical with the truth, but this is perhaps a slightly cheap and easy shot. As the BBC's chief political editor, Ann Sloman (1999), suggests, the media are largely constrained to report either what they are given directly by politicians or what they hear (and then interpret) in debate, either on the floor of the Chamber or in committee, or, of course, in the lobby, and if the politicians don't like what they read or hear, then it is their responsibility to change the message. So, both sides believe in their own virtue, blaming the other for twisting or distorting reality. Women Parliamentarians suggest that the media are only really interested in sensation—another feature of the "dumbing down" and tabloidisation argument—and that in order for, say, a backbencher (the status of most of the women whom I interviewed) to get *any* kind of publicity, they must say or do controversial things, especially if they take a line which is against their own party. Women easily recognize that for all backbenchers, not just women, and for members of minority parties, the media's general interest in them is minimal:

The media are always looking for an angle, a story and therefore the way in which they report is to sensationalise everything that comes up. Or they try to find an angle which fits the editorial perspective of the paper . . . so they want pictures, they want spicy stories. So whatever you say, it's not enough to be making good points. You must be prepared to say inflammatory things, to rant and rave, before you'll get column inches. (Hilary Armstrong, Labour, UK)

They're not interested in backbenchers. They are only interested in Ministers and even they, they're selective . . . the only time they're interested in backbenchers is if they want us to leak what happens in the Party Room or they'll try and get a comment on that. I could be on the front page of every major daily newspaper tomorrow if I was to come out and make extremely derogatory remarks about the Prime Minister or the Treasurer. (Fran Bailey, Liberal, Australia)

I'm too bland for them, I'm too ordinary. I am a housewife and a mother. I've been married to the same guy for nearly 40 years, two ordinary children, five ordinary grandchildren. I can't even boast a divorce or a death. (Elizabeth Grace, Liberal, Australia)

If I were interested in getting my face on the box, which is the only realistic way of being noticed in politics, I would have to make a noise, say embarrassing things, say controversial things, talk about National Apple Day, sing "Yellow Submarine" in Latin. Do any kind of stunt that people notice. Anything but be a sober politician making a reasonable, decent and interesting point in the Chamber, and that's wrong. Politics is being turned into an entertainment. (Angela Eagle, Labour, UK)

The media's approach to minority parties is to give them a bit of a look in, like they'd give them a tag at the end because it's a predominantly two-party system, so you might get a little bit of a tag at the end in the last paragraph ". . . and the Democrats said . . ." or if it was a very big conflict-oriented balance of power issue you would get a lot more focus. But, you know, over the years, these young unsophisticated journalists, all they would ask is "are you going to block this?" That was their only interest, their only interest—not in the substance, just in your action. (Cheryl Kernot, Labor, Australia)

In an emerging democracy such as South Africa, the media have an even more crucial role in accessing the polity to the workings of the government they have campaigned to bring to power. It is therefore of even greater frustration for many of the ANC women interviewed that the media seem so intent on reporting only negative aspects of the government's performance:

We haven't had a democracy for very long and people's understanding of it is so minimal, there is therefore a bigger obligation on the part of the media to explain the executive . . . you need to show that things have changed and progress has been made. (Gill Marcus, ANC, South Africa)

I think there is some justification for the way it [the media] portrays politics and I think that very much, this place reeks of patronage and privilege and people being given various favours, such as promotion to the front bench or other goodies or chairs of committees, not necessarily on the basis of merit or ability but on the basis of who they are in favour with. I think the media has, rightly, played a part in making the public far more aware of the sleazier side of politics and I'm very much in favour of changing the nature of politics and developing a far more participation-based politics which is participation by more members of the public. But I do think that the media sometimes focus too much on people's private lives and I am concerned that the media is dominated by soundbite reporting of politics and we're losing the art of investigative journalism at its best. (Rachel Squire, Labour, UK)

Increasingly, consumers also complain about the "dumbing down" of news, as the infotainment bandwagon trundles on bringing with it countless "newzak" programmes, talking heads and journalistic interpretations of news events which must serve as proxy for real, live debate from Parliamentary chambers or "serious," challenging productions. Often, journalists will try and encourage a combative exchange between politicians as a way of trying to enliven the proceedings, even when such antagonisms are not authentic:

I've actually sat in a radio station where I was trying to be very even-handed, I was debating an issue with the then Minister—she was in another State—and the presenter of the show that I was on, while the ads were playing, was egging me on to "go for her: don't just sit there, go for her." That's what they're interested in. (Fran Bailey, Liberal, Australia)

Quite often, the multi-item news reports which do not allow for topic discussion further exacerbate the freeze-frame nature of political discussion, so that the still image of a politician, offset, top left as background to the story, could be the only unmediated part of a news report which otherwise comprises interpretation, conjecture, and paraphrase. The problem is that soundbite journalism rarely allows for anything other than a brief pass across the original story or event, and so content becomes almost entirely subordinated to image. As part of a general worry about the increasing tabloidisation of political news coverage, there is a concern over the way in which news has become just another entertainment genre and that the media's preoccupations and interests come to dominate and shape the news agenda. Moreover, by talking to only a few sources, their views on what is important are limited, and thus it is scarcely surprising that what is reported is highly partial and particular.

> When people see you on television, they don't have time to absorb what you're talking about, but they do notice how you look, so increasingly people say it's how you look that's important and if you're ugly, you can never get to be president of the US and in a curious way, we're all locked into this, it's like a little hamster wheel and none of us can stop and get out. I find it very offensive and it is particularly tyrannical for women because women's clothes are very visible and people in my constituency are really pleased at how often I'm on television locally but it's depressing how often they don't remember what I was saying! (Jean Corston, Labour, UK)

However, there was an acknowledgement that not all journalists are just out to deliver a quick and dirty story, that some will do the necessary background research and talk to a range of sources before writing their piece. "There are a few journalists who are quite good and who will come and seek out background information and write that, but there are others who you just think, 'were you at the same function as me?'" (Sue West, Labor, Australia). Equally, there is a certain sense of some journalist corps being better than others in their professionalism, but to some extent, the grass is always greener:

> When I go to Britain and read the papers there, like the *Guardian*, *Observer*, etc., one is just so impressed with how informed the journalists are and how they can actually give you the background and analyse the problem in a very short article. We can't do any of that here. Our reporting is at the crudest level. They do report a speech but they don't analyse it, don't put it into any kind of context, they don't give any background and so on. (Mary Turok, ANC, South Africa)

If backbench women Parliamentarians experience a particularized interest in them by the media, women who achieve senior Parliamentary positions, in the cabinet or shadow cabinet, are even more scrutinized by the media, and their standards of behaviour, as well as their policy statements, are all vulnerable to the investigative notebooks of journalists. It is almost as if their stepping outside the norms of "appropriate" female behavior by becoming Parliamentarians at all is just about bearable, but taking up positions of authority lays them open to a highly critical form of scrutiny which is entirely gender-specific. When Carmen Lawrence (Labor) became Australia's first State Premier (of Western Australia), she experienced what she describes as the "sore-thumb" phenomenon—"I just stuck out and so your actions, for good or ill, are often exaggerated and they are seen as more significant than they really are, which means that you can fly higher but you can also fall lower."

THE POLITICAL INTERVIEW AND THE CULT OF PERSONALITY

However, as Bird (1998) argues, the storytelling style of much newscasting is in danger of usurping a more rational and considered news delivery so that the journalist/newscaster as messenger has as much, if not more authority, than the original source for the particular story. In Steele and Barnhurst's (1996) study of journalistic language during election campaigns, the authors argue that journalists have become more dominant, controlling (and increasing) their share of airtime with shorter, more pacy reports. As elsewhere, the shift towards the celebrity interviewer/journalist who expresses authoritative opinion on the pronouncements of elected representatives confirms the growing trend in journalist-centered rather than news-centered programming. The focus on journalists and their opinions may well turn newscasters into personalities, but it does little to increase the public's knowledge of the political process. Many women were extremely frustrated with the news industry's hyper-inflation of the importance of its own practitioners, most obviously manifest in the show*man*ship of certain key "celebrity" journalists who have become famous for their aggressive interviewing style and technique with politicians. Political programming of the *Question Time, 20/20, 60 Minutes, Dateline,* and *On the Record* variety also feed into the perception of politics as an abidingly aggressive and combative arena where politicians are interrogated to identify the degree of their lying rather than interviewed to hear their views on policy. The way in which the "cult of the interviewer" as one woman phrased it, has invaded political reporting is seen as antithetical to a true democracy as star interviewers such as Barbara Walters, Dan Rather, Jeremy Paxman, Mike Wallace, and Diane Sawyer are given much more credibility and accorded considerably more political acumen than many of their political subjects:

> I think there is now a huge confusion between discussion and entertainment. Witness the enormous emphasis there is now on the person interviewing—the Dimbleby interview, the Walden interview.

> What are the viewers tuning in to see? Are they tuning in to see the
> interviewer or are they actually tuning in to see why it is that a
> politician of whatever party it is promulgating the view that he [sic]
> is promulgating. (Ann Widdecombe, Cons, UK)

As the journalist, Anne Karpf (1999), points out so persuasively,
the most that the political interview usually achieves is to demonstrate
the terrier-like tenacity of the interviewer and the extent to which the
politician under the spotlight can avoid answering what are often deliberately provocative questions. What this format patently does *not* do is
give anything to the public which is genuinely informative and useful as
a basis on which to make an informed judgement. The political interviewer decides what the people want to know, contributing to, if not
entirely setting, the agenda, enabling certain issues to be aired in preference to other, perhaps equally important and pressing topics. And, of
course, the politician in question must show her- or himself to be
amenable to any probing, to show oneself in a good light, particularly in
the highly visible event of an interview during a general election. Winter
(1993) suggests that there are two principal functions for the political
interview: in the first instance, it is about an exchange of ideas, at least
superficially, between interviewer and interviewee, manifest in the
question-and-response format of traditional interviews; second, the particular image of the politician which she or he wishes to create is also
managed through the interview process, and in particular, the way(s) in
which the politician relates to the questioner. The politician's facility
with interviewee tactics such as evasion, avoidance, interruption, attack,
and promotion, and the skills employed in executing any and all of these
with minimal detection by the audience, all contribute to the way in
which the audience perceives the veracity of those responses and, by
extension, the integrity of the politician. However, politicians themselves believe that the use of these tactics by the interviewer, especially
in the context of an aggressive broadcast interview functions to undermine the credibility of interviewers, always trying to place the interviewee on the back foot or to make him or her take a defensive stance. In
Winter's (1993) study of political interviews, she found that women
interviewers were much more likely to work with, rather than against,
an interviewee, recognizing the turn-taking, question-response strategies which are the traditional characteristics of the political interview:
"the female interviewer maintains her questioning interview style and
thus cooperates with the interviewee in their mutual understanding of
the context" (p. 137). Male interviewers, on the other hand, were much
more likely to be competitive in their interview technique, being less
interested in information gathering and exchange of ideas, and more
interested in asserting their authority and control over the interview.

Studies which have undertaken microanalyses of political interviews and conducted extensive discourse analyses on interview transcripts will often point to a large repertoire of strategies which politicians routinely use to avoid answering awkward questions and/or ensuring that they get across the particular and crucial point they want to, irrespective of what the original question is (Greatbatch, 1986, 1988; Winter, 1993). Indeed, Beattie's (1982) study found that interruptions accounted for nearly half of all attempted changes of "turn" in political interview situations and Bull and Mayer (1988) argue that interviewer interruptions are often the consequence of politicians talking at length but *not* answering the question, so that a reformulation of the same question is then proposed, often as an interrogative interruption. These nonanswer strategies are usually seen as deliberate acts of evasion to manipulate public opinion although some commentators (notably Bavelas, Black, Bryson, & Mussell, 1988, 1990) suggest that the "answer" to many political questions is inherently negative and thus the no-win situation provoked requires the politician to still give an answer while trying not to offend anyone. However, this argument seems a little thin given the scale of research "evidence" to the contrary. Bull and Meyer's (1993) analysis of interviews conducted with Margaret Thatcher and Neil Kinnock during the 1987 general election includes an impressive typology of nonreplies to questions, ranging from "ignores the question" and "acknowledges the question without answering it," through to "questions the question," "attacks the question," "attacks the interviewer," and "declines to answer," "unwilling to answer," "makes a political point" and "apologizes" (pp. 656-661). Such a complex array of evasive strategies is unlikely to be other than fully conscious, if not deliberately manipulative, then certainly self-defensive. But Economou (1997) puts a much more generous interpretation on why politicians seem to be evasive, since he argues that this has more to do with their lack of awareness that the rules of engagement have changed than deliberate acts of misinformation. For Economou, the shift towards the adoption of less deferential positions of journalists *qua* politicians has meant that politicians are sometimes led to give the "wrong" answers because of their failure "to establish common communicative ground," and the journalist continues to enjoy the upper hand since she or he is able not only to frame the discussion as it develops but can also edit it in post-production to fit the desired particular frame (p. 101). While this thesis has some merit, its presentation of "politician as hapless victim" is implausible as a generalized theory. But as Hamilton (1998) cogently argues, the issue is less about being "fair" to a political interviewee than about whether, having asked a difficult (or unfair) question, the journalist is prepared to listen to the answer. It is probably not worth spending too much time fretting over the various merits of differing concepts of fairness when discussed in the context of either politics or the media and especially when discussing the impact of one on the other since that which different professional groups hold to be "fair" is likely to be considerably different as well (Romano, 1998).

Of course, media practitioners themselves take an altogether different view on what their function is, so that the BBC's highly popular principal presenter, John Humphrys, of the channel's flagship news programme, *Today*, can say, completely straight-faced, that journalists like facts,

> but it seems to me that that is the beginning middle and end of it. If we assemble the facts as best we can they will speak for themselves, and the audience must make of them what they will. To move beyond that is dangerous. Emotion does not have a political dimension. (cited in the *Guardian*, 30 August 1999)

That journalists simply put the facts together and leave the rest of us to get on with our own interpretation is so fatuous as to almost beggar belief, but clearly, it is a myth that the media insist on peddling in the face of considerable evidence to the contrary. Perhaps Humphrys believes he can make that kind of comment precisely because he knows that all "facts" are contingent and that his version of "the facts" are as open to contestation as those espoused by the politician whom he happens to be interviewing. Even so, its audacious lie is nonetheless impressive.

That politicians and governments recognize the need to "manage" the media, both in terms of their own personal presentation but also attempting to limit the media's political output, scarcely needs to be said; spin doctoring was already an established concept in the lexicon of political terminology in the late 20th century and, arguably, it has been this very publicly paraded tendency to artifice which has encouraged an already apathetic polity to become more knowingly cynical. While television is an excellent medium for getting a political message across, it is also merciless in its ability to confront politicians with their own, often empty, rhetoric. The examples are legion, but perhaps the best is captured by George Bush's now infamous "Read my lips, no new taxes" statement, which he lived to regret ever saying. More recently, the relentless media (and public) scrutiny of Bill Clinton during the "Lewinsky" scandal made obvious that, once committed to tape, public utterances are indelibly recorded and ready to be replayed *ad nauseam*. Nonetheless, contemporary politicians understand very well the power of the media in getting their message across, and the rapid rise of politi-

cal consultancy agencies demonstrates the grave importance attached to
having the right media angle and the right media relationships, if not of
the politician themselves, then certainly their assistants and "briefers."
For governments, entire departments or units usually exist through
which to manage the communication process, and in Britain, the
Government Information Service which performs this function has
around 1,200 staff, many of whom are employed solely to manage the
news (Watts, 1997).

> A couple of years after I was elected, I was at a friend's house who
> manages quite a big company and is politically aware, and he said to
> me, "Val, I worry about the Education Committee, what is it really
> like?" So I said to him, "I am really the most unqualified person on
> that committee. We have four professors, the heads of three univer-
> sities, lecturers, school principals, inspectors." He looked at me
> amazed and said, "I can't believe it." Because the way it's portrayed
> in the media is that everyone is stupid, this is the sort of portrayal
> that comes across, it's all about race. (Val Viljoen, ANC, South
> Africa)

GENDER ON THE AGENDA: FRAMING WOMEN

The ways in which the news media privilege the dominant socioeconomic paradigm of capitalist patriarchy ensures a male-ordered and
global system of social and economic control in which women are situat-
ed in highly gendered and specific contexts. If it has become merely a
commonplace to argue that broadcast media (especially, but other
media, too) regularly and routinely perform an important affirmatory
function in reinforcing dominant norms and values to "the public" and
confirming the cherished and comfortable beliefs of most of their consumers, it is no less true for the repeating. Existing and unequal social,
economic, political and cultural relationships are routinely (and unprob-
lematically) promoted through both fictional and factual programming
strands, and the ways in which women (particularly, but also other disadvantaged groups) are represented on and in broadcast media send
important messages to the public about women's place, women's role,
and women's lives. The sadness and frustration is that after more than
20 years of documenting the media's representation of women so little
has changed (see, for example, Tuchman, Daniels, & Benet, 1978; Root,
1986; Soothill & Walby, 1991; Creedon, 1993; Ross, 1995a, 1995b; Ross &
Sreberny-Mohammadi, 1997; Carter, 1998; Wykes, 1998). Much contemporary research effort on broadcast media has focused on analysing the

ideological effects of television, that is, how the dominant ideology is mobilized by the media, and especially television, to produce an apparently shared, uncontroversial, and unproblematic understanding of the world. (See for example Dines & Humez, 1995; Eldridge, 1995; Fiske, 1996.) But within this more general project of identifying how ideologies work as conveyors of meaning, how they constitute specific belief systems, who believes them, and what circumstances continue to support them, lie particular questions of gender.

As Mosco (1996) rightly points out, communication scholars began to use a politico-economic approach to understanding media institutions when press, electronic media, and telecommunications began to transform from small, single-business enterprises to multinational and even global amalgams, controlled by very few (male) hands (Danielian, 1939; Smythe, 1957; Herman & Chomsky, 1988). Such has been the pace of change, particularly through amalgamation and conglomeratization, that analyses of media industries have been forced to abandon traditional boundaries such as single-media foci towards an appreciation of those very large enterprises which comprise examples across all media forms (Schiller, 1989; Downing, 1990; Pendakur, 1990; Wasko, 1994). While it almost goes without saying that politico-economic studies of communication organizations have largely been about powerful men, there has been some interesting research undertaken which has looked at the gender dimension, most often looking at the position of women as workers in media industries, since actual media ownership is extremely rare, other than one or two feminist publishing houses.

But generally, work on the gender dimension of political economy as it relates to media industries has not been prolific although, over recent decades, a body of woman-centered theory has begun to look critically at the way in which political and media institutions function to exclude or limit women from their operational orbits, both as specifically gendered "subjects" of public policy but also as professionals within the industry itself. (See for example Fraser, 1989; Benhabib, 1992; van Zoonen, 1994, 1998; Holland, 1998; Steiner, 1998.) However, rather less work has been undertaken on the intersection of women, media, and politics. The mediated visibility of scandal can threaten those in public power, who are more often men, but scant attention has been paid to the systematic ways in which media construct "women" in their gender-politics discourse, the ways in which the media undermine their status as politicians in myriad small—but important—ways, their use of cartoons, their use of specific language strategies, and so on. One of the principal means by which gender and politics *do* come together to excite the media's interest is when there is a "sleaze" story (see Wheeler, 1997; Connell, 1998; Ross, 1998b; Stephenson, 1998) and then the debate about media intrusion into the privacy of *male* politicians gets played out, raising questions about the relationship between private morality and public competence for office. If the media articulate the "political" within the "public" sphere, then representation does matter, and the ways in which women and men are portrayed, their differential access to media outlets, and the differentiated visibility of women and men as active agents with authority and/or expertise *all* matter too.

Women politicians are clear that there is a specifically gendered news discourse which comes into play when journalists report on activities and events involving them and women colleagues, not just in campaign terms but more generally, as everyday occurrences. Crucially, aspects of their sex are routinely incorporated into what should be "ordinary" stories of politics; they are mundanely framed as women first and then, maybe, as politicians. When 120 women were elected to the British Parliament in 1997, the front page headlines figured them as "Blair's Babes." While, in retrospective, British women see that perhaps they should not have agreed to have Blair pictured in their midst, their victory was trivialized instantly, not just by the possessive-implied "his" but as damningly "babes." Framing serious women politicians in this way might be seen as merely irreverent or even playful, but it signals a dangerous tendency to trivialize and neutralize the potency of women to be actors and leaders on the political stage. While some women take a generous view of the media's interest in them as "novelties," others see an altogether more insidious side to the media's propensity to treat them differently to their male colleagues:

> I think there is still a bit of a novelty about us . . . when a number of women came into the Parliament in 1996 there was a lot made of it, photographs with the Prime Minister, which I thought was pretty patronising. I'm sure many of those women didn't feel differently to the guys, they just looked different. When I was elected, there were five or six other women and they [the press] wanted to know what schools we had gone to and our ages and I objected on both counts. It was all about whether you were a private or public school kid. In the end, they wore us all down and threatened to run a story on how we wouldn't cooperate, so we all capitulated. But there was no interest in the new men. It was a girlie job and I found it offensive. (Jeannie Ferris, Liberal, Australia)

> Women are a much more interesting story. They/we have a human interest factor that men don't come anywhere near and that automatically changes the dimension of the story and how it's presented. Women are multi-dimensional beings, far more than men . . . and we all bring a little bit of a story to this place. (Kate Lundy, Labor, Australia)

And women point out that they often find ways of getting their policy points across almost by default, as a consequence of the media's interest in them as women, but then discovering that they have important and interesting things to say which are not necessarily about gender:

> When I was first here, in the 1970s, I was questioned repeatedly about burning bras, and that actually ended up with me having huge publicity because they [media] realised that I could string two or three words together and that I wasn't a token, and that I was there for serious political reasons. (Kathy Sullivan, Liberal, Australia)

To be sure, women in significant numbers in any Parliament (other than in the progressive Scandinavian countries) is still a rarity, but that is surely no reason to treat them in ways which are qualitatively (negatively) different to men. Women argue that the media often appear to be operating double standards when considering women politicians, almost as if they expect "better" standards of behaviour, higher moral values, more honesty, integrity, loyalty (see also Chap. 2). What seems to happen is that women are often set up as paragons and are then "unmasked" almost as quickly as having feet of clay; the point is, they never said they were perfect in the first place, so it is a doubly unfair trial by media:

> Women are still unusual and therefore interesting and as soon as they [the media] put them up there, they then work very hard to chop them down, so it's the old tall poppy syndrome. To some extent Natasha [Stott Despoja] has that problem and people say that she's a policy flake and maybe she's not as strong on policy as she could be but . . . (Sue Mackay, Labor, Australia)

> . . . if you have certain weaknesses, it's like, "after all, she's just a woman" and as a woman you are not expected to perform well. If you do perform well, you also draw eyebrows, it's like, "what kind of a woman is she? She's tough, she's arrogant, she's a minotaur." There's always this negative aspect. (Koko Mokgolong, ANC, South Africa)

> Bronwen Bishop was going to challenge John Hart for the leadership and the media followed her all over the country saying, you know, how wonderful she was, and then she didn't do well in a particular pre-selection and she was absolutely vilified. Men in comparable situations are much more able to retain credibility. You know, they might be regarded as bad, tough guys, but everybody sort of secretly admires a bad tough guy in politics, but a bad tough girl in poli-

tics is just bad. A soft wimpy but good guy in politics is often respected for having that other side to him, but a soft wimpy girl in politics, you know, you've had it. There are so many double standards. (Margaret Reynolds, Labor, Australia)

Ironically, as Amanda Vanstone (Liberal, Australia) comments, the media is always interested in stories which play to discrimination within political parties: "Some media want you to do 'poor me, they're picking on me because I'm a woman' stories and it would be easy, I would have the media dripping off my fingers for weeks on end, but I rejected those proposals because I think that's a bad position to take." Even if there is that element in play, unless one can prove it, which is almost impossible, it simply comes to be seen as whining and special pleading, that somehow women just aren't up to the cut and thrust of political life. Of course, particular opprobrium is reserved for those women who are highly capable and thus even more threatening to the possibility of a different kind of politics. Gertrude Fester (ANC, South Africa) uses the analogy of the "witch" as a way of describing something of the media's revulsion for strong women: "I find the witch image a very strong one. The modern witch is strong . . . sophisticated, educated, you know, the woman who threatens."

> Women politicians, particularly at cabinet level, tend to be knocked, judged, assessed, by a criteria that is incredibly harsh, relative to their male counterparts . . . it's not that the media wouldn't want to focus on men when mistakes are made but it is more relentless and with women, it's personalised in a way that it isn't with men. (Janet Love, ANC, South Africa)

The ways in which powerful women are routinely denigrated for their politics by specifically gender-based attacks are brought into sharp relief by a brief discussion of specific examples of the media's coverage of particular women during the fieldwork period in Australia and South Africa. In both cases, although the interviews were undertaken a year apart, it happened that particular women had recently been or were currently being given considerable negative media coverage, and many of the women I interviewed spoke about the reasons behind the tone and style of that coverage. In Australia, Carmen Lawrence (Labor), Cheryl Kernot (Labor) and Pauline Hanson (One Nation Party) were placed in the public eye for very different reasons, but the way in which they were reported was remarkably similar in that there was always a gendered double standard in play. In South Africa, Nkosozana Zuma (ANC) was persistently attacked for her policy positions on health. In both countries, the media's subtext was clear: women should know their place and conform to "public" expectations. If they insisted on flaunting the conventions of femininity by daring to become politicians, then the least they should do was to act like women and not interfere in the *real politik* of business and corporate affairs. Women as both spokespeople for and representatives of government as Ministers (in the case of Zuma and at one time Lawrence) or as outspoken opposition politicians (in the case of Kernot and Hanson) are soft targets for political point-scoring, where their perceived weaknesses *as women* stand as proxies for wider criticisms of their respective party's policies.

Many of the Australian women had things to say about the media's response to Pauline Hanson, the Leader of the One Nation Party, which had had an unexpected success in the 1998 Queensland State elections and who, at the time I was undertaking the Australian fieldwork in the spring of 1998, was gearing up for the general election later in the year. One Nation campaigned on a broad nationalist agenda, and pledged, among other things, to curtail inward immigration and not to settle Aboriginal land rights claims; Hanson was the only woman who was regularly in the media's eye in the run-up to the general election. In some ways, looking at the media's framing of Hanson is to understand two fundamental aspects of the media's relationship to women politicians: one is that journalists appear to operate a kind of serial monogamy when it comes to women, so that at any one time, only one woman can be the focus of the media's interest; the other is that there appears to be a propensity for setting women up as saviours, prophets, or Madonna figures (the pedestal model), only to find them unable to live up to the media's own unrealistic and entirely fabricated expectations, and thus become targets for opprobrium (the falling from grace model). "They've [the media] sort of created her and now they're trying to undermine her" (De-Anne Kelly, National Party, Australia).

With Pauline Hanson, part of her early appeal (among voters and media alike) was, arguably, the casting of herself as an "ordinary" woman from the Bush, who had been encouraged to stand for election on a platform of basic values and a common sense agenda. That it was a woman apparently taking on the might of business-as-usual politics made her seem almost like a folk hero, and her red hair, the catch in her voice, her clear discomfort at public speaking, all set her up as being truly in touch with "real" Australians because she was, resolutely, one of them:

> There is something inherent in the Australian psyche, of a resistance to authority of, you know, "up yours jack," and the major political parties are seen as part of that almost conservative mass of MPs, so they [the media] are promoting her as being a maverick. (Fran Bailey, Liberal, Australia)

> She is tapping into a group of people who are probably increasing in number, who just feel left out of everything that's happening. (Amanda Vanstone, Liberal, Australia)

> She has a vulnerability about her, she has a way of speaking that is not that clear, if I might put it that way, and its quite endearing and of course she's female, she's red-headed, she's very attractive in a sort of strong way, and that's helped her immeasurably. (De-Anne Kelly, National Party, Australia)

That she was an attractive woman promoting politically incorrect policies which actually caught the mood of many Australians who were becoming fearful about the "Asian menace" meant that she was guaranteed media coverage. The fact that her policies didn't actually stand up to any serious analysis was irrelevant in the early phase of the media's flirtation with Hanson:

> The media understand men putting hard, ultra right-wing messages and they know how to react, but I don't know that they quite comprehend that same message, that same ultra right-wing, that really fascist nonnurturing type of position, can come from a woman, because it is such an antithesis. (Sue West, Labor, Australia)

For a politician like Nkosozana Zuma, a Zulu woman Minister (of Health when the South African interviews were being completed but later of Foreign Affairs under Thabo Mbeki), both gender and race come into play in trying to interpret her media coverage. For most of her colleagues, these two factors were inextricably linked and doubly implicated in fueling the negative media response to her and her policy actions. For some women, though, it was more an issue of the vested interests which were being targeted by her strategies on health, suggesting that a man promoting such policies would not have been similarly treated. But this latter was very much a minority view and, interestingly, no black women advanced that thesis. For Gill Marcus, there are no doubts about the reason for Zuma's resoundingly negative media coverage, and she argues that those who have the biggest problem with her are those for whom she represents the maid at home talking back to the master. The dual drivers of gender and race embodied in Zuma produce a level of cognitive dissonance that whites simply cannot transcend; she is both too different and simultaneously too familiar to be allowed to do her job without persistent antagonism:

I have no hesitation in saying that if she was a white male, she would not have the problems she has got. There are a number of factors and it might be a bit crude, but the people who give her a hard time have the notion of an average black South African woman as someone who is slim, made-up and a black version of a dolly. She [Zuma] is the maid—they expect her to come in her apron and dook [mob-cap]. Now she is stylish and does dress well and takes care of herself, but she is their image of an African maid who was always their domestic. So when they see her with this level of authority and competence and articulation and the ability to stand and talk back to them, it shocks them totally. "What is this maid talking back to me about?" This may be crude but that's why she's got these problems. They still have a maid in their kitchen, so if Zuma can do it, so might their own maid. It is almost surreal for them, because they have a mental picture and a practical reality that don't mix. (Gill Marcus, ANC, South Africa)

I think there is a lot of respect for Dr. Zuma, an acknowledgement of her stubbornness but the major reason she has had bad press is that there has been so much money involved. She is taking on organisations in a way that no-one else has ever dared before. (Val Viljoen, ANC, South Africa)

I'm sure you know that, if you're assertive, a woman and assertive, whether you're a Minister or wherever you are, you would get that kind of reaction from people and . . . her [Nkosozana Zuma's] ministry touches on very serious issues that effect big business, for example, and big business is men mainly and mainly white men . . . and here she is, this black woman saying, "no more smoking in public places," like, "how dare she?," you know, that kind of thing. But she does dare. She is very brave. (Ntombazana Botha, ANC, South Africa)

Patricia de Lille (PAC) implies that one of the problems with Zuma is that her political inexperience manifests itself in her not questioning the information that she is given by her advisors, so that she becomes the scapegoat for decisions based on faulty intelligence. As de Lille is a political adversary to Zuma, this is a generous reading of the situation and demonstrates the power that common cause has over party politics:

But you know, she has people from the old order in her department, advising her and bringing information to her, the civil servants, and sometimes she just receives the information the way they bring it to her, rather than looking at the context within which they bring it and that sometimes makes it embarrassing for her. But comparatively speaking of all the ones we have had in the past, she is the best.

Talking about the media's continuing denigration of Nkokosama Zuma, but also extending her analysis to other women, one of her political opponents, Suzanne Vos (IFP, South Africa), is clear that one of the reasons for the media's continued negative interest in Zuma has been her stoicism in the face of their attacks: "There's no doubt that because she has refused to wilt in front of the onslaught, the media have been extraordinarily unforgiving . . . [they] are far more forgiving to the men, there's no doubt about that." Women cannot make mistakes, apparently, and they certainly shouldn't be out in the world when they have children to look after. Many women commented on the media's interest in their gendered identity, usually in relation to how they manage to juggle family and work, what their families think of their success. If they have young children, there is usually a barbed question which is ostensibly about childcare arrangements but where the subtext is almost always condemnatory. While this is scarcely a phenomenon peculiar to women Parliamentarians, they are nonetheless irritated at the insistent framing of them as women first and then politicians:

> When I became Premier, all this stuff came out, [using my] first name, wanting images of me shown in domestic situations and references to my family and all that stuff that comes out with women . . . you rarely see a man described as Joe Bloggs, 54, father of three. . . . (Carmen Lawrence, Labor, Australia)

> The day after I got pre-selected, most of the reporters and radio people asked me: "how are the family going to cope? What are you going to do with little Kate?" They didn't ask that of the men. (Trish Crossin, Labor, Australia)

Crossin goes on to suggest that in her particular campaign to achieve pre-selection, her male opponent used the fact that she had a two-year old daughter in *his* campaign as a reason for not voting for her:

> At meetings, lots of their [the opposition's] supporters had been worded up to ask me the question, "so, you've still got three children at home between the ages of two and sixteen, your husband's a trades union official and he works long hours—have you talked about this with the family and how you're going to cope?

This kind of underhanded tactic is something which women who take up the political call must get used to and frame adequate responses in advance so as not to get wrong-footed every time such sexist questions are asked:

I'd say, "First of all, I resent you asking me these questions because
it's absolutely my business and secondly, do you think I'd just nomi-
nate for pre-selection and not talk to my family? You must be very
silly if you think I've just done this and my family and I haven't had
a serious discussion." (Trish Crossin, Labor, Australia)

And women were also very sympathetic to the plight of women
who have felt the media's temperamental treatment of them as first
saints and then sinners, particularly in the case of Pauline Hanson. The
empathy expressed by women was on the basis of their shared gender
and recognition that it could be themselves in the media spotlight, and
they were able to simultaneously empathize with Hanson's predicament
while at the same time abhorring the politics she espoused:

It's infuriating, the way they [the media] say she couldn't have
dreamt this up by herself, that these blokes are behind her, but I
don't believe that, she can't be that stupid. (Jenny Macklin, Labor,
Australia)

From a political point of view, I'd love that [downfall of Hanson] to
happen, but from a human and compassionate point of view, no,
because I admire what she's done. She's fought through some very
tough odds, she's a tough cookie. (Elizabeth Grace, Liberal,
Australia)

But the Hanson phenomenon has knock-on consequences for women in
political office more generally, as Margaret Thatcher's Premiership also
had, which are both negative and positive—positive because both
women demonstrate that it is possible to lead a party, so there are role
model cues available for other women. But also negatively, since both
women, among many other things, have provoked a sexist knee-jerk
reaction which brackets all women together and says, "Never let a
woman near power because, see what happens!" Interestingly, the
media's efforts to pull Hanson down were temporarily halted after a
particular interview, when a journalist asked a question about xenophobia and Hanson said, "I don't understand, please explain." The interviewer and the media more generally roundly ridiculed Hanson but, as
Kathy Sullivan (Liberal, Australia) argues, the public don't like "smart
alec stuff": "Ninety per cent of the viewing audience of that programme
would not have known what 'xenophobia' meant and when she was
ridiculed for saying, 'please explain,' the public felt that they were also
being patronised." Her ratings soared after that programme although
they dipped subsequently.

DOES THIS MAKE HER BOTTOM LOOK BIG?

When asked about the most frequently reported aspect of women politicians' lives by the media, most women believe that their outward appearance is the focus of both more column inches and airtime than anything that they might say and that such a focus is more likely to apply to women than their male colleagues. Women mentioned repeatedly the way in which the media always include the age of women politicians, what they look like, their domestic and family circumstances, their fashion sense, and so on:

> The one thing that always does happen, no matter what the context, when being introduced as a speaker they always, without fail, say what year I was born. I saw a news report from a Buenos Aires news paper on my punishment suggestions and it starts off, Elizabeth Peacock, 57 years. Now I can't for the life of me think why this is important. If this was a man, they wouldn't dream of saying that. It's almost that they're saying, here she is, and she's so old and she's still here, sort of thing. This interest in how old we are and what we are wearing comes up time and time again, and I don't understand why. (Elizabeth Peacock, Cons, UK)

Work on newspaper photographs recently undertaken by the Women in Journalism group (1999) revealed that, although it is clear that "men outnumber women in public life . . . the analysis shows that the way newspapers use images of women is at best old-fashioned and at worst complacent" (p. 12). Older women recognize that while they themselves may no longer excite the media's interest in them as sexual objects, this priapic propensity is still a problem for younger colleagues:

> I remember sitting with Dawn [Primarolo] and when she got up to ask a question, there were all these sexist remarks coming from the opposite benches. When we compared notes, I got the "old bag" yells and I said, you can't win. (Alice Mahon, Labour, UK)

For some women, dressing in particular ways is a conscious strategy designed to both subvert normative considerations of what a politician *should* look like but also to assert individuality in a context where conformity is the expected line. Many women politicians were intensely irritated with the media's inappropriate focus on their personal sartorial style—with the preoccupation with their hemlines, color coordination, and fashion sense—and the spurious link made between outward appearance and ability to do the job. Fiona Mactaggart believes that the media's fascination with sartorial style is partly due to the view that how women dress is a much more important indicator of who they are and what they stand for, than is the case for men. The emphasis is made to undermine women; it is *not* an unconscious process:

> A lot of men in this place have never sent their suit to the cleaners and nobody ever says, "have you noticed the smell?," which is a perfectly reasonable question to ask. And it's done [focusing on women's externalities] to make women feel vulnerable, that's the purpose . . . I'm afraid, I don't think they are completely naïve. (Fiona Mactaggart, Labour, UK)

> I don't know whether it is deliberate or it's so ingrained, but a woman's appearance is always commented on, her age is always commented on, her style of dress is always commented on. That never happens to male politicians, ever, unless they have made a particular point about their style, like Nicholas Fairbairn who has made a particular point of presenting himself, but they are presented as extreme, exceptions that prove the rule. We are always approached as being suspect women if there aren't certain rules of presentation that are observed. (Glenda Jackson, Labour, UK)

Women are very conscious that they are always on display, they are always a potential target for the media's scrutiny, even in their leisure time. Jeannie Ferris (Liberal, Australia) takes a pride in looking good for her constituents as well as for herself, and she dresses carefully as a pre-emptive strike for any off-duty journalist who might catch her wearing a tracksuit to the supermarket: "I am very conscious that wherever I am, people will know me, I feel that I have to maintain a certain standard in the way I dress, even in my leisure time, I don't think a female politicians is ever off duty."

> Women are never the right age. We're too young, we're too old. We're too thin, we're too fat. We wear too much make-up, we don't wear enough. We're too flashy in our dress, we don't take enough care. There isn't a thing we can do that's right. (Dawn Primarolo, Labour, UK)

> I followed Shirley Williams in Stevenage and I remember when I was selected that I was told two things. Make sure you arrive on time and comb your hair. Well, this isn't exactly the most important political advice to be given as a newly selected candidate and yet that was the perception that was most remembered about Shirley Williams, her appearance. But I could take you into the House of Commons anytime and show you a whole load of men with dan-

druff all over their collars, their suits all over the place, not sure if they should have the waistband of their trousers over or under their paunch so it moves about all over the place, their hair lank and dirty and their suits looking as if they've slept in them. If women were to appear in the House of Commons in that state they'd be on the front page of all the newspapers, asking, "do you want someone like this to represent you?" or, "this is bringing politics into disrepute." (Judith Church, Labour, UK)

I see the guys coming into Canberra with me on a Sunday night and they have a suit pack over their shoulder. We always have suitcases because if we wore the same clothes everyday, as the men do, it would be noticed and there would be a story about it. (Jeannie Ferris, Liberal, Australia)

We're judged on how we look. We're expected to look better than the men in here, to have a broader range of clothes, to not have a hair out of place. All that sort of thing. There are some of us who don't go along with that, but we do have to maintain a certain style. And you also have to put up with having the shape of your legs described rather than the shape of your mind, and that does go with the territory. You challenge it all the time but you can't spend your whole time challenging what's written about you in the press. I find that on TV news, I'm treated as an ordinary Member of Parliament. A couple of times a cameraman may shoot your legs but I've never had anything outrageous. Sooner or later they'll forget we're women and just think of us as politicians who happen to be women rather than other way round. It will come with familiarity and more women MPs. (Angela Eagle, Labour, UK)

Similarly, in Peake's (1997) British study of Parliamentarians and Prospective Parliamentary candidates (PPCs), she found that her sample revealed a common view that perceived levels of attractiveness were much more important for women than men and, moreover, that looks alone could determine the outcome of women's success in achieving elected office. Peake (1997) cites the view of one Conservative woman PPC: "Well, being short and fat . . it's going to be a hard slog getting a good seat," and another Labour woman PPC: "this sounds dreadfully arrogant [but] one of the closest competitors said to me afterwards, when you walked into the room and I saw that dress and that jacket, I knew you had won. I was very careful in terms of sheer presentation" (p. 14). A number of Australian Parliamentarians spoke of the "red dress" incident as a good example of the way in which the media's double-standards are made manifest. On the one hand, they are always interested in discussing women politicians' sartorial style; on the other, when a woman does a lifestyle piece which frames her as a gendered being, then

the rest of the media immediately castigate her as making politics frivolous. Cheryl Kernot (Labor, Australia) agreed to do a magazine interview
for *Women's Weekly* which included photographic illustrations, one of
which pictured her in a red dress and feather boa, reclining on a chaise
longue. In hindsight, Kernot admits that she might have been more circumspect in agreeing to wear that particular outfit, but she insists that
most "ordinary" people thought she looked great and that she "human-
ized" politics. However, the media did not have this view and they used
the "red dress" photograph on a number of front pages to demonstrate
Kernot's lack of political judgement. There was no story attaching to the
photograph itself, nor any mention of its context within the longer magazine article which hadn't even been published at that time:

> It was very dishonest of them, because it was done completely out of
> context . . . the headline was, "Labor's scarlet woman," but as you've
> never seen her before. No story, just the picture. I tell you, I had to
> keep my patience . . . [the media] said it was a great big lapse of
> judgement, as though, you know, somehow because I put on a red
> dress everything else I've ever done or might do in the future is all
> gone.

Of course, women choose to dress provocatively because they
can and because it is a way of achieving a media presence quickly. This
strategy is useful for women in opposition and especially in minority
parties because they would otherwise find it very hard to get any exposure. Often, women will do or wear or say something unexpected in the
hope that they might be able to slide in a policy position along with the
expected quote and picture. But there is also a political point in expanding the scope of our perceptions of who politicians are and what they
look like:

> When I was sworn in, I was wearing Doc Martens [workboots] and I
> got more publicity for that in my first few months in office than any-
> thing I said and its funny really, because my party has radical poli-
> cies, like decriminalising marijuana . . . but it's the shoes the media
> focus on. (Natasha Stott Despoja, Australian Democrats)

While Stott Despoja recognizes that the kind of publicity she attracts,
both as a consequence of deliberate sartorial strategies but also because
of her continuing label of "youngest Senator," and the fact that she is an
attractive and articulate women, is as likely to parody her as it is to do
her "straight." She believes that such is the price she pays for gaining the
public's attention. Often, members of minority parties, such as the

Greens, offer the media plenty of opportunities for stories, especially when the members themselves leave the way clear for a particular line of attack. Just before Dee Margetts (Green Party, Australia) arrived in Parliament, she had been an impoverished student and had little money for clothes, so she made her own, which immediately made her a figure of fun for the media when she wore these home-grown efforts in the House:

> When Christabel [Chamarette][1] and I were both in Parliament together, a comedy programme called *The Late Show* did a spoof on us and had a go at our clothes, saying that we had passed the budget in 1993 because the government did a deal offering us a new clothing line called "the Christabel and Dee line for women who want to look like 1980s maths teachers."

Some women suggest that the objectification of women politicians as subjects for the male (sexualized) gaze is symptomatic of the way in which women's bodies are commodified in mainstream society, that women are viewed principally as sexual objects, no matter what their profession, no matter why they are otherwise "newsworthy." A woman politician is always described as a *woman* politician, her sex is always on display, always the primary descriptor. She is defined by what she is not. She is not simply a politician (male as norm), but rather a special kind of professional, a *woman* politician. It is women's bodies, not their minds, that fascinate the boys (Ross, 1995a, 1995b). Dawn Primarolo (Labour, UK) argues that women are "never free of our bodies . . . because of the continued presence of pornography, soft porn and pin-ups."

> I think that men's sex hardly enters into it when they're in politics. No one thinks of them like that until they've transgressed, then suddenly there's a moment when something to do with sex happens and men are in the public eye, but only when they've been caught out. All the rest of the time, they are mainstream serious politicians and sex has nothing to do with it. But I think that [with] women politicians, the minute anyone wants to be critical in any way, their looks or the fact that they are a woman instantly sexualises them and so their sexuality is part of them all the time that they are being commented on, for good or ill. They [the media] might say "attractive" or "unattractive" or "lumpy" or "man-hating" and she might be talking about policy on Northern Ireland. Of course it's all linked to the idea that women are their bodies for men and men fancy them or not. (Clare Short, Labour, UK)

---

[1]Senator Christabel Chamarette was a Western Australian Senator (for the Greens) from March 1992-June 1996.

The media also undermine women as serious political actors by framing them in sexual situations with male colleagues, a strategy which has a particular potency when used in cartoon form. Many women talked about being pictured in this way, especially when they were suddenly taken up as a news item because of a particular prominence. For example, when Cheryl Kernot crossed the floor of the Australian Parliament in 1997, giving up her leadership of the Australian Democrats to become a Labor candidate, the media responded, in picture-form, by cartoons of her in bed with Kim Beasley (Labor Leader). Similarly, when Pauline Hanson was dominating public discourse in early 1998 because of her spectacular success in the Queensland State elections, she was immortalized in cartoons showing her in bed with a variety of political colleagues, as well as pictured as a puppet, with men pulling the strings. She was thus characterized as a "not very bright woman who's being manipulated and is too dumb to even know that she's being manipulated" (Sue West, Labor, Australia). Such presentations convey several negatives simultaneously and sometimes even contradictory messages: that women are being "used" by men; that they are in thrall to and carrying out the orders of men; or that they have used their sex to advance their political careers. "It's almost as if you can't think of a woman without thinking of her sexuality simultaneously" (Carmen Lawrence, Labor, Australia).

A woman politician is always described as a *woman* politician in the media; her sex is always on display, always the primary descriptor. She is defined by what she is *not*; that is, she is not what is expected of a politician who bears no gendered descriptor, masquerading as a neutral "it" but clearly marked as male if the label "woman politician" is to make sense (Ross & Sreberny-Mohammadi, 1997). In a recent radio show, *Week in Westminster* (Radio 4, 5.2.2000), the political commentator Anthony Howard talked about different leadership styles of prime ministers, referring to "Callaghan," "Wilson" and "Major" but pointedly talking about "Mrs Thatcher," adding a gendered reference when there was absolutely no possibility of the audience *not* knowing that Thatcher was female. Not only does he name her as woman, he also names her as wife. If elections are won or lost in the public gaze of the media, as the media itself has often claimed, then it is easy to argue that the privileging of form over function, presentation over policy, means that *all* politicians are subject to the tyranny of telegeneity and must surrender to inappropriate sartorial scrutiny, not just the women. While this is, in principle, true, the objectification of male politicians in this way is noticeable because of its infrequency. With women politicians it is, on the contrary, the rule.

Even for women in positions of considerable power, such as previous Prime Ministers Golda Meir, Indira Gandhi or Margaret Thatcher, they nonetheless received broadly similar media coverage, suggesting that, although there was very little that was traditionally "feminine" about these women nor anything very similar about them apart from their shared gender, the "woman politician" frame was used as a handy catch-all, regardless of their differences. "If women leaders are described in a common way in the news, despite these differences, this suggests the media are viewing women through a sex stereotyped lens" (Norris, 1997, p. 155). However, Norris goes on to suggest that the evidence of her own study rejected the proposition that journalists employ simplistic (en)gendered stereotypes, perhaps because the amount of material readily available on such women militates against the necessity to trade such lazy shots. What did emerge from her study, though, was the disclosure of a number of similar thematic frames which positioned emergent women leaders as breaking the mould, as the outsiders winning against the odds, and as agents of change. These are all very "positive" frames at a superficial level, but the first two at least are unsustainable over the lifetime of a woman leader's career; they are no longer possible once she is an established rather than a "new" leader. The third frame is equally problematic since it could, by its emphasis on change (from the barren desert of "politics as usual") set women up to fail, unable to achieve the inevitable, unrealistically high expectations. Fowler's (1995) work with women politicians also found that press interest with women's appearance was a source of constant complaint among her respondents, including a recognition that such preoccupations could lead to women and their achievements being trivialized. Elsewhere, in a study of women members of the Israeli Parliament in the early 1990s, Liran-Alper (1994) reports that her respondents criticized the way in which national media marginalised women in precisely the same ways as discussed above.

THE GENDERED DISCOURSE OF POLITICS

Beyond the media obsession with the physicality of women politicians, the gendered assumptions about politicians are manifest in the discourses used. The differential use of language signals the media's opprobrium against women who transgress the orthodox boundaries of what "real" women are and what "real" women do. What they don't do, apparently, is become politicians:

If a woman goes out at 6'o'clock in the morning to clean offices to keep her family together, to raise her children, she will be presented as a heroine. If she wants to run that office she will be presented as an unnatural woman and even worse, as an unnatural mother. (Glenda Jackson, Labour, UK)

They like us as a change from the chaps, as long as we aren't as grey as most of them. They like us to fulfil their obligation for a "token woman." But they usually trivialise us unless we are Cabinet Ministers. Women with brains and balls are still an anomaly but at least we get more "shouts" than the men. (Theresa Gorman, Cons, UK)

In a study undertaken by the British group Women in Journalism (1996), analyses of stories were undertaken which compared the news media's treatment of comparable personalities in comparable situations in order to examine what differences, if any, could be seen in reporting strategies, where tone, style, and language were all explored. One of the case studies they undertook was the "defection" of two Conservative MPs—Emma Nicholson and Alan Howarth—to other parties, Nicholson to the Liberal Democrats, and Howarth to the Labour Party. When the researchers used quantitative measures, they found that the number of news stories in each case was about the same, and the number of column inches was broadly similar as well. Where differences did emerge, however, was in the tone and style of the reporting, especially in the use of negative quotes from previous colleagues, with Nicholson being written off as a "vain and silly woman [with a] plummy, affected voice," "muddled," "pseudo-feminist," treacherous," frightful bitch," at an emotional age," while Howarth was praised as a man of principle and a moral crusader, "conscientious, intelligent and committed." A selection of quotes from the newspapers that the authors monitored makes the point well:

On Nicholson:
"Prostitutes her views around the House for some months" (John Carlisle MP, quoted in the *Observer*).
"She and her husband, who was married to someone else at the time, 'fell in love at a lunch party'" (*Daily Mail*).
"Has been known for years in right-wing Tory circles as the Wicked Witch of the West" (anonymous Tory MP quoted in the *Observer*).
"Emma Nicholson is an admirable woman but not a serious politician. Her defection is a dramatic gesture, gratifying to her personal opinions and fulfilling a psychic need but it will have the opposite effect from the one she wants to make" (*Guardian*).

On Howarth:
"Unquestionably one of the most thoughtful, intelligent and inde-
pendent-minded people in the whole House" (*Observer*).
"The Howarth testament insinuates itself into the party bloodstream
and will dominate its body politic at Blackpool" (*Guardian*).
"Disillusioned" (*Daily Mail*).
"An extraordinary man in extraordinary times" (*Guardian*).
(Women in Journalism, 1996, p. 15)

The researchers argue that, although Nicholson was occasional-
ly afforded the courtesy of being considered as conscientious, it was the
catalogue of failure (in career terms) within the Tory Party, as well as the
wellspring of spite suddenly unleashed upon her by her erstwhile colleagues, which dominated coverage of Nicholson stories rather than the
principles by which she stood. Her aristocratic lineage, her millionaire
husband, and her adopted child all featured prominently in news stories, while such personal features were entirely absent in the coverage of
Howarth. Interestingly, though, the media exercised considerable
restraint in not drawing attention to the fact that Nicholson is hearing
disabled, and even her colleagues were discrete on the matter, indicating
that certain personal characteristics are still regarded as forbidden topics
for discussion, even for the tabloids. When Nicholson's husband died
recently in circumstances which might have accelerated his death,
Nicholson was again in the news, but even though she had crossed the
floor more than five years previously (in 1995), she was given the label
of "defector" in a number of news reports. Howarth, on the other hand,
disappeared without a trace onto the backbenches, never to be heard of
again. This kind of negative-positive framing when matching women
and men across story types was also very clear in my own work on the
Labour leadership campaigns in 1994, where Tony Blair was framed as
an up-standing family man while the only woman in the contest,
Margaret Beckett, was described in universally unflattering and grossly
personal terms (Ross, 1995a, p. 502):

Mr. Blair is a man of rare ability. Rarer still in modern politics, he
has an unblemished reputation for honesty and integrity that com-
mands the respect even of his most committed opponents . . . that
Labour were able to recover so well between 1987 and 1992 was in
no small part due to Blair's contribution from the front bench in
moderating the harsh socialism of the early 1980s Labour Party . . .
he is happily married to fellow-barrister Cherie Booth . . . and they
have three children . . . Blair is a devoted and active father . . . committed to family values. (*Daily Mail*, 13.5.94)

> Deputy leader Margaret Beckett, 51, has the task of leading Labour
> through the European elections. But her spell in the limelight is like-
> ly to be short-lived . . . since her election as deputy two years ago,
> most Labour MPs admit she has been a disaster . . . and has even
> been ridiculed for her lack of fashion sense . . . Smith didn't look like
> the man to lead Britain . . . particularly with that gargoyle Margaret
> Beckett in tow . . . if Labour is still loathe to sever all links with the
> past, it should dump the gruesome and insincere Beckett and
> replace her with John Prescott. . . . (*Sun*, 13.5.94)

Unfortunately, Beckett stuck it out and was rewarded with a
promotion to Secretary of State for Trade and Industry in Blair's 2001
Government. Confounding the limits of "normal" female aspirations
and role-types carries with it specific penalties which speak in the register of hysteria and aberration. Numerous studies which have looked at
social responses to women's refusal to conform to (gender) type demonstrate the labeling processes which immediately come into play (see, for
example, Gilbert & Gubar, 1979; Showalter, 1985; Tavris, 1992;
Daughton, 1994), where "deviant" women are regarded as sick, unnatural, or mad. The women politicians whom I interviewed for this book
identified a number of language strategies which were routinely
employed by the media to describe them and their activities. Carmen
Lawrence (Labor, Australia), commenting on the time when she was
Premier of Western Australia, suggests that, because she was Australia's
first-ever female State Premier, the media were constantly finding new
ways in which to signal her gender and her novelty, mostly because they
simply didn't know how to cover this unique situation. She is well
aware of the ways in which the use of her first name is always a mixed
blessing:

> At various times I got labels like Lawrence of Suburbia, although
> I'm anything but a suburban mum . . . my first name was routinely
> used in reference to my being a premier or aspiring to it or whatev-
> er, and you don't see that with men. I mean admittedly I've got a
> somewhat unusual name, but I've seen it happen with other women
> too . . . they become familiar very quickly. Now that's a double-
> edged sword because on the one hand it means you can be seen as
> friendly, approachable, one of the family in a sense, but it also is a
> way of diminishing your significance as a public figure.

One British politician mentioned her surprise at the way in which con-
testants in a by-election in which she was standing and in which she was
subsequently elected, were reported in the press.

> Fighting in a by-election . . . I was struck by the barrage of sexist comment. Because three of the four candidates were women it was described as the "menopausal contest" by a number of commentators [and] the most vicious articles written about me then, and since, were written by women journalists. (Helen Liddell, Labour, UK)

The *Guardian* carried an article on the by-election proclaiming, "Gender scrap for Smith's seat" (16.5.1995). Liddell won and in 2001 became Secretary of State for Scotland. Sheila Camerer (New National Party, South Africa), believes there is a deliberate culture of undermining women politicians through particular framing techniques, and she suggests that part of the reason lies in the hands of male journalists who continue to perpetuate a discriminatory regime:

> The media tend to stereotype women from all the parties and I have been the butt of it often. I've been called "blondie" and "the dumb blonde of politics," even if I make a serious statement that they approve of, the picture they print is me in a frivolous hat, you know . . . So I have had a lifetime of gender stereotyping in the media and it irritates me tremendously. They way they go for Winnie [Mandela] or any prominent women of any party, they can't resist sexist remarks and gender stereotypes. I think it's because most of the editors are men, of the daily newspapers, so there is still a culture that is gender unfriendly when it comes to women in politics.

Women Parliamentarians also argue that they are often described in highly emotional and much less favorable terms than men: "I don't know how many times I've been described as having my claws out, instead of saying here's a woman being robust, which is what they would say about men. Who would describe a man's claws being out?" (Ann Clywd, Labour, UK). Similarly, in her final speech to the Victoria Parliament in 1994 as outgoing Premier, Joan Kirner emphasized her decision-making toughness, rejecting the media's insistence on casting her as "soft, furry, cuddly and polka-dotted and not being able to make tough decisions" (cited in Reynolds, 1995, p. 120)

The sentiments expressed in the examples above echo findings from other academic studies. Looking particularly at the way in which newspapers frame women in their narratives, Fowler (1991) argues that

> women are represented in an unfavorable light and men are characterized by mentions of occupational and political success . . . taken all together, the discourse of the newspaper media handles men and women in terms of different sets of categories, different stereotypes [and] it seems very likely that discrimination in discourse helps maintain intellectual habits that promote discrimination in practice. (p. 105)

"Women are less quoted in newspapers, projects that female ministers are involved with are less likely to get reported on" (Janet Love, ANC, South Africa).

Patricia de Lille (PAC, South Africa) makes it clear, though, that the invisibility of women in political coverage is not always a consequence of deliberate decision making on the part of journalists since women have to be making news in order to be covered. She articulates that which many of us already know: that sexism in political parties contributes to the already poor coverage of women Parliamentarians more generally. Somehow, both political parties and the media need to consider how this skewed portrayal of women politicians impacts upon the democratic process:

> You will find some key conferences taking place and invitations are sent to a political party. The party decides to send some of their good guys, prominent guys, and it is the same people over and over. It is at that point where we need to rectify things, because you can't expect the *Cape Town Times* to write about Matambu, if her party hasn't put her on the invitation to represent them.

5

Acting Up: Women and Media Negotiation

I know I'm a lot to blame. I don't do enough with the media, but I just don't want to. I don't want to risk having my privacy invaded, for me and my family. (Joan Ruddock, Labour, UK)

INTRODUCTION

It is a truism that being in the public eye means that one is always vulnerable to media scrutiny, often under the spurious guise of "the public interest." While women politicians discussed in this book certainly believe that the media's interest in them as specifically women politicians goes with the territory, they also recognize that putting themselves in the public eye inevitably invites the kind of interest which can and often does lead to a more intrusive scrutiny. This has resulted in women being circumspect about taking up media opportunities when they are presented. Dawn Primarolo (Labour, UK) recalls being asked by a breast cancer campaign group to launch a new screening initiative which would require her to wear a T-shirt with the message "do more for your breasts than any bra can—examine them" emblazoned across her chest. Although she wanted to support the campaign, she was well aware of the way in which the media would cover the launch, and so she declined to appear. Other women tell similar stories about wanting to promote themselves and their parties but feeling anxious about the type of "expo-

101

sure" which could result. Cheryl Kernot (Labor, Australia) describes very well what it's like to live under the media's persistent spotlight and illustrates precisely why many women politicians are very anxious about letting journalists get too close to them. While many are relatively philosophical about being targets of media attention themselves, they are very concerned with the levels of intrusion which can affect their families:

> I was stalked at home, by the media. I couldn't go out of my home . . . they sat across the road . . . on one occasion, my daughter had to leave—my husband was meant to take her somewhere—and people advising me said "don't let him leave the house, because they'll come back if they see him leave," so friends had to come and collect my daughter from the front . . . it's just disgraceful. Now my husband and daughter have a very negative view of the media. My husband said he'd never felt so powerless as getting up day after day. He'd appear in the doorway of the bedroom like the grim reaper with the daily newspapers. I had to finally say to him, "I think this is a very bad way to start the day, we're all feeling totally vulnerable. Let's not let them rule us like this." My daughter was 14 then and a headline would be "Kernot's sexual past: whose business is it anyway?" She saw the stalking and she saw the level of invasion and intrusion . . . but my daughter's 15 now and she's entitled to grow up without that glare. I mean she gets enough of it when we go out and people just point all the time, but I don't want her made, being public property. (Cheryl Kernot, Labor, Australia)

> I have a rule that I don't have my children photographed. Whether that is a gender issue or whether that is more . . . it started off being a security issue, secondly a very deliberate point not to expose the children to my public life. We had a lot of coverage at the beginning of the ANC and my children did not like the onslaught of cameras in their faces, coming to the house, etc. My husband's grandfather was a previous prime minister in SA and was regarded as the architect of apartheid. The family has always had a fairly high profile in politics going way back. (Melanie Voerwoerd, ANC, South Africa)

> I have done a magazine piece . . . but there was a lot of negotiation and eventually I said OK. It is important for women to speak about the difficulties involved with politics and family life, but I am careful not to complain too much about this because I've had a lot of flack about that, told that at least I have a decent salary and can pay for someone to look after my children. (Dawn Primarolo, Labour, UK)

What I know will get me into women's magazines is if I involve my
daughters and I am not prepared to do that, so at the moment, the
magazines aren't interested, so that's the price you pay. They want a
family story . . . I am a single parent and they want a family-type set
up . . . well, I'm not interested in that and I've paid for it. (Meg Lees,
Australian Democrats)

Women's circumspection about making themselves too accessible to the media is most often related to their fears that their family
would suffer intrusions in privacy, but it's a hard line to tread. If too
much effort is made to protect one's family, this can then give rise to an
escalation in media interest since there could be an ulterior motive for
such secrecy:

They don't know where to draw the line and they become very
intrusive so I obviously sort of worked all the time to try and maintain a level of privacy in my own life but doing nothing which could
be used to suggest I was hiding something. (Carmen Lawrence,
Labor, Australia)

The way in which the media are able to manipulate the statements made
by political actors makes women cautious about taking up media opportunities: "It's meant that we're far less forthright with the media. I am
very cautious about taking any of them into my confidence and talking
about the problems and difficulties we may have" (De-Anne Kelly,
National Party, Australia). But women are nonetheless hungry for the
exposure, so choices have to be made about which appearance or interview will yield maximum publicity at the same time as providing minimum potential for disaster and intrusion. Most women reported preferring live interviews where there was limited scope for creative editing,
and studio discussion programmes where there was a genuine sense of
debate. However, some women who had had experience of the interro-
gation-style interview believe that presenters will often see women as
easy targets for intimidation and bullying, particularly as women have
generally had far less match-practice than men and are more likely to
follow the rules, unlike the men who, when interrupted, will simply
shout more loudly. For example, during a broadcast of *Question Time*,
Clare Short was treated very rudely by the programme host, David
Dimbleby, and was so outraged that she felt compelled to publicly
remonstrate with him. She felt that the programme carries with it under-
tones which were about class as well as gender and that, although there
was another woman on the panel, she was not a politician and was
therefore only on the periphery of the debate. Short, on the other hand,
was contesting the "serious" political space and resisted attempts to "be

put back in my box." It was this act of resistance which lay at the root of Dimbleby's antagonism as he and the other men attempted to wrest control away from "the woman."

> Well, I must say, I haven't been treated like that for a very long time and there was something peculiar going on. It was very much a group of aging, declining public school boys together and I was just a complete outsider. I don't think it was just about being a woman, it was also about class. I think he [David Dimbleby] was insufferably rude and I had about 50 or 60 letters afterwards from members of the public saying, I'm not Labour but what a rude man, and people stopped me in the street and said what's he got against you? I think it was remarkable but I felt that they were all being terribly clubby and there was one aspect of it that was pathetic. They're all getting older, they're all second-rate players and they were all making these remarks and I wasn't meant to be there. The net result, certainly from the mail, is that it did me more good than harm. They give you a hard time and they think they're so clever. They can goad you into aggressive behaviour and then turn round and say, isn't she aggressive?! They put you on the spot behaving like that, but then people find out what you're made of. (Clare Short, Labour, UK)

As well as these kind of intimidation tactics, the inexperience of many women politicians when they appear on high-profile political programmes such as *Question Time* means that they will often stick to the rules while the battle-hardened male guests constantly elbow and shout their way to the front:

> I can remember one programme I was on, where we were each told the rules, that you will each have two bites of the cherry and over and above that, you will be free to come in as you want to, with the contributions you wanted to make. I remember that I stuck to the rules and I didn't interrupt because I'd been told that they would come back to me and then the presenter didn't. And then you're faced with a situation where you suddenly find that even in the course of a programme, the rules are being changed and you have gone back to this adversarial style. Because a man butted in and hijacked the agenda, you've got no choice but to ignore the rules and do the same. (Joan Walley, Labour, UK)

> You can be jolly strong, very determined, but you can't outshout them [men]. If you start shouting back you sound shrill and the physical difference is a huge advantage to them. All your media training tells you that you must not interrupt too much, so when they interrupt you, you try to carry on and then you sound terrible.

You hear it on *Today*, when they interrupt the women they shut up but when they interrupt the men, they just speak louder. (Margaret Hodge, Labour, UK)

Television appearances are possibly the most dangerous arena in which politicians perform since they provide a highly visible opportunity for elected members to be questioned about specific policies, in "real-time," so audiences can see exactly how they respond to what can often be awkward or provocative questions and measure the consistency and coherence of the reply. They are also dangerous because they are public and a matter of record, and attempts by party spin doctors to downplay or even undo the words uttered by politicians often follow after a particularly damning television appearance. For example, shortly after the 1997 general election in Britain, one of the *Guardian's* political columnists, Matthew Norman, waged a highly personal and damaging campaign in his regular column against a newly elected MP, Helen Brinton, after she had made a rather over-zealous appearance on the television programme, *Newsnight*. Norman accused Brinton of being a robot because she insisted on giving a comprehensive and highly detailed party political answer to every question put to her, giving a very good impression of being an eager and humorless apparatchik. For whatever reason, Norman took strongly against Brinton and her performance on that programme to such an extent that she became notorious as the person against whom the infamous "on message" taunt became most frequently used (McDougall, 1998a).

Despite their misgivings about the media's intrusion into their lives, women politicians recognize the crucial role played by broadcasting and the press in giving publicity to them and their colleagues, particularly backbenchers, and they are all too aware of the consequences of not conforming to what the media wants of them. In McDougall's (1998b) work with the incoming group of British women MPs in 1997, she argues that the majority of women she interviewed believe that the media treat women politicians differently from men, "and they all wished it was not so" (p. 80). Generally, there was a clear acknowledgement of the mutually dependent relationship which exists between politicians and the media (see, for example, Franklin, 1994) but for many women, they are obliged to play by the media's rules and not the other way round, while media professionals will often argue the precise opposite. The highly regarded and experienced interviewer, Sir Robin Day (1987), for example, argued that politicians use the media as a party political mouthpiece, answering however many different questions with the same, completely unrelated political point—and to some extent, that was Matthew Norman's point as well—lamenting the good old days of the 1960s and 1970s when he claims that politicians did at least answer the questions they were asked instead of using techniques such as "broken record" to simply repeat the basic message they actually wish to convey.

Yet, there is always caution about recorded appearances because of the media's propensity to edit politicians' speeches and use only one or two sentences which do not make sense out of context, so that the speaker ends up appearing stupid or confused. While Franklin (1994, 1997) may well be right in suggesting that the burgeoning of media outlets has created many more media opportunities for politicians to sell slickly-packaged messages, more access also means more chance of misrepresentation.

> The approach is invariably that you are trying to hide something, that you are concealing something, that you are a phony . . . on many occasions I have wondered why I bothered to give an interview at all because they didn't really need me. They had already written the piece. (Marion Roe, Cons, UK)

Questions about the appropriateness of doing soft media such as magazine interviews also exercised many women, largely because such exposure often carries with it accusations from the "serious" media that women are making politics too frivolous, and for many women, it is always a judgement call. Magazines have a very high circulation, often three or four times higher than a prime circulation daily newspaper, so the reach is huge, but the low-brow nature—especially those aimed at women—means that politicians have to be careful about the slant and focus of any piece they agree to:

> I was sitting in an airport lounge the other day and opened a magazine and there was Cheryl [Kernot] and the conservative politician sitting next to me, who hates democrat women said, "don't worry, love, no one will read it," and I said, "you're joking aren't you, a million women read this every week," and he didn't believe me. They just don't get it. (Natasha Stott Despoja, Australian Democrats]

> While you are not known and wanting to make a place for yourself, then it has got to be very tempting, but it is naïve, this business of women politicians being sort of the sex symbol type it's not my style, I pass, but I wouldn't be critical of others doing it, they might be right, it might be fine. (Margaret Reid, Liberal, Australia)

> I don't think there is anything basically wrong with letting people see that you are a human being, that you have a family and you play soccer or whatever . . . but if you want to treated as a serious player in policy and in shaping what happens in this place, you have got to be very careful to balance it out. (Judi Moylan, Liberal, Australia)

While many women are rather equivocal about doing soft media for lifestyle pieces, there is rather more support for using magazines to get important policy and health points across to an audience who would otherwise not hear the message. Thus, magazines are seen as useful political vehicles when the emphasis is on policy, but as more questionable as a tool by which to publicize oneself. However, even here there is ambiguity, since "self-promotion" is also seen as providing role models to other women, that they, too, could organize work and family in a satisfactory way:

> Women's magazines have been unbelievably helpful, in their portrayal of women MPs, and the problems they have and the ways they are addressing those problems. So you can't forget the magazine section. Nearly all of them have covered these women who have achieved, and they hold them up as role models. Your life and what you do outside politics informs your political opinions, I don't think you can see yourself as being totally apart from one or the other. (Val Viljoen, ANC, South Africa)

> I think it is important for us to be more imaginative in the ways we use the media. I don't think we use women's magazines enough. I would like to do something for, say, *Cosmo*, because I would be talking to many women who I wouldn't otherwise reach. But it would have to be issue-based—I wouldn't do a lifestyle piece. What on earth for? (Fiona Mactaggart, Labour, UK)

Mactaggart is keen to "burst out" of the straightjacket of daily newspapers, instead encouraging magazines to write seriously about parental leave and welfare benefits and thus providing access to a wider base of the population on knowledge about social policy issues. "Many women have very strong political views but they don't see themselves as political and they are not interested in those particular bits of the newspaper." She is clear that there is little point in having policies on, say, teenage pregnancy if that policy isn't communicated to teenagers in a form and in a forum in which they are likely to be listening and receptive.

WOMAN-ON-WOMAN RELATIONS: SISTER JOURNALISTS?

It would be heartening to think that perhaps women journalists would bring new and different perspectives to their reporting of politics and, for our purposes, the reporting of women MPs. However, content analysis and anecdotal evidence provided by women themselves suggest that women journalists often resort to even more macho reporting styles than their male colleagues as if to prove their professional mettle and, of course, in order to get their material past the sub-editor. Quite often, women interviewees will be more forthcoming to a woman journalist because the discursive space which opens out between two women will often generate an atmosphere of collusion and then that woman-shaped bond will often render the woman interviewee more candid and more expansive than she would (or should) be with a male interviewer:

> There was an article about me in the *Guardian* by [a woman journalist] and it was a perfectly sympathetic piece and she wrote something that was meant to be flattering—that I was sexy or attractive or something—and I thought, good heavens, this is a *woman* journalist [original emphasis]. Women don't talk about each other like that. They might say, wears striking elegant outfits or something, we might say that about each other, but this was her writing like a man. It was an extraordinary thing to do. She obviously felt she had to take on that [male] stance. (Clare Short, Labour, UK)

> I think that women journalists can be very spiteful, I have been the butt of [. . .] she and I don't see eye to eye politically, and she managed to say something nasty about me putting on lipstick . . . I was probably suffering from dry lips because of the air conditioning or something. So I think it is the case that there are . . . some women who are not principled enough not to do this [attack women]. I think in her case she . . . used it [gender] as a political weapon to denigrate me and devalue any contribution I might have been making to the debate on the Truth Commission. But there we are! That is her choice but I think it is unprincipled of her, actually. Because she does tend to line up with the gender lobby and so on. (Sheila Camerer, New National Party, South Africa)

> They always get women to write nastily about women, and I think they do it deliberately so we can't complain that it's sexism from a man. (Angela Eagle, Labour, UK)

Women journalists are often much more hostile in their reporting of women politicians than their male counterparts, and many women represented in this study believe that women journalists are used deliberately by news producers to either disarm interviewees and thus encourage them to disclose more than they want, or else to write bitchy women-on-women pieces which are given a spurious authenticity because the journalist and politician share the same sex. Clare Short argues that it is not even as if women journalists betray the trust of their female interviewees, that they don't tend to reveal views which are supposed to be "off-the-record," but rather that one woman talking to another inevitably leads to a lot more disclosure than is generally good for the interviewee. "I've noticed myself ending up having a chat as one does and then reading the copy afterwards and thinking, Oh my god, I was a bit self-revelatory there" (Clare Short, Labour, UK). Ann Lesley, a journalist for the *Daily Mail* rejects absolutely the charge that some women politicians make, that women journalists are simply "obeying orders." "[That's] utter piffle. There isn't an editor born who could make me write something I don't believe. When I write that Harriet Harman is a bossy little milk monitor, that's what I believe" (cited in McDougall, 1998b, p. 94).

In Wales, where resistance to the Labour Party's pro-women strategies has been particularly marked, further hostile fuel has been poured on the fire in the mountains by the journalist Anne Carlton, who wrote a number of critical pieces for both the national and local press. She was provided with precious column inches because she had formed a "women against quotas" group, albeit that group membership is scarcely as high as the number of participants of a typical Labour Party branch meeting. That Carlton is married to Denzil Davies, Labour MP for Llanelli also probably contributed to her dissenting voice being privileged over less hysterical outpourings. Looking at women journalists from a more sympathetic position, Clare Short suggests that, like women politicians, women in the media have to compete in a man's world, and they often have to play by the big boys' rules if they are going to survive. This inevitably means adopting the male-oriented ethos of the newsroom and taking on a determinedly masculine gaze when writing about women. Women in this study were scathing in their criticisms of media organizations which are scarcely exemplary in their recruitment of women, suggesting that the relative invisibility of women in news media has the effect of maintaining a male-oriented view of what constitutes "news."

However, women did acknowledge that some women journalists have tried to bring some balance to political reporting, particularly in the face of the worst excesses being played out against women Parliamentarians: "There are a lot of women in the gallery who find this disgraceful and say it is outrageous and wouldn't happen to men" (Sue Mackay, Labor, Australia), but unfortunately, most of them are not in positions of authority or have power to reframe the gender agenda:

> The print media is controlled by the editorial departments and even
> if you get a sensitive journalist who writes good stories, frequently
> they will be butchered by the time you see it. Even if there is a

female journalist who seems to be responsible, sometimes it's just the way a headline is put together by a sub that can swing the opinion from the beginning. (Meg Lees, Australian Democrats)

One of the things that I've noticed is that some women wrote about it [a "positive" story about women MPs' achievements] and their pieces got scrapped, so it's not enough to get women in the lobby engaged in something, we've actually got to do something about the editors of newspapers. (Fiona Mactaggart, Labour, UK)

And in a kind of political double-bluff, sometimes it is one's own "side" which will make damaging comments to the media under the cloak of anonymity, as was clear in the Labour leadership elections in 1995 when much of the negative material circulating about Margaret Beckett almost certainly emanated from inside the Party (Ross, 1995a). Clare Short, in a devastatingly candid interview with Steve Richards for the *New Statesman*, more than hinted at the practice of selectively "leaking" information from Party headquarters to the media and Richards (1996) argued that "It is well known that some of them [Tony Blair's advisors] 'briefed against' her . . . political correspondents were told she was unreliable and a maverick" (p. 24). More recently, the small controversy which raged over Mo Mowlam's relegation to the unappetising and strictly backroom post of Cabinet Coordinator, also known as "the enforcer," after her high-profile and mostly successful job in Northern Ireland is shot through with a scarcely veiled "whispering campaign" reported in the media, which surfaced again when she announced her intention to stand down at the next election in 2001 (see *The Observer*, 3 September 2000): "So, who is behind the whispers, and why are they gunning for Mo? Mowlam is convinced there is someone, somewhere in Downing Street (not Millbank) trying to get her. Some ministerial colleagues agree. So do some backbenchers" (White, 2000, p. 2). It is noteworthy that Michael White, one of the *Guardian's* pre-eminent political journalists feels he must make the point that Mowlam believes that members of her own side are responsible for the slurs rather than the massed ranks of the media—"not Millbank." The responsibility for ruining the careers of politicians is often laid at the door of the media, especially journalists, for their unwavering interest in the more salacious elements of politicians' private lives, and it is in recognition of this perception that White presumably feels the need to exonerate himself and his collegial corps. But even as it is difficult, especially for backbenchers and more especially women backbenchers, to achieve the oxygen of publicity, when it does come, the woman in question is still likely to be on the receiving end of critical comment from her own colleagues. When Ann Clwyd MP staged a sit-in at the Tower Colliery in her Welsh constituency, which was being threatened with closure, her fellow MPs were less than supportive. Rather than congratulating her on her campaign, her colleagues could instead be heard muttering, "that bloody woman's at it again" (Sedgemore, 1995: 127).

PROACTIVE STRATEGIES WITH JOURNALISTS: CULTIVATING STRENGTH

In order to take a more proactive approach to media coverage, a number of women have adopted the strategy of not only being circumspect in their choice of media engagements, to maximise impact and minimize likelihood of skidding on banana skins, but also of cultivating relations with particular journalists (McDougall, 1998b). Those journalists can either be lobby or mainstream political journalists, but they are usually trusted by politicians to deal sensitively with whatever story they bring to them.

> I don't have the same fear of the press that perhaps some of our members do, because I know the individuals concerned, and I haven't been as upset as some people have by the negative publicity that we have had. But it is about making the personal contacts, getting to know the reporters. With regard to the lobby journalists here it is difficult, because of the lack of time, but I have been lucky here in that a lot of the journalists I have known, for example [. . .] I have known him since he was a boy. It s like the old boy network but in a different way. (Val Viljoen, ANC, South Africa)

> You have to form relationships with people and you have to get to know the individual journalists and they have to get to know you. You have to establish your credibility on the issue and then you have to consistent and service them with information. But it's very much a people thing. (Kate Lundy, Labor, Australia)

> There's no doubt that it's extremely valuable to have those [media] contacts because you find that they are the contacts that tend to phone you back if they're not sure of a point, they will listen to you more carefully, they will come and collect your documentation . . . but newspapers have not gone out of their way to make contact with women politicians. They have made contact with key party people, probably on the instructions of their financial managers. (Suzanne Vos, IFP, South Africa)

When the British politician Clare Short was reunited with her son, Toby Graham, whom she had given away for adoption some 25 years previously, she knew that the story would be picked up immediately by the media. To head off potentially harmful versions of the meeting and the events leading up to it, she gave an exclusive interview to the feminist journalist Suzanne Moore. There was an overwhelmingly sympathetic response from the public when Moore's piece made the front page of the *Independent* (17 October 1998) with other newspapers following Moore's lead and putting a "happy" spin on the story. This form of direct news control has worked well for other politicians keen to ensure that their version of particular events gets covered in the least damaging way. Many women are extremely proactive in the way in which they manage their media strategy, identifying both specific media and individual journalists as targets for their stories and reactions. They recognize that for many backbenchers, they need to be constantly pushing for attention, and the more they can "feed" the media with easily digestible stories and soundbites, the more likely they are to become a regular source for comment. Importantly, they need to be able to extemporize on policy points, and this requires high levels of knowledge across a range of issues. For many women Parliamentarians in South Africa, especially members of the ruling ANC, radio is often the communication medium of choice, not only because it has the best reach—continuing high levels of illiteracy across South Africa means that newspapers are mostly read by whites and television is still not the ubiquitous medium it is in the West—but because it is less likely to have a negative-orientated agenda and is more likely to genuinely engage with the community at large.

> Radio has been a really good medium. It is the best medium to get your message across. It is supposed to reach something like 97 per cent of the community, particularly community radio. For example, this particular one sent me through this tape because there was a particular discussion on some legislation that we are dealing with. They sent it through so that we can hear what the people phoning in thought, and I wish we could get more of that because we are missing out on a lot of this community discussion. It is a big problem. We have to find a medium where people can be heard and I think radio is the best, but we don't use it enough. (Vil Viljoen, ANC, South Africa)
>
> Radio is by far the most powerful medium in South Africa, but only certain radio stations. If I was quoted on an African language station, I would have at least 20 or 30 people remarking on it the next week. If it was on the Afrikaans radio station, I would be lucky if

one or two of my colleagues would say something, or on the English stations, the same thing. Talk radio is now popular and a good way of understanding how people feel and think. I make a point of phoning in to the stations and building up relationships: when they know you are willing to talk, they will keep coming back to you. (Melanie Voerwoerd, ANC, South Africa)

Similarly, Patricia de Lille (PAC, South Africa) is clear that being a woman and a spokesperson for a minority party means that one has to be very strategic in looking for media coverage and to consciously seek out journalists and cultivate relations:

You know it is all about being strategic and tactical in your political life, and it applies to men and women equally, if you want to make a breakthrough in the media. For me it has taken years to build up a good relationship with them: I have learnt not to fight with them anymore and sometimes they misquote me, and they do whatever else. But to get into the newspapers first of all, you have to make news: they are not going to put you there because they like your face. I make sure I am accessible 24 hours a day to the media.

Because she is one of only three MPs from her party in Parliament, de Lille tries to keep herself up to speed on as many aspects of policy as possible so that she can always respond to the media's requests to give a comment on new initiatives. She argues that turning the media away is never a good strategy as they might not come back; for her, keeping informed by reading background reports, attending and being part of numerous portfolio committees, and trying to read and listen to as much news media as possible is part of her general media strategy. Crucially, an important aspect of her media strategy is being succinct: "They [journalists] say, 'one reason that we write about you, is that you have sound bites, not long stories.'" Is that an indictment of their attention spans or of ours?

Because achieving publicity for policy positions or initiatives is very difficult for most women, they often work hard at trying to develop good relations with their local media. Not only does this mean that their constituents at least get to know what their elected members are doing (and that they are working on their behalf), but it also has the effect of ensuring that they remain in the mind of the public who will be turning out to vote at the next election. "You must have a good relationship with them [local media] because that's where people, you know, they're going to reach their electorate, that's where you do your real grassroots work" (Helen Coonan, Liberal, Australia). This is a good strategy since local media are usually especially interested in their local politicians and often have less of a "hidden agenda" in terms of trying to get a sensational scoop or biasing story tone. "I think the local media tend to home in on a local issue and give it a local slant rather than trying to beat up the story underneath" (De-Anne Kelly, National Party, Australia), and again, "it's more my local press that I have to be nice to" (Elizabeth Grace, Liberal, Australia). "I will fax a copy of my speech through, I talk to them, let them know what I am doing, and where I am going to be" (Val Viljoen, ANC, South Africa). However, there is a conundrum. On the one hand, local media are interested in their local politicians, but the latter are often more interested in getting exposure in the national media, so there is always tension between the two, especially when the local media is commercial and therefore seen as more low-brow. "We all know that 3AW [a Victoria radio station] reaches thousands of times the audience that ABC has, but because ABC is serious, we kill to be on ABC and don't go out of our way to get on 3AW" (Lyn Allison, Labor, Australia).

But there can be a downside to good relations with journalists when those relations sour because the politician does or says something which puts them out of favour. When Cheryl Kernot stepped down from being leader of the Australian Democrats in 1997 to fight for Labor, there was an immediate and mostly very negative response made to her decision by journalists, and she suggests that part of the problem was that she had always had good relations with several key journalists who, on hearing of her decision, seemed to have felt betrayed, almost in a romantic way, and also that she had made a considerable error of judgement. These two emotional responses were then reflected in the tone, style, and language of much of the media reporting of that event. This is not to say that journalists would not have responded in the same way if Kernot had been a man, but it is unlikely that many would have used quite the same patronising tone. Kernot's comments make clear the importance of having good relationships with journalists, but also indicates their fragility and the payback which can arise when a politician falls foul of particular journalists:

> There was one who was formerly a friend of mine who has written really vitriolic stuff . . . and the day after it [the "defection"] he wrote, "This is the worst mistake you've ever made in your life"— that was the headline—and he rang me up and told me that I was a stupid, stupid woman and that Labor would use me and exploit me like they've done every other woman and . . . I said, "that's your opinion, I actually have a greater view of my own capacity to fight some of these things. I know Labor's done this in the past but I'm actually coming to them in a different way, from other women, and I intend to use that" . . . And then a senior staff member told me that

on the day it happened, this particular male journalist came down to her office to kind of express his concern to the lot of them and she said he behaved like a jilted lover. So there was a lot of that in the press that's flowed on. (Cheryl Kernot, Labor, Australia)

Kernot's experience provides a good example of why women politicians are circumspect about getting close to journalists. It is always a double-edged strategy and of course for some women, positive media strategies mean *not* cultivating relations with journalists, for a variety of reasons, but mostly because such relations are often contingent and fragile:

Well, the politicians who do best often have close relationships with the media but that can also blow up in their faces if, for some reason, they don't deliver or they're seen as not having performed on a particular issue and they get a whack from their favourite journalist. I've never developed a relationship like that and . . . that may be a mistake, but I've tried to keep a professional distance. I regard them as having a job to do which is not mine in a sense, and to be able to adjust my approach depending on the sort of response you get, that can be difficult. (Carmen Lawrence, Labor, Australia)

I think it is a matter of making a conscious decision about the place of the media in your political career . . . I don't place a very high value on personal media. (Judi Moylan, Liberal, Australia)

It is also important that women recognise the different skills they have and use them to their best advantage. Lyn Allison (Labor, Australia) is the first to admit that she does not feel comfortable in face-to-face situations with journalists and consciously shies away from media opportunities:

I don't seek it out . . . I'm not very witty or good at being clever on chat shows and things, I don't enjoy it. It isn't me, but [other women] handle it much better and I think it's good for women to be portrayed as everything along a continuum.

The context in which politicians get to "deal" with journalists is also one which is sometimes awkward or otherwise off-putting to many women, again predisposing them against cultivating relations. For Fiona Mactaggart (Labour, UK), considerable discomfort is felt about the traditional forms of information-exchange which take place between politicians and journalists in the lobby, where the latter hope to be picked up by the former to be fed snippets of information. "The awful thing about the lobby journalists is that they have to hang around like tarts and I don't think that men have the same views that women have, about standing around in the lobby waiting for the pick up." However, more recently, she has begun to form relationships with some of the women lobby correspondents although they tend not to meet in the bar:

> One of the reasons why women MPs don't have great relationships with the lobby is because the places in which most of those relationships are nurtured are horrible places for women to be, smoky bars. And I can't spend very long in a smoky atmosphere, I can't bear it. (Fiona Mactaggart, Labour, UK)

Some women even put up their own funds in an effort to circumvent the media's insistence on interpretation, instead getting their own media voice by writing their own press releases and other written material about what they stand for and what they've been doing on behalf of their constituents, going out directly to their local community:

> I'm going to print a newsletter that is an insert in the local paper, so it looks like part of the paper and that's going to have things about what I'm doing and I'm paying for it, and hopefully, people will read that, as if it was an article, rather than the rubbish or the nonreporting that happens in the rest of the paper. (Elizabeth Grace, Liberal, Australia)

A similar strategy was played out in South Africa, where Tersia King (New National Party, South Africa) paid a newspaper to allow her to promote her own policies in the run-up to the general election:

> I'm actually doing a two-weekly promotion thing, in which I can really speak as much politics as I want and I pay for it myself, so they have to publish it, and then I get reactions from the public, especially from the opposition parties, and then that gives me the opportunity to return again.

Other women adopt the strategy of always issuing press releases and then only repeating precisely what is in that press release when asked to comment further. "If you do a radio interview, the best way to ensure that what you want to say comes out, is to say exactly what's in the press release and go no further" (Jeannie Ferris, Liberal, Australia).

Many women are very cautious about their dealings with the media, often preferring to only go to the media with a story or a policy line or a statement on very specific and focused issues. Their strategy is to provide only occasional soundbites to the media so that when they are despatched, then journalists know that the politician really does have something to say, as opposed to a more scatter gun approach, with policy statements on numerous issues, although for minority parties, this latter is often their only chance of ever getting coverage. Women's approaches to managing their media is, as I have demonstrated, highly diverse, but at least there is a growing recognition that being proactive with the news media is one way of exercising more control over their representation: it doesn't always work, but it is surely better than being misquoted, trivialized, or made invisible.

> I manage my media tightly, but it's an efficient way because when I do put something out, people know that I'm saying something and that it's not frivolous. And the chances are that this might be the only thing they see from me this week and it has some value. (Kate Lundy, Labor, Australia)

6

Women, Politics and News in an Election Climate

Cameras are not directed the same way if you are woman . . . for instance, when you get out of a car, the cameras are focused on your legs . . . it never happens to a man. (Edith Cresson, cited in Liswood, 1998, pp. 71-72)

INTRODUCTION

If the participation of the public in political life is the *sine qua non* of democratic government, then that public needs to be as informed as they can be in order to exercise their basic democratic rights, not least at the ballot box. But, as Thomas Jefferson argued so eloquently nearly 200 years ago, if the public "are not enlightened enough to exercise their control [over society] with a wholesome discretion, the remedy is not to take it from them but to inform their discretion" (cited in Buchanan, 1991, p. 19). So, if the public is to be able to discriminate between different candidates and their policies and thus make an informed choice about who they want to lead and govern them, then they must "acquire sufficient information about matters under public discussion to avoid being easily duped about the facts by self-interested candidate misinformation or distortion" (Buchanan, 1991, p. 22). What Buchanan is implying here, although not quite saying, is that the political "default" position is one whereby the category "politician" (all are pretty much the

119

same) is more likely than less to manipulate the voter/public, so the latter needs to be awake to evidence of the willful intent to deceive.

But of course, Joanne and Joe Public can very easily be derailed from a "proper" understanding of the political process, in its widest sense, simply by virtue of their own ignorance and apathy. Perloff (1998) summarizes a series of studies and surveys carried out over a decade in the United States and reveals alarmingly low levels of political knowledge; for example, in 1987, more than 7 years after the Congressional debate on aid to Nicaragua, only one-third of respondents to a survey knew that Nicaragua is located in Central America; in a 1989 survey, less than half of the respondents knew which party then had a majority in the Senate (both examples taken from Delli Carpini & Keeter, 1991); and that in a 1995 survey for the *Washington Post*, nearly half the respondents could not name the (then) Speaker of the House of Representatives—Newt Gingrich (Morin, 1996). However, some caution does need to be exercised when trying to make causal links between the public's lack of knowledge of certain political "facts" and their/our knowledge (or lack thereof) of other political "facts." As Popkin (1991) has observed quite properly, such surveys (or as he puts it, the "incompetent citizen" literature) are good at telling us what people do *not* know, but are rather poor in providing insights into what they/we *do* know. Lippmann's (1922) classic work on public opinion still has considerable salience to the contemporary news scene of the early 21st century: political opinion is not shaped by the direct experience of politics, but is rather a consequence of the images which we are given via news accounts of politics. As Bennett (1997) questions pertinently, the fundamental conundrum to unravel is how journalists and therefore news organizations more generally—acting in fierce competition with each other—nonetheless manage to construct a political "world" which is both standardized across the sector but also believable enough to form the baseline for the public's political understanding.

As the politician and the journalist play out the delicate dance of the "fool-me-fool-you" two-step, each courting the other in an endless bid to "really" tell it like it is, the inevitable casualty of their dalliances is any kind of reality check which actually provides the electorate with a clear grasp of the particularity of specific political agendas. Real information about policies and priorities falls in the gap between the traditional campaign strategies of the politicos who are keen to square the seductive circle of promising nothing but offering everything, and the journalistic desire to expose precisely the same thing. Most elections are remembered not for the quality of their political debates but for the tedious display of political antagonism vented by each party against the others. They are remembered not for what each party actually has to offer the electorate, but for the interminable news and current affairs programmes which show the same few (male) faces hauled out to argue why everyone but they themselves is unfit to govern, and where most "news" is about the election itself, not about the issues on which it is allegedly being fought.

That television continues to play an important role in elections, at least significant ones such as general, national, and Presidential elections, remains unquestioned, despite the considerable impact that the world wide web has had on information dissemination. In Australia, for example, there was, until quite recently, specific legislation (the Broadcasting Act 1942: section 1.1.6: subsection 4) which enforced a ban on the media's reporting of election issues and party promotion precisely because of the media's putative power as an influential force on public opinion (Winter, 1993). Yet, undoubtedly, the medium of television has changed over the past 30 years, and Hallin (1997) suggests that one indicator of change is the length of a soundbite. The average soundbite has been shrinking over the past few decades, from 40 seconds in 1968 to less than 10 seconds now, and in concert with the diminishing soundbite comes the interpretative voice-over. The polity doesn't need to read or listen to boring speeches made by politicians when we can receive edited highlights straight from the journalistic voice-box in a handy, predigested form:

> Today those words [of candidates and other newsmakers] rather than simply being reproduced and transmitted to the audience, are treated as raw material to be taken apart, combined with other sounds and images and reintegrated into a new narrative. (Hallin, 1997, p. 61)

Not only has the form of political and campaign reporting changed, but so too has its tone, and Hallin's (1997) study of CBS coverage of elections in 1980s America showed that reporting became more negative as the decade wore on and that this negativity was closely allied to the diminishing size of the soundbite. Negativity is also strongly correlated to voter disillusion and growing cynicism, provoking greater levels of political disengagement among ordinary voters who are turned off by campaigns which function solely to discredit political opponents rather than to promote ideals and values (Watts, 1997). But as Kavanagh (1995) notes, despite the evidence which suggests a response of revulsion rather than attraction among its audiences, advertising agencies that are recruited by political campaigns will insist on using negative messages. This is not because of their perverse whimsy but rather because all parties strive for the same basic things, such as safer communities, economic improvement, and a more efficient health service, and it is therefore easier to construct a negative message about the opposition than a positive one about oneself since all parties will promote similar goals. Moreover, because political slogans need to be short, snappy, and avoid charges of libel, their message is often inferential and double-handed: the Labour Party's "New Labour, New Britain" has a very obvious upbeat message about the thrusting, revamped Labour Party of the 1990s moving itself (and Britain) with the times, with a subtle "Old Tories, Old Britain" inference of stasis and stagnation.

While it would seem to be a positive trend that journalists no longer simply report drearily on what politicians say and want the electorate to hear, but that they rather engage more proactively with our elected (and putative) politicians and call them to account, that pendulum seems to have only two maintainable positions which are at either end of the continuum of passive reporting versus aggressive interpretation. Healthy debate is good for democracy and information flow, but the political process is not really helped if the electorate is unable to hear for more than a few seconds at a time what the politicians actually say, but rather are treated to a sustained commentary and critique by a journalist of a long speech or debate made by a politician or party or, more likely, given an overview of how a particular political party has "done" in the polls, or whether their election tactics were the right ones to employ at any given stage in the process. As Gitlin (1990) points out, the audience becomes inured both to the blandishments of politicians and the cynicism of much of the media, but in the end, it has no alternative but to accept both the construction and the critique since they are at least versions of some kind of reality.

As Perloff (1998) suggests, there is, of course, an opposite side to the persistent lamentations of the propensity of the press to both trivialize the political process and to act as interpreter of political events rather than rapporteur. He argues that the charges against the press for treating politics as a game are entirely misdirected because politics *is* a game, and "[presidential] candidates, being ambitious people, spend considerable time trying to figure out the best way to win it" (p. 326). But Perloff goes on to give perhaps a little too much quarter to the journalistic imperative for sniffing out a good story, arguing a little too hard for the "obligations" which journalists apparently have, to cover dirty tricks and gaffes, in order to provide the "voters with the facts, and let them make the call" (p. 326). This innocent command to duty is surely naive as presented, as if journalists have no *real* appetite to cover the things which go wrong or those things which someone hopes to remain concealed, but rather are merely fulfilling their professional obligation to keep the public informed with no other "lower" goal or aspiration in mind. The interest in political campaigning has, in recent years, taken a comparative turn, as scholars have sought to capture evidence of global "Americanizing" tendencies, including mapping of campaign "styles" (Gurevitch & Blumler, 1990; Negrine, 1996; Swanson & Mancini, 1996). It now seems clear that there is indeed a good deal of similarity, at least in democratically oriented contexts, in terms of the use of increasingly professional communication strategies, campaigns aimed at a mass media audience rather than more traditional forms of voter address, and the growth of "image" politics which sees voters as mere consumers (Scammell, 1998).

The agenda-setting power of the mass media has been well documented over the past few decades (Entman, 1989; Iyengar, 1987; Ansolabehere, Behr, & Iyengard, 1991), to a point where it is now accepted that the media's impact is less about actively changing values and beliefs than about determining what issues are important, and the extent to which media scholars cede power to media organizations has also shifted considerably. In fact, some commentators put up so many caveats to media influence as to make almost any impact impossibly contingent, such as " . . . this study argues that agenda-setting studies . . . document that some kind of public learning does result from some media content under some kinds of conditions" (Shaw & Martin, 1992, p. 903). The agenda-setting push is important to understand in general terms, but the everyday power play which is a routine part of the political-media dance is thrown into even sharper conflict when the stakes are raised as they are in dynamic situations, such as in elections. Recent research studies exploring more precisely the contours of that relationship and the media's potential and actual role in influencing voting behaviour have identified a complex set of effects, with variables such as gender, party, education, and ethnicity all playing a part (LeDuc, 1990; Kahn & Goldenberg, 1991; West, 1991). For example, it is not simply the way in which news media choose to frame a particular topic, but also important is its position in the newscast itself, as lead story or backstop (Iyengar, 1987). And the negative framing of domestic and international news not only encourages a negative view of politicians, but it also undermines public confidence in political leaders (Hayes & Makkai, 1996). In Britain's general election coverage in 1997, it was clear that there was considerable dissonance between what voters reported were their key policy concerns—health, education, law and order—and what the media actually chose to focus on in their coverage—Europe, taxes, and the economy (Burns, 1997). It is scarcely surprising, then, that the electorate feels that they have insufficient information to make informed political choices (Sancho-Aldridge, 1997), since information on the policy positions which they want to hear about from the political contenders are mostly ignored by the media in favor of the topics *they* are interested in covering. What is a little less clear-cut, though, is the existence of any cause and effect relationship between exposure to political campaigning and voting decisions, although most studies suggest that the media is more likely to reinforce existing attitudes than change them and therefore has a negligible real effect on influencing final outcomes. What seems, in principle, to be an interesting political conundrum, however, is the fact that media messages appear to impact on women and men differently, since women's voting behaviour over the past two or three decades has remained stable, while men have migrated very obviously towards conservatism. Do women and men read the media differently? Are they affected by the same messages differently from men? Are they less susceptible to media manipulation? Are they affected by women and men candidates differently?

MOVING TO A DIFFERENT DRUM—GENDER AND CAMPAIGN THEMES

Most work which has focused on the gender dimension in the campaign strategies of candidates tends to suggest that there are very real differences in the ways in which women and men operationalise a campaign, for example, the kinds of issues they choose to focus on, their style, and the ways in which the electorate respond to them (Fox, 1997; Kahn & Gordon, 1997). The importance of issue priority and visibility on voting decisions can be seen most easily with reference to the American "Year of the Woman" presidential campaign in 1992. In that year, the Anita Hill-Clarence Thomas hearing was going through the courts, focusing attention on sexual harassment and abuse; the Family and Medical Leave Act was again being debated, bringing issues related to women's working lives to the fore; and abortion law was again being considered for reform (Dolan, 1998). All of these issues, with their focus clearly on women and rights, captured public and political attention, and probably not by coincidence, that year saw a record number of women candidates standing for office (119 standing as major party candidates for both the House of Representatives and the Senate), with a very creditable 53 women achieving success, bringing the number of Congresswomen to an all-time high of 10 per cent of elected House members (Center for the American Woman and Politics, 1993). The point is that, although 1992 will be remembered for its great success story for women politicians, perhaps more importantly, many of the women candidates were standing on a gender-ticket, playing precisely the gender-card in their appeal to voters as honest, hard-working women who identified with ordinary people. In particular, women candidates sought to appeal to women voters who, as much research evidence shows, were more likely than men to vote for a woman (Hershey, 1977; Burrell, 1994).

While the orthodox reason given for this trend is women's more liberal-leaning proclivities, some research (see, for example, Plutzer & Zipp, 1996) suggests that there is also an element of identity politics at play, with women voters acting out a woman-on-woman support vote, especially if the voter is a feminist and the female candidate is pushing a feminist agenda. Going further, Paolino (1995) suggests that women voters are attracted to women candidates when they address issues which are especially important to women's lives, such as sexual harassment and abortion, and moreover, women candidates are regarded as more competent in handling such issues. What Paolino appears to have discovered, then, is the interconnectedness between issue salience, gender, and competence, so that if the salient issue is gender-related and there's a woman candidate pushing it, she is likely to be regarded much more favorably by women (and possibly men) voters than a male contender. In the 1992 American elections, more women than ever before were elected to Congress, 24 to the House and 4 to the Senate, bringing the total number of women in each chamber to 47 and 6 respectively. Yet, as Dolan (1998) remarks, those women did not achieve political success just because of their gender, but because "they appealed to coalitions of voters and to the demographic, attitudinal and issue characteristics of these voters" (p. 288). Just as importantly, many campaigned as (and *were*, quite genuinely) outsiders and as women, keen to capitalize on voter apathy and cynicism with the "business as usual" style of politics, and pushing a welfare and social agenda at a time when the electorate were also concerned with those issues. In an interesting experimental study on the effectiveness of political advertising during the 1992 American state and the 1994 gubernatorial elections in California, Iyengar, Valentino, Ansolabehere, and Simon (1997) found that, when women candidates included issues of particular importance to women, they did well, but when their messages focused on crime, they were less persuasive. Conversely, when comparing the relative effectiveness of a woman-man pairing, when the campaigns of both candidates converged on issues relating to education or employment, the woman candidate was viewed more favorably than her male rival, but as the campaign wore on and crime came to the fore, the male candidate took a lead and eventually emerged as the successor.

A gradual shift in policy, to incorporate as legitimate concerns those issues on which women had always campaigned—women's health, domestic violence, working motherhood, and childcare—has been identified by a number of political researchers in successive American Congresses since at least the 1970s (Flammang, 1997). This shift was, arguably, a consequence of a growing radicalism on the part of women's pressure groups for equality and reform, their improving relationship with women politicians, and the election of more (though still very few in relative terms) women to Congress (Freeman, 1975; Tinker, 1983). Many of the women who began to make their presence known in Congress identified themselves as representatives of their constituents in general and of American women in particular, and two particular features of their conduct were a studied indifference to becoming "incorporated" into the male culture of parliament (one of the boys), although they neither played up their femininity nor played it down, and active campaigning on "women's issues," arguing that they were best placed to draft legislation which affected the lives of other women. "They raised the consciousness of male colleagues, politicized issues which had until then been considered private rather than public . . . and began to alter the national agenda" (Gertzog, 1984, p. 248). As Boles (1991) argues, both women and men politicians recognize that the presence of women Parliamentarians makes a difference to the way in which issues are discussed and privileged, so that women can and do campaign for specific reforms from within, rather than simply from without the Chamber, pushing forward different priorities and bringing different views to policymaking.

Yet, despite these developments at the policy level, women's issues have never been high on the media's reporting agenda. For example, in Kahn and Goldenberg's (1997) study of Senate campaign coverage in the mid-1980s, the authors found that women's issues were rarely discussed in news reports on campaigns and only two per cent of all issue-based coverage was concerned with "women's issues" such as the Equal Rights Amendment. As Kahn and Goldenberg (1997) point out, "Because the public's issue priorities are largely shaped by the media, the lack of attention to women's issues in the news does little to push these issues to the top of the agenda" (p. 156). Similarly, the 1997 British general election was supposed to be the one which would speak to "women's concerns," since it had been recognized, at last, that women voters held the key to winning elections. But the concerns which women have identified in a number of studies (see, for example, Women's Communication Centre, 1996; Stephenson, 1998) were again ignored. For example, in my own work on monitoring the gendered dimension of election coverage, only 3 of 136 news items which appeared in one week of broadcast news during the campaign period of the 1997 election, addressed the key issues which women themselves say are of concern— child benefits, childcare, parental leave, pay/conditions for part-time workers, the minimum wage and poverty in older age (Ross, 1998b).

POLITICS AS BIOLOGY: GENDER AS AGENCY

The kinds of experiences which women will have already had as daughters, mothers, and workers are likely to give them perspectives on social and other policy areas which are absolutely different from those of their male colleagues (Okin, 1990). Not only may those experiences be actually true for certain women, predisposing them towards the adoption of particular policy stances on so-called "women's issues," such as childcare or nursery education, but also the continuing dominance of sex-role stereotyping encourages other people to view women and men in specifically gendered ways, not just as ordinary people, but also as political candidates (Kahn & Gordon, 1997). In work carried out by Emily's List Australia in 1998, it was found that women are keen to see more women candidates since they believe that women will better represent their interests because women politicians have a better insight into the lives and experiences of "ordinary" women:

> [Women voters] don't want them [women candidates] to be caught up in the political game, so at that level, there's a desire on the part of the female community to see more of themselves in politics because they think that would mean there'd be more politicians who understood what it was like to do the things they've got to do, in balancing work, family, responsibility. They think they're more straightforward, more co-operative. (Carmen Lawrence, Labor, Australia)[1]

Lyn Allison (Labor, Australia) also sees considerable support for Labor women candidates among women voters, both because they want more women in Parliament, and because "our policies are more inclined to appeal to women who are very opposed to big budgets for defence, for aggressive economic rationalist policies." The views that voters have towards women candidates are broadly assumed, by feminist political scholars, to be largely stereotyped and consistent with the "global woman" category although this could be because their exposure to the ideal type "woman politician" might be very limited and therefore their experiential context could be similarly restricted. While much research shows that voters often have quite rigid and gender-stereotyped perceptions of the "ideal" politician (Hewitt & Mattinson, 1989), the media also play an important role in providing (and of course denying access to) information about political contenders. The majority of studies which have explored the extent to which the sex of political candidates is a factor in voter choice have concluded that there is no evidence of any discrimination against women candidates (Leeper, 1991; Burrell, 1994;

[1]Carmen Lawrence is Chair of Emily's List Australia.

Chaney & Sinclair, 1994; Darcy, Welch, & Clark, 1994). However, Fox and Smith (1998) suggest that small-scale research in experimental settings might be obscuring real biases against women which do exist, but which remain hidden, and which can go some way toward explaining why women are still grossly underrepresented in both the Senate and the House of Representatives, and have always been so.[2] In Fox and Smith's (1998) experimental study with college students, they found that, contrary to much research, there was obvious evidence of discrimination against women candidates and that the geographic location of voters (students) made a difference in their attitudes towards women and men candidates. They conclude that dismissing gender discrimination as a contributor in the nonelection of women politicians is ill-advised and that larger studies with more representative samples need to be conducted in order to tease out precisely how gender bias on the part of voters actively works against women candidates.

However, the explanatory strength of suggestions that voters reject women candidates on the grounds that they provide an impossibly counter-intuitive model to the traditional presentation of the ideal type of "politician-as-male" is not entirely convincing since role models for women as political actors have been available for many years. For example, Cirksena (1996) suggests that the news media themselves have been carrying stories which have highlighted women's growing participation in both formal and informal politics throughout the last few decades, and even as early as the mid-1970s, the volume of news reports in just one influential newspaper, the *New York Times*, on women and/or women's issues had increased sevenfold—from approxiamately 200 to 1,400 articles—over the decade since 1964. So, it is not simply that voters don't believe that women can be competent politicians, but it is that their adjudged viability is much more context specific and complicated. Iyengar et al. (1997) make the important point that, in an election context, the average voter "lacks the motivation to acquire even the most elementary level of factual knowledge about the candidates and campaign issues" (p. 79). (See also Buchanan, 1991 and Popkin, 1991.) This means that visual cues such as gender take on an increasingly important function in influencing voter choice, no matter how arbitrary those cues actually are and no matter how stereotyped (and therefore, possibly ill-informed) voter expectations might be.

If gender is a significant *negative* criterion brought to bear on making ballot box decisions—for example, the view that a woman is no good as a leader—then we really do get the politicians we deserve. Fortunately, voting decisions, for most people, are probably based on

---

[2]However, the fact that women struggle to get selected by their parties, and onto the ballot papers in the first place, is the other part of the equation.

something a little more considered, and as Kern and Just (1997) argue, women and men are likely to bring different perspectives to their viewing and understanding of the same campaign message, leading each to be more or less persuaded for different reasons. Yet, voters do seem to believe that male politicians are more likely to deal competently in "hard" financial areas, such as the economy, and tough foreign policy areas, such as defence and arms control, whereas women candidates are seen to be better at dealing with "softer" policy areas, such as civil rights, education, poverty, and childcare (Huddy & Terkildsen, 1993). What those sex-based competencies suggest is that women are passive, emotional, and caring, whereas men are aggressive, rational, and protective. While at some base level that might be true for a majority of women and a majority of men, the problem is that those characteristics are not valued equally, either in human beings generally or in politicians more specifically. If they were, then one could hypothesize that all of our parliaments and congresses would be staffed with equal numbers of women and men, providing mutually complementary skills, expertise, and perspectives with which to govern wisely and fairly. That this is not the case anywhere in the world—with the possible exception of some Scandinavian countries—is eloquent witness to the fact that something else is at play when we, the people, go to the ballot box.

While gender stereotypes are pernicious and unfair, they are hardly unexpected because they are simply extrapolated from the private domain of women's experiences to public issues and concerns, making the easy glide from private to public in the minds of voters and journalists alike. This is lazy thinking at its most damaging. But, as women are trying to subvert the traditional assumptions made of them by stressing their competence in orthodox "male" areas of both behaviour and policy, men are busy doing the same thing for themselves, capitalizing on precisely those positive attributes of leadership for which their biology, apparently, makes them uniquely qualified. As Daughton (1994) points out, all of the American presidential candidates of recent decades have been men, and they have tended to define the role of president in strictly male-ordered terms. In her analysis of both Democrat and Republican convention speeches over two decades, she argues that, "first and foremost, the president is the national patriarch: the paradigmatic American Man" and that handling the economy (unless there's someone to go to war with at the time) becomes the principal preoccupation of incumbents and challengers alike (p. 114). This focus on economic efficacy is unsurprising, given poll data which suggests that the most favored definition of "masculinity" among the American public is being a "good provider for his family" (Faludi, 1991, p. 65). Yet, such an insistence on the virtues of testosterone have not gone unchallenged. In Britain, The

Rt. Hon. Clare Short, as Shadow Minister for Overseas Development, accused Tony Blair's advisers of trying to reinvent Blair as "macho man" instead of promoting him as the decent principled person he really is (cited in Hencke, 1996, p. 10). On the other hand, Bill Clinton's presentation of himself in the 1992 election was seen as a conscious attempt to brand a kinder, less macho President for the more sensitive 1990s:

> Arguably the person who did the most to feminize political rhetoric in '92 was Hillary's husband. Bill Clinton became the Oprah of presidential politics, embracing not only women's issues but women-speak. (Salholz, Beachy, Miller, Annin, Barrett, & Foote, 1992, p. 21)

Yet, Clinton and other men have sometimes had to contend with attacks which judged them to be not man enough and, even worse, as feminine, subverting the "public" expectation of robust masculinity as a basic requirement for occupation of the Oval Office:

> American political figures since Thomas Jefferson (who was accused of "timidity," "whimsicalness" and a weakness for flattery) and Andrew Jackson (referred to as "Miss Nancy" and "Aunt Fancy") have fought against attacks from opponents for any indication of femininity in their public persona. (Wahl-Jorgensen, 2000, p. 55)

It is ironic, in the post-Lewinsky twilight of Clinton's incumbency, that Bill's own brand of "sensitive" masculinity was, at the time of his first presidential campaign, considerably panned by pundits who accused him of being "squishy" (Klein, 1992), an "old maid in britches" (King, 1993), and was derided for feminizing the Democratic Party. Yet, as Wahl-Jorgensen (2000) points out, these criticisms never hit home with voters since Clinton was always careful to balance this "sensitive" side with equal evidence of a more rugged masculinity which accorded more closely to public (and media) expectations. Time has shown that Clinton has been no more willing to tackle equality issues or "the woman question" than his predecessors, and, as elsewhere in the English-speaking world, America's record on the recruitment and promotion of women to elected political office remains dismal.

Of course, it isn't just a simple question of negative gender stereotyping at play when it comes to candidates promoting what might be called their "issue competence" among voters since women candidates can choose to deliberately highlight particular "known" gender attributes in order to emphasize their difference from male contenders. For example, many women will use slogans which emphasize how "in touch" they are with ordinary people, especially if they are mothers and they can use that experience to both pull in other mothers—we all know what it's like bringing up kids, eh?!—but also to signal a "natural" instinct for looking after each other and the planet, thus making the world a better/safer place to live in. When Pauline Hanson was campaigning in Queensland during Australia's state elections in 1998, she consistently emphasized her working-class roots as a welfare mother who had raised a family single-handedly and who ran a small business, claiming that she wasn't a "professional" politician like those other guys, but rather someone who had a lot of common sense and who had been persuaded to stand by her friends as an antidote to the "usual suspects." And for Pauline Hanson, that strategy worked. When she campaigned on employment policy, she used her own experience of welfare to highlight problem areas and possible solutions. Although her crucial policy platform was entirely racist—her One Nation Party, which she led, was committed (among many other things) to immediately halting immigration from the surrounding Pacific Rim countries and disavowing Aboriginal land rights—it was couched in the language of a nurturing mother wanting to do the right thing by Australia's true (white) people. Hillary Clinton, although campaigning on an explicitly democratic, antiracist, pro-choice platform, also appealed to the electorate as a mother and wife, as have countless other women contenders.

Because women are expected to be more caring, and more compassionate, more interested in social, educational, and environmental issues than are men, they clearly see benefits in emphasizing precisely those particular policy agendas in their campaigning, and Kahn's (1993) work on political advertising shows exactly those kinds of gendered emphases. Indeed, as discussed in Chap. 3, the issues on which women candidates campaign are not just hauled out at election time to try to attract voters, but tend to be the same ones which women will support once they have been elected to office. In work on legislative priorities, researchers found that women were more likely to introduce legislation orientated towards the traditional domains of women's concern, that is, health, welfare, and education (Carroll, Dodson, & Mandel, 1991). This echoes other work which suggests that, as a gendered group, women politicians tend to be more "liberal" than are men (Poole & Zeigler, 1985; Darcy, Welch, & Clark, 1994; Kahn & Gordon, 1997). However, this finding could also be the consequence of the kinds of portfolios which are given to women once they become elected. Even in Australia's Parliament, which has seen quite a creditable inclusion of women ministers over the past two decades (Reynolds, 1995), given their relatively small numbers overall, there still appears to be a belief that women can't be responsible for key ministries such as finance, defense, internal, and foreign affairs:

Portfolios in which women have most often been appointed are
those responsible for the status of women and family/community
services. Appointments in this group occur at about twice the rate of
the second group of portfolios, which includes consumer affairs,
local government and environment, followed by education, the arts
and ethnic affairs. (p. 109)

However, these gendered priorities are always contingent upon
the wider political and social agenda of the day at any given time. When
Tony Blair's Labour Government introduced a new bill which would
restrict, and in some cases halt, welfare benefits for single parents, his
then Social Security Minister, The Rt. Hon. Harriet Harman, was called
upon to lead the debate and, obviously, defend and support the proposed legislation. The sense of outrage and betrayal among "ordinary"
women was immediate and intense, that a working mother could promote such a bill, barely 12 months after being elected on a family-friendly platform. For many women, this was the first serious intimation that
electing more women Parliamentarians than Britain had ever seen
before (in the 1997 general election) was no guarantee that women's
brand of politics and/or their policy agenda would necessarily be different just because they were women. On the other hand, as Langdon
(2000) points out, perhaps it was simply that women were not confident
enough to challenge government policy so early on in their political
careers. Although some Scandinavian research and one or two American
studies have suggested that women politicians do tend to be more supportive of a liberal agenda on welfare, most studies which look at their
impact on shifting the agenda have revealed a rather more patchy performance (Sawer & Simms, 1992; Ross & Sreberny-Mohammadi, 1997).
The news media were particularly aggressive in their reporting of
Harman's defense of the new bill, echoing precisely the public's question: "How can a mother do this to other mothers?" Of course, such
questioning cannot bear even the tiniest scrap of scrutiny since fathers
do reprehensible things to other fathers and mothers all the time, but it
is in capturing the "mother-as-nurturer" motif and suggesting a mutual
inclusivity which makes the reporting of its opposite an incitement for
repulsion. When women Parliamentarians have actively campaigned on
a specifically gendered ticket, though, it is hardly surprising that they
are criticized for supporting a policy which would affect single parents
(mothers) so severely.

In the event, such was the public outcry that Harman was quickly relieved of her ministerial office and relegated to the backbenchers;
the legislation, naturally, became law shortly thereafter. It is ironic then,
that it has been Harman herself who has been pushing a women-friendly agenda to her own party executive as the key to winning the 2001

election. In an address to her colleagues, she commented that, "we won the support of women at the last election by holding ourselves out as 'women-friendly.' If we slip back in our commitment to women, women will see us as having been cynical last time and punish us" (Harman, 2000) This view is finally being echoed by Conservative women in Britain too, and in an influential report by senior women in the party, William Hague and the rest of the executive are given a clear warning, "The party has managed to lose touch with women voters . . . a party which still appears to hanker for the days of the subservient family woman and whose public face is almost exclusively male is not going to attract their vote" (Keswick, Pockley, & Guillaume, 1999).

But the point is that, in a different political climate with a less prosperous economy, public sensibilities could have reacted very differently, and it may be to women's considerable advantage to promote a "tough" policy stance in order to show their competence in so-called male areas of expertise. One highly successful politician, Margaret Thatcher, took exactly that approach. However, she was one of very few women politicians who dared to break out of the straightjacket of traditional femininity, and the path she chose to take was, for many commentators, one which was entirely devoid of any gendered understanding of the different social realities experienced by women and men:

> Except for a very brief period when Baroness Young was Lord Privy Seal, she [Margaret Thatcher] has run a Cabinet in which she was the sole woman . . . the tendency of both Mrs. Thatcher herself and of colleagues to project her as the "best man available for the job" has the effect of singling her out as a wholly atypical woman . . . (Carter, 1988, pp. 131-132)

More generally, though, elections until quite recently were usually seen as too volatile and too important for many women to experiment with and confound voter expectations, and work on political advertising during the 1980s shows women candidates continuing to stress their traditional "feminine" traits, such as warmth and compassion, and traditionally female areas of policy concern, such as health and education. In any case, following what Iyengar et al. (1997) describe as the "resonance" model of campaigning, whereby messages which confirm public expectation are more likely to succeed than those which create dissonance, promoting a gender-stereotypical policy platform could be successful. Yet, "given the importance of the campaign context, women candidates may be well advised to consider public priorities when choosing among campaign themes" (Kahn & Gordon, 1997, p. 75). This is because, unless those particular issues happen to be already prominent on the political agenda, they are unlikely to find the same kinds of appeal with voters or attract the same kind of interest by the media as a televised "head-to-head" on the economy involving the leaders of the main political parties, which give plenty of opportunity for aggression but, perversely, little scope for real discussion of real policy.

POLITICAL ADVERTISING AND THE POWER OF PERSUASION

Given the routine cry of media manipulation by political actors, especially during events such as elections, one of the few ways by which political contenders and parties can get their messages across without the constant interference by the news media is through political advertising. The proportion of campaign funds dedicated to such activities has grown year by year since the very first televised political advertisement in 1952 (Jacobson, 1992), and advertising accounted for between 60 and 70 per cent of the total campaign budget for the 1992 elections (West, 1993). Interestingly, single party election broadcasts during campaigns have experienced a decline in their impact as voters increasingly look to the allegedly more impartial form of political descriptions offered by television news and current affairs programming (Harrison, 1992). Scammell (1990) found, for example, that given a choice, viewers vote with their remote controls, ". . . on average one quarter to one third of the inherited audience turns off or switches over when a party [election] broadcast comes on" (cited in Scammell & Semetko, 1995, p. 19). But of course, this supposed impartiality is also a mythic "truth" since journalists now routinely interpret the speech and exhortations of politicians rather than report it straight, much to the wailing disgust of politicians themselves, who continuously reprimand the lobby hack for her or his deconstructive rather than journalistic tendencies. However, the power of party election broadcasts should not be underestimated, and Scammell (1995) warns that, despite the turn-off factor, most people will see at least one party election broadcast during the short lifespan of a general election campaign and as such, they ". . . remain the only opportunities for exclusive party control of the airwaves, and they achieve a greater national audience than any other direct party publicity, such as newspaper ads or billboard posters" (p. 39). As Jowett and O'Donnell (1992) point out, in a more general discussion on propaganda, "Media utilization is vital to a propaganda campaign. Access to and control of the media literally means access to and potential control of public opinion" (p. 267).

The power of party election broadcasts to focus and influence opinion (both negatively as well as positively, as it turned out) was palpably demonstrated with the Labour Party's controversial "Bulldog" party election broadcast in the 1997 campaign, designed, allegedly, by Peter Mandelson, which not only appealed quite overtly to a muscular and definitively macho patriotism—witness the highly evident male genitalia of the star performer dog and the male arm of the "handler"— but which also, more insidiously, promoted Labour as the Party which could return Britain to a triumphalist (nationalistic) order with all that that concept implies. The controversy generated by that particular party election broadcast was, in many ways, anticipated by political commentators several years earlier. Scammell and Semetko (1995), for example, suggested that campaign messages would continue to employ ". . . more . . . shock tactics and close-to-the bone emotive material" (p. 41). This appeal to emotion rather than logic, as exemplified by many party election broadcasts, is borne out by comparative analyses of political advertising across Western democracies which suggest, among other things, that "Despite the emphasis on issues and positivity, most leaders and parties rely on emotional, rather than logical, proof to make their points" (Kaid & Holtz-Bacha, 1995, p. 223). In the British general election campaign of 2001, the Labour postes most criticised by the opposion was a head and shoulder portrait of a morphed image of William Hague dissolving into Margaret Thatcher, complete with hairsprayed hairdo and earrings. The inference was clear and the appeal emotional: vote Hague, vote Thatcherism.

The dominance of leader profiles in political campaigns in the 1997 British elections was a relatively new phenomenon, starting, arguably, with the 1992 election campaign when John Major was conspicuously featured, almost to the exclusion of discussing the party's manifesto agenda; he even featured on the manifesto's cover, something that Lady Thatcher deliberately vetoed for fear of appearing "too presidential" (Scammell & Semetko, 1995, p. 35) during the 1983 campaign, an interesting twist given her emulation of the American leadership style in other areas of political diplomacy. And British political campaigning has moved inexorably closer to the U.S. style of presidential electioneering, arguably as a response to traditional contagion theory (Duverger, 1954; Epstein, 1967), but where instead of the left/right driver, the act of emulation is more in line with the bit-player copying the super-power. In fact, the trend identified more than 30 years ago, whereby parties were increasingly toning down their distinctive ideological messages in order to appeal to a broader-based constituency continues apace, as witnessed by the current political environment in both the United States and the United Kingdom where centrist tendencies among the left and the right converge on more or less identical policies, even while parties retain *some* distinctive policy positions to make their differences more overt to the public.

Yet, perhaps the most important element in any political advertising campaign is the "attack" ad (Hitchon & Chang, 1995) and although the public are deemed to dislike ads which are emotionally aggressive towards political opponents, some researchers argue that they are nonetheless highly efficient in "moving votes" (Pfau, Parrott, & Lindquist, 1992). That political advertising matters is at least one of the truisms that have emerged from research on what "works" in election terms, and there is a growing body of evidence to support the contention that ads are an important source of voter information (Scammell, 1998) and that the judicious repetition of key ads can have an influence on subsequent voter choice (Just, Griegler, Alger, Cook, Kern, & West, 1996). The proposition that, of all political advertising, it is the negative ads which wield the most influence is a little less clear-cut, and it is even less clear which style of negative advertising has the most impact. Apart from anything else, advertising strategies which work in one country have no guarantee of similar success elsewhere, especially if the political structures are very different, as in the United States and the United Kingdom, where the latter doesn't officially allow sponsored political advertising. However, as Scammell (1998) suggests, despite very profound differences in what is "allowed" to be conveyed about political candidates and parties through the media during election campaigns, the last three general elections in Britain have all witnessed an enthusiastic embrace of marketing principles and strategies, with the Conservatives especially enamoured of the virtues of negative advertising, although this latter approach has consistently worked against them as far as voter attitudes are concerned (Scammell & Semetko, 1995; Sancho-Aldridge, 1997). Despite the significant evidence which shows public hostility towards negative advertising (see, for example, Lau, Sigelman, Heldman, & Babbitt, 1997), political parties, strangely, continue to use them, and the parties which tend to use them more (Republican, Conservative, and other right-of-centre campaigns) are the very ones which are hurt most by them. In Lemert, Elliot, Rosenberg, and Bernstein's (1996) study of the 1992 American Presidential elections, they argue that, while many voters did not appreciate "attack" ads, no matter who was attacking whom, they worked particularly disastrously for the Republican (Bush) campaign and had done so in the previous election in 1988. "Bush was the only candidate whose own attack ads seemed to hurt him and help his Democratic opponent. In contrast, Clinton's attack ads seemed to achieve their purpose of damaging their target's election prospects" (p. 271).

The lack of actual information in presidential advertising campaigns is one of the most serious issues to emerge from political advertising, with the complaint that ads are more about "mudslinging" than about real policy differences being almost ubiquitous. In Kern and Just's (1997) experimental study, they looked at the way in which voters actively "construct" political candidates as a response to the media's coverage and their messages about them. Among their findings, they suggest that women react more strongly to negative "attack" advertising and tend to invert the preferred reading by attacking the author of the advertisement rather than supporting the message, that women and men's gendered social positioning influences the way in which they construct the political persona, and that all voters "draw heavily on emotional advertising, including negative advertising, in their construction of candidate images" (p. 111). But Pinkleton, Austin, and Fortman (1998) argue that negativism towards the media's coverage of political campaigns can have the effect of reducing media use among consumers and that in turn, a cynical polity reduces the effectiveness of governments and thus compromises the democratic ideal. In an interesting study of German politicians and self-presentation as performance, news audiences were shown a series of clips from broadcast interviews and asked to rate the interviewees' performances (Schutz, 1998). Aggressive behaviors in the form of interrupting questions, deflecting criticism, and making personal attacks on political opponents were all regarded negatively, as were displays of aggression and loss of control, whereas cool responses under provocation were regarded very positively. In a global context, this study is interesting since it reverses the roles of politician and interviewer, where the latter is increasingly seen as having the upper hand in what are regarded as public contests of political authority.

And it is not just the political "attack ad" which is largely off-putting to the voters, but the media themselves add to voter hostility by their own persistent negative framing of politics and elections. For example, Liebes and Peri's (1998) work explicitly shows the ways in which the media can serve to further undermine the credibility of politicians: by making it their business to contest political rhetoric; by undertaking extended "disaster marathons" and other melodramatic strategies designed to destabilize serious political debate; and by degenerating debate to tabloid levels which again reduce the potency and seriousness of political messages. Barnhurst and Mutz (1997) also develop the social problem frame as a specific thesis, suggesting that providing a social problem context to a given story enhances its chances of being reported on as news and enables a greater level of journalistic commentary outside the actual event or phenomenon being reported. Journalists themselves identify two key responsibilities as being a channel of news dissemination to the public: delivering news as quickly as possible and "investigating" government claims (Weaver & Wilhoit, 1997). Clearly, this latter responsibility is important for my purposes, but there seems to be some equivocation about how journalists actually fulfil this responsibility since, contrary to expectations, journalists in Weaver and Wilhoit's study claimed that they are not really interested in taking an adversarial approach to politicians, and across different media contexts, print journalists tended to want to be the most aggressive. Interestingly, journalists refuted the suggestion that they are increasingly taking the role of agenda-setters and only 4 per cent of Weaver and Wilhoit's sample believed that such a function is very important for a journalist to perform.

The media are in an extremely powerful position to determine the relative visibility of political candidates and to rehearse the particular arguments of particular candidates. Moreover, television is used much more frequently as the medium of choice in statewide and national campaigns by political parties. As Goldenberg and Traugott (1987) reported more than a decade ago (and there's no reason to believe that things are very different now), more than half of all campaign expenditures in Senate races were spent on the production and broadcasting of television ads. So, although much research suggests that television ads have minimal impact, their persistent use means that we have every reason to study them. White (1994) argues persuasively that women candidates often have difficulty in portraying themselves symbolically, let alone actually, as effective leaders in political advertising since they are constantly running to subvert the traditional conventions of women (housewife-madonna-whore) by promoting themselves as possessing the qualities of orthodox masculinity. Analysing political ads from a Maryland Senate race—two women and one man—White argues that while the man (George Bush) was easily able to position himself in a routinely symbolic "father" figure role, ready to lead the country, the two women (Linda Chavez and Barbara Mikulski) adopted very different strategies in their campaigns. Chavez took the more conventional route, portraying herself in relation to patriarchy, figured as wife and mother and glad to be so. Mikulski, though, played an altogether more risky hand, stressing the strength of her great-grandmother and wishing to follow in her brave footsteps, simultaneously carving out a new way to be a woman politician, a new symbolic space from which to campaign. So, it is possible to fight on a platform which is not about compromising innovation for the sake of convention, but it's always a gamble, and with electorates which are generally conservative, it is a high-risk strategy. As White (1994) herself points out, "the collapsed nature of commercials makes it difficult to create a satisfying and full political imaginary to 'ensnare' the voter to support women's candidacies" (p. 68).

While the majority of gender-based studies on political ads argue that women are usually less successful than men because of stereotypical assumptions of what makes for a "good" politician, there has been the odd dissenting voice arguing the opposite. For example, Kaid, Myers, Pipps, and Hunter (1984) found that, in an experimental study of women and men candidates, women were rated as highly as men when the "setting" was the same and more highly when women were placed in specific male environments. Although the researchers admit that they did not expect the results to be so positive for women, one possible explanation was that it was precisely women's subversion of the expected failure to perform, especially in a male domain, which provoked an excessively positive reaction. Conversely, in this study, women candidates speaking on traditional female platforms, such as education and children, did particularly badly, almost as if voters had high expectations of them and when they performed only moderately well, they were "marked down." As Miller, Wattenberg, and Malanchunk (1986) have pointed out, the public dismay with "politics as usual" means that women's higher ranking on the integrity continuum can stand them in good stead in certain campaign situations, such as when running for state governor rather for a Senate seat, where the former is viewed as a more domestic (female) post and where women are generally much more successful than in their pursuit of the latter (Kahn, 1994). Yet, problematically, the media seem compelled to concentrate on women's looks and not their issue priorities. Kahn (1996) found that, although women's campaigns were just as focused on "issues" as those of their male counterparts, the media appeared to discard the issue content in the former and instead focus on personality characteristics, appearing "to echo the campaign messages of men candidates, while they largely distort the messages sent by women candidates" (p. 132). Thus, the media's misrepresentation of women's campaign messages have very clear (negative) consequences for their overall effectiveness and, therefore, on women's potential to achieve elected office. Lower media visibility and access, coupled with skewed coverage when women's campaigns are reported, combine to produce an election environment which significantly disadvantages women.

In Khan's (1996) study, she compared a dataset of television ads from both women and men candidates, as well as analysing press coverage of elections over the same time period—1983-1988—and she suggests that women's access to political office, "may be limited by people's stereotypical views of women's capabilities and liabilities" (p. 131). Her concern is with the notion of "stereotype" and how the strength and endurance of gender stereotypes in the public imagination continue to hamper women's aspirations to achieve political power. And, it is not only the electorate and the media who are responsible for the pernicious circulation of gender-biased assumptions which continue to keep women stuck in the same old groove. Women themselves attempt to play the stereotype game to their own advantage, both rising to the expectation that the public has of them, as well as trying to subvert some of the more pernicious ones, but it is a hard game. On the one hand, they must emphasize precisely those character traits and issue concerns which are traditionally associated with women, and on the other hand, they must demonstrate their competence in areas more routinely associated with men and men's concerns. Sometimes, the zeitgeist acts in women's favor, if the pressing issues of the day also happen to be those "softer" ones which are more oriented towards women's concerns— health, poverty, education—and voters are therefore more likely to support women at the polls (a phenomenon more likely in local or regional rather than national elections).

Often, the problem with women candidates appearing in ads is that, because of the orthodox views of voters towards the viability of women politicians, a contradiction persists in their viewing a political actor and that actor being a woman, two attributes which are counterintuitive to their own beliefs about "appropriate" gender roles (Hitchon & Chang, 1995). In addition, viewers can choose which bits of any particular promotion they can elect to believe, ignoring any aspects which they find too challenging to absorb, so that some aspects of a candidate's address will be "consistent with expectations about men candidates [but] will be inconsistent with expectations about women candidates, and vice versa" (p. 435). Perhaps unsurprisingly, levels of physical attraction are also influential features of voters" preferential attitudes; yet while for men, physical attractiveness is always a positive attribute, it is a much more ambivalent feature for women (Sigelman, Thomas, Sigelman, & Ribich, 1986) and in at least one study, attractiveness was actually found to be detrimental to women's electoral success (Rosenberg, Kahn, & Tran, 1991). Because of the propensity of viewers to recall information from political advertising (and obviously elsewhere) which resonates with their own beliefs and values, there is often more accurate content recall from male candidates' ads than those featuring women because viewers are constantly challenging the fundamental basis of a woman's claim to political viability, almost to the exclusion of listening to and agreeing or disagreeing with her message (Hitchon & Chang, 1995). However, what viewers recalled more accurately from women-featured campaigns were the aspects of the candidate's personal and family life which they revealed, suggesting that such elements were entirely consistent with the ideal (stereo)type "woman."

THE GENDER GAP-MYTHS AND REALITIES

The relationship between women, politics, and news finds its most potent expression in the way in which those variables interact at crucial times in the democratic cycle, that is, during election years. Numerous studies over the past three decades have sought to understand the characteristics of that nexus of variables, so that it is now possible to map the trajectory of women's involvement with the political process, as represented by the media, through successive studies on election campaigns. One consequence of this interest in the gender dimension, at both a general political level but also with a specific focus on the media and news coverage, is a number of "facts" about women and politics which mostly serve to obscure what might be called the *real politik* which actually *does* concern women and policy. A number of these facts are debunked as myths by Seltzer, Newman, and Leighton (1997) as a way into exploring the salience of gender as a political variable. For example, the authors suggest that while there is, undoubtedly, a difference in the American context in the way in which women and men vote, this difference often accounts for no more than 10 per cent (women are more likely to vote for the Democrats than the Republicans), and gender is therefore actually less important than many other voting variables such as class, race, and age (Kaufmann & Petrocik, 1999). The propensity for women to be more "liberal" (and vote for the Democrats) relates to the so-called gender gap on issue priority since it is as likely to be political beliefs about the role of government in, say, supporting welfare programmes which determines voting behaviour, as is the sex of the voter. Similarly, women are often accused of voting less frequently than men, but Seltzer, et al. (1997) argue that comparing the number of women voting in 1994 with 1992 (fewer in the former) is to miss the point since fewer men voted, too, because 1994 was not a presidential election year. Moreover, they point out that the turnout rate for women has been higher than for men for every election since 1980.

The existence of a gender gap had been accepted for a number of years, since the analysis of successive election campaigns demonstrated that, in general, women and men had different political priorities from each other and that they were therefore inclined to vote for parties supporting particular positions on particular issues (see Klein, 1984; Thomas, 1994; Ladd, 1997). Of increasing importance was the strength of association with specific policy agendas, with women tending towards a more liberal, socially inclusive agenda (and therefore inclining towards a Democratic Party stance) and men being more supportive of "tough" regimes which manifested in a more Republican position (Kern & Just, 1997). While that may be broadly true, clever marketing can easily subvert those gender-based behaviors. In work carried out on George Bush's 1988 political advertising campaign (West, 1993), women were found to have been far more influenced by a campaign targeting increasing crime than were men, causing women to report crime as a serious problem. But this is less about substance than degree. Ladd (1997) suggests that crime is consistently mentioned by both women and men as the most pressing problem facing America. However, this anxiety takes the form of supporting the wider use of the death penalty for men, while women want better systems of personal security and favor penalties other than capital punishment.

Early explanations for the newly "discovered" gender gap, especially in the Reaganite 1980s, centered on different attitudes among women and men on defence issues and on the use of military force more generally (Francovic, 1982; Gilens, 1988). However, more recent work found that defense had become a much less salient issue by the 1990s (Chaney, Alvarez, & Nagler, 1998), having been replaced by social welfare as a more pertinent focus for women's political liberalism (and men's conservatism). Reagan's antipathy towards higher welfare spending, coupled with his overt disapproval for the feminist movement and women's campaign concerns—especially reproductive rights—contributed to a loss of Republican support among American women which still shows no sign of return in the early years of the 21st century (Smeal, 1984; Conover, 1988; Kaufmann & Petrocik, 1999). In Britain, however, there has been almost the opposite tendency, not because British women are less "liberal," but because the party espousing an inclusive and social welfare-oriented policy—the Labour Party—was simply seen as too "masculine" (Short, 1996). In fact, it took the concerted efforts of a number of women both inside the party and outside (via pressure groups) to convince British political parties that women's votes were important (Fawcett Society, 1996; Lindsay, 1999). The jury is still undecided as to whether women are more or less likely to vote for women candidates since it is impossible to control for the other factors involved. For example, if women are more likely to vote for a Democrat, and Democrats are more likely to field women candidates, then the woman-on-woman vote is coincidental and is determined by party rather than gender. Seltzer et al. (1997) write that their own exit poll data analyses suggest that the women's vote for Democratic candidates increased by several percentage points if the candidate was a woman, but women's support for women standing as Republican candidates fell when compared to their votes for a male candidate, standing for the same party. This suggests that Democrat women are more likely to support a woman candidate, and Republican women are less likely to support a woman, which at the very least, makes the glib assumption that whether

whether women will or will not support women candidates is a much more complex issue than it initially appears. As elsewhere, women simply cannot be bracketed together as a bloc and, once again, political allegiance seems to be at least as important in voting behaviour as gender, which is probably, in turn, much less important than other variables, such as age, race, and class.

In Australia, the election of two women as State Premiers in the early 1990s gives the lie to an electorate hostile to women leaders although, interestingly, the two women—Joan Kirner (Victoria—1990-1992) and Carmen Lawrence (Western Australia—1990-1993)—both took on the job at a time when their governments were the subject of public disapproval because of alleged economic mismanagement, and Reynolds (1995) argues that the media at the time were full of images of the homely mother figure being brought in to clean up the boys' mess. Ladd (1997) also argues that, although gender is an important variable in considerations of voting behaviour, the divide it suggests is probably less significant than that which exists between members of majority and minority ethnic communities, between different religious affiliations, and between members of different socioeconomic backgrounds. "We rarely write of the 'education gap' in this context . . . even though educational groups differ more substantially than do men and women" (p. 113). So, although the gender gap tends to increase if the Democrat candidate is a woman fighting against a male Republican candidate, it tends to decrease when the position is reversed (Smith & Selfa, 1992). On the other hand, Rosenthal's (1995) study of voter preferences *did* find that men were more likely to vote for male candidates and women for women candidates, but most other studies indicate that gender is a neutral factor in determining voting behaviour (Darcy, Welch, & Clark, 1994) or is at least neutral in predicting final outcomes for candidates since gender preferences cancel each other out at the final count. There are more discernable gender factors at play in the areas of policy which voters believe women and men are more likely to support or more competent to decide on (Burrell, 1994), a point discussed elsewhere.

Interestingly, what has also been known for some time is that the gender gap, at least in the United States, is a function of the changing political partisanship of *men*, since the political attitudes (and voting behavior) of women have remained largely constant over the past two decades and certainly since the "discovery" of the gender gap during Ronald Reagan's election year in 1980 (Wirls, 1986; Miller & Shanks, 1996; Box-Steffensmeier, DeBoef, & Lin, 1997; Kaufmann & Petrocik, 1999). However, despite agreement on the broad principles of men's movement and women's stasis, there is some difference of opinion for the causes of the contemporary position. While most commentators would argue that women's attitudes have simply remained constant, others (for example, Wirls, 1986; Box-Steffensmeier & Lin, 1987) argue that women are also retreating from the liberal democratic view, but their rates of defection are much slower than those of men. However, there is little evidence of women's (even incremental) move to the right, so what is interesting to ponder is why it is that political discourse and research continues to focus on and stress the importance of *women's* political behaviour and voting power rather than men's when it is men who are actively engaged in using their political muscle by shifting party. What is going on?

MEDIA, VOTERS AND IMPACT

In Britain, there is a considerable body of work which has focused on the phenomenon of the general election, and since at least the early 1970s, research teams have undertaken both primary research and secondary analysis on the various datasets emerging from the British Election Studies, exploring the relation between media coverage of elections and voter behaviour. Early work, such as that of Butler and Stokes (1974), began a trend in better understanding the electorate's viewing habits during election campaigns. Sanders and Norris (1997) suggest that subsequent studies, while closely replicating the initial set of questions, also added new research issues, such as attitudes towards bias in news coverage as this became a bigger issue (see, for example, Ansolabehere & Iyengar, 1997). While those research studies certainly revealed voter attitudes towards political campaigning, they did little to improve our knowledge about the impact that such viewing has on voter's positive or negative ratings of parties. Sanders and Norris (1997) thus set out with the specific intention of trying to map the existence (if any) of a cause-and-effect relationship between the tone of political advertising and voter perception of party, arguing that in designing their study they made two basic assumptions: that television news is an important informational source, and that voters will modify their political preferences and attitudes in response to the information which they receive about parties. Linked to this second point are two further working assumptions: that although significant shifts in political ideology are only likely to occur after audiences experience sustained and prolonged exposure to media messages which challenge their beliefs, more limited exposure could produce small but important perceptual shifts; and that some people, such as those who claim to be "undecided" or a "floating voter," are more likely than others to shift their position as a consequence of quite small but obviously persuasive doses of information. What Sanders and

Norris found was that exposure to positive party coverage by the news media provoked a positive response to that party by voters; on the other hand, exposure to negative coverage provoked inconsistent responses. Importantly, the study also found no evidence of what the authors term a "collateral" effect; that is, negative coverage of one party did not encourage voters to view other parties more favorably. Looking at the print media's involvement in the same election and its impact on voter choice, Burns (1997) argues that the media's much more overt support for the Labour Party, especially in the tabloid press (with its considerably bigger circulation than the more centrist or centre-left broadsheets) probably contributed to Labour's success, again giving credence to the suggestion that positive coverage improves voter perception of parties. This is hardly news, but it does add further weight to the contention that news media do play *some* part in shaping voter attitudes and that they can materially affect a party's standing (and ultimate success) by deliberately choosing to frame that party in a positive or negative way—by their choice of story, their slant, their perspective, and so on. If, as appears to be the case, campaigns continue to be covered in ways which give the media as much power to control the message as political parties themselves, then their claim to be able to make or break politicians (and parties) is still one to take seriously.

Voters who actively seek out political information from the media are persistently thwarted by the media's insistence on covering election process issues, such as competitor league tables, and who is doing the best character assassination on whom (Hart, 1994) rather than discussing policy positions. In the United States, and in other countries like the United Kingdom which emulate American-style politics, the media's persistent framing of elections as a "horse race" means that coverage is much more oriented towards the gamesmanship of the principal actors/parties than in any real engagement with the particular policy or issue positions of candidates (Kiousis, 2000). Not surprisingly, most studies of voter perceptions of election coverage produce highly negative results since campaigns, which are arguably about trying to provide voters with policy information upon which to base their ballot box decisions, signally fail to do this, instead focusing on personalities, sleaze and/or public relations battles (Hart, 1987; Patterson, 1994; Just, Crigler, & Buhr, 1999). As Patterson (1993) notes, rather cynically, the "United States is the only democracy that organizes its national election around the media" (p. 28), and the veteran BBC news correspondent, Nick Jones (1995) makes the relation between politics and media very clear when he says that "the state of a governing party's relationship with the news media has always been a useful pointer to its chances of electoral survival" (p. 220).

Of course, what passes for "news" during elections is often little more than opinion poll "research," often carried out for broadcasters and newspapers themselves, which provides spurious evidence to support whatever claim individual segments of the media might be making at any one time. Fletcher's (1996) work on polling suggests that polls are not necessarily helpful in the democratic enterprise because their myriad failures—to take into account the intensity of individual preferences, to give the same credence to informed and uninformed opinion alike, and their tendency to discuss single issues in isolation—militate against their having any real utility. And, if politicians and candidates are unhappy with the ways in which the media frame political stories during election campaigns, opinion pollsters are equally frustrated with the casual use of the data and "story" which the polling companies have been careful to ensure is as reliable and sober as possible. Broughton (1995) suggests that the news media's insistence on simplification means that the contingent nuances of much poll data is ignored by journalists keen on putting out sensational copy, and it contributes to the fact that polls are seen as increasingly unreliable predictors of voting behaviour. However, it is probably not just the media which are implicated in missing the polling point, but the electorate itself, who will not necessarily tell the truth when asked about their voting intentions.

Yet, the ways in which the media have been seen to be an active element in political campaigning—and specifically, their role in affecting voting behaviour—have changed over time as the methods of gauging effects have become more sophisticated (Ansolabehere, Iyengar, & Simon, 1997). Initial alarm over the propagandist possibilities offered by a national medium such as television—assuming a passive polity ready to believe any message provided that it was slickly packaged—was initially assuaged by early effects studies which suggested that the media exerted minimal effects on voting behaviour, other than making voters more committed to their preselected candidate/party of choice (see Lazarsfeld, Berelson, & Gander 1948). However, what has become clear is that surveys are not sufficiently sensitive as research instruments, and opinion polls are often unable to detect the effects of particular "advertising" strategies. Ansolabehere et al. (1997) suggest that at least two recent theories of political campaign "effects" have better explanatory value. The "resonance" model posits the view that voters can be persuaded by carefully constructed messages, but it inserts a contextual index into the equation relating to pre-existing political preferences and the extent to which political messages conform to voter expectations. The "competitive" model is mooted by the authors as the most sensitive approach yet developed for measuring campaign effects, a model which acknowledges the interrelationships between political competitors and the importance of criticism and refutation in the "game" of political persuasion and vote catching.

Yet, the point of political campaigns is to achieve a specific focus, to make one issue of paramount importance in terms of an election platform (Popkin, 1997). In the 1992 elections in America, Clinton's camp attempted to focus the essential difference on change versus the status quo (and in fact Blair's message in 1997 was not so different), whereas Bush wanted to use a more frightening specter to distinguish his claim, namely to suggest that people could trust the Republicans, but the Democrats would raise taxes—trust versus taxes. In Britain's general election campaign of 1997, the Labour slogan of "education, education, education" made clear the party's principal issue priority, and in 2001, the Party attempted to convince the electorate that consolidation was important with its slogan, "Labour is working." Lippmann's (1922) classic work on public opinion still has explanatory relevance to news stories in the late 1990s; political opinion is not shaped by the direct experience of politics, but rather emerges as a consequence of the images which one is given via news accounts of politics. As Bennett (1997) questions pertinently, the fundamental conundrum to unravel is how journalists—and therefore news organizations more generally—acting in fierce competition with each other nonetheless manage to construct a political "world" which is both standardized across the sector but also believable enough to form the baseline for the public's political understanding. Yet, even journalists themselves can't resist having inter-sector squabbles about the virtues of one medium over another. One of the BBC's most respected political journalists, John Humphrys, who works for the flagship radio 4 programme *Today*, is critical of the way in which television news has become infatuated with its own clever tricks—which have everything to do with style and very little to do with improving access to real information:

> Television news does too many things because they are possible rather than because they are necessary . . . vast amounts of money were spent on a new set by Channel 4 so that [Jon] Snow could emerge from behind his formidable desk and show us his socks. It was bad enough being able to see ties. (Humphrys, cited in the *Guardian*, 30.8.1999)

While this could be seen, to some extent, as sour grapes on Humphrys' part, since television news has considerably higher audience ratings than its poor radio relation, it probably isn't, since the *Today* programme is singled out by many British politicians as being an important show to both listen to and to perform on, regarding it as being of particular relevance and interest (and therefore potentially highly influential) to elite decision makers, especially the heavyweights in the corporate sector. Humphrys' point is well made, and his substantive argument is made repeatedly by the politicians I have interviewed in my own work: that the infotainment elements, clever graphics, and aesthetically pleasing but totally irrelevant image backgrounds, all contribute to television news being increasingly viewed as a quasi-entertainment genre which also, unfortunately, has to convey unpleasant messages about the social, economic, and political world. For Barnhurst (1998), these high-tech sets, fast paced and frenetic cutaways to an outside broadcast, and similar strategies are attempts by journalists to try to make up for the "growing and inevitable dreariness of journalism filled with their own opinions and interpretations by disguising and dressing up news in visual excess" (pp. 202-203). This is news as spectacle, as performance, and even newspapers are busy changing their image to make themselves more sexy, more attractive, and more interesting, with fancy banners, postmodern fonts (Nerone & Barnhurst, 1995), and a handy two-minute digest for those too busy (or too lazy?) to read even the front page.

Conventional wisdom has had it that newspapers are a superior source of information during election campaigns to broadcast media, especially television, since the latter is regarded as providing merely superficial infotainment, whereas newspapers devote considerable space to political stories, including background and context, allowing the reader to go through the material at her or his own pace. This folk wisdom has been "corroborated" by numerous studies which have shown that people who mostly use newspapers are more likely to score highly on comprehension and recall tests than are those who mainly use television as their information source (see, for example, Robinson & Davis, 1990). But the specific medium is not the only variable here since it may be that media consumers who mainly read newspapers are more literate and more highly educated, not just that newspapers constitute a better information source (Bennett, Flickenger, Backer, Rhine, & Bennett, 1996). In any case, more recent work on the newspaper/television debate is beginning to show that television news can, in fact, have as much impact on voter understanding as newspapers (see Neuman, Just, & Crigler, 1992; Zhao & Chaffee, 1995) and that *attention*—as much as *exposure*—to news items appears to be crucial. Admittedly, viewers have to be sufficiently motivated by a news item to watch it attentively and to thus actually take in and process the information which is being given out, but that is also the case with newspapers.

Of course, different media produce different effects, and numerous studies over the past years have indicated that print media are more strongly associated with the acquisition and retention of political knowledge than television (Becker & Dunwoody, 1982; Kennamar, 1987; Miller, Singletary, & Chen, 1988), so that individuals who use "print media to follow politics rather than solely television or no media are more knowledgeable about politics" (Strate, Ford, & Jankowski, 1994, p. 168). Part of the distinction between the two media in terms of knowledge and information giving has to do with television being a highly visual medium, unsuited to dealing with complex debates but more likely to deal with simple concepts which can be easily represented, such as with graphs showing who is doing better than whom in the horse race. It is ironic, then, that it is television which is seen increasingly as the most important source of information about the world rather than newspapers. Other studies find that voters' attitudes towards news media coverage of elections are strongly influenced by their level of party identification, so that individuals who are strong supporters of a(ny) party tend to believe that the media are especially biased against "their" party (Mughan, 1996). Similarly, in an exploration of relations between media use frequency, media importance, political disaffection, and political efficacy, Pinkleton and Austin (2000) report an association between newspaper use and low cynicism and news magazine use and higher cynicism, where the variable of cynicism itself is strongly directed both at the media and politics. Interestingly, their study also demonstrated that voters who believe that newspapers are the most important sources of political information are much more skeptical and negative about politics than frequent users of television. Overall, the researchers argue that the most significant variable in their study was satisfaction with the media, suggesting that voter dissatisfaction with the media could be a more significant inhibitor of active political participation than hostility toward negative political campaigning. But as Perloff (1998) points out, the newspapers versus television debate is largely academic since most people use a mix of sources to meet their information needs, and not just traditional outlets such as newspapers, radio and television, but also new media such as cable, satellite television, and the internet.

Yet, do women and men view the media's political messages differently from each other, and how salient is the volume and mode of delivery of news stories on perceptions towards both the practice of politics and the efficacy of the media? In Kennamar's (1986) telephone survey of residents of Madison County, he found that, although the media featured strongly as an influential feature in men's attitudes toward particular policies, women's attitudes appeared to be determined more by their political allegiance generally and by their level of education. Interestingly, while contemporary campaigns allocate a sizeable portion of their funds to television advertising, Kennamer found that it was print rather than broadcast media which actually had an impact, although that situation is likely to have changed somewhat in subsequent years. Other research paints a similar picture, that while the media's coverage of elections can have a contributory influence on voting decisions, this process is gendered such that it appears that only men are susceptible to media impact (see Hayes & Makkai, 1996).

There are any number of reasons why women might appear to be less influenced by mass media coverage of political campaigns in terms of impacting on their final voting behaviour, and Hayes and Makkai (1996) posit at least three explanations. They suggest that women are more likely to be involved in local political activity and to make personal investments in achieving local ends, and are thus likely to be more interested in local rather than national issues and, by extension, local rather than national elections. In addition, women are more likely to rely on and give credibility to political information and material which is personally and anecdotally derived, eschewing the conventional and constructed political "spots" of television campaigning. A third reason could be that women are more disillusioned with the failure of mainstream politics to address the key issues of concern to them and are thus more hostile to the "media circus" which has become the accepted style for election campaigns. Any and all of these factors could contribute to women's greater reliance upon and loyalty to party preference, using "party identification as an easy mechanism to determining their voting outcome" (Hayes & Makkai, 1996, p. 66). In Cirksena's (1996) study of women and political persuasion, she found that women who are relatively high consumers of news media are more likely to be involved in trying to encourage other people to share their own political views than are low news consumers. This suggests that women who have more (and possibly wider sources of) political information may be more confident in their knowledge levels and are therefore more likely to become politically engaged. Women politicians themselves recognize the problem of the media's singular interest in portraying the worst of the political process to the electorate. "There is internal party intelligence, from both the major parties, that show that women are turned off by the combative environment of Parliament and the sledging [barracking] that goes on" (Sue Mackay, Labor, Australia). Out on the campaign trail and supporting other women candidates, Cheryl Kernot (Labor, Australia) suggests that women voters recognize precisely the ways in which the media try to marginalise political women, and she comments on the attitudes of support and understanding which flow between women in different relations to politics and media:

I've been campaigning for women candidates in marginal seats and there are some fantastic ones, women have come up and said to me in huge numbers "don't take any notice of it, we know what they're trying to do." One woman said "it's OK if you leave, we really want you to be there, but we don't think you should have to put up with this crap if you don't want to. Don't feel you have to for women." I thought that was a wonderfully generous thing to say.

Although we now have many more column inches and broadcast minutes devoted to election coverage, what we get from this barrage of information is less, not more. We are now, in the early 21st century, in the absurd and entirely perverse situation where the volume and sources of news material concerning election campaigns has increased significantly over the past two decades, including the more recent development of 24-hour news channels which are achieving a global reach, while at the same time "real" information about what candidates actually stand for becomes increasingly elusive. We are turning on its head the truism that the more we know, the less we understand; we understand very well exactly what we don't know, and we blame the media—not politicians—for the gaps in our knowledge and for our increasingly cynical approach to politics more generally (Lasora, 1997; Cappella & Jamieson, 1997). While public confidence in politicians continues its downward trend, the situation is little better when the media industry is targeted as a source of information integrity, where public trust has been in serious decline for at least the past three decades (Patterson, 1994; American Society of Newspaper Editors, 1998), with newspapers being the focus for particular skepticism. A significant element in this public disenchantment is, arguably, the overly negative slant of news in general and political news in particular, especially during election campaigns (Owen, 1997; Klotz, 1998). In some ways, the persistent interpretative lens through which journalists seem determined to mediate messages from political actors, refracting their efforts to address the polity directly by their casual use of an interrogative style to suggest a hidden agenda if not a downright lie, is part of a wider phenomenon of news as infotainment. The tabloidizing tendencies of all media are well documented and have been noted by politicians and polity alike. The news media thus find themselves in rather an awkward place. On the one hand, they allegedly (and self-referentially) pander to the craven appetites of the mass audience, but on the other hand, they are roundly condemned by that same audience for not providing them/us with straightforward reporting. Is there a happy medium? In his work on what he calls "boomerang" effects, whereby the number of cynical stories and the volume of stories overall are negatively correlated to public confidence in the press, Kiousis (2000) suggests that such effects *do* exist, albeit tentatively concluding, given the limited nature of his sample material, that one way to combat poor public perceptions of news media is for the latter to change their reporting conventions.

GENDER AND EFFECT

While the media are generally predisposed towards downplaying women candidates' campaign messages in a straight fight between a woman and a man, there is some evidence to suggest that, in contests which pitch women against each other, news reports take on a rather different complexion (Braden, 1996). In the New York State primaries in 1992, the media suggested that Elizabeth Holtzman had waged a campaign war which had sunk to new political depths because, as Braden argues, she had dared to attack her sister Democrat contender, Geraldine Ferraro. While male opponents can be as sleazy, personal, and grubby as they like when slandering and libeling each other under the acceptable auspices of robust electioneering, women cannot do the same thing without being targets for all manner of gendered exhortations which mainly center on the fact that women are supposed to be nice to each other: ". . . as the primary campaign heated up, some media observers expressed concern that the women weren't acting the way women were supposed to act. They were behaving more like traditional male politicians" (Braden, 1996, p. 134). Ferraro herself recognized that the gender dimension was an important element in the media's sustained coverage of the allegations against her perpetrated by Elizabeth Holtzman since negative attack advertising has always been a routine part of any election campaign. Yet, in this case, there was something qualitatively different about the media's coverage: "They [the media] had to report it—there was nothing you could do about it . . . they loved that type of thing . . . the fight going on between these women" (cited in Braden, 1996, p. 136). Interestingly, the acrimony and viciousness which pervaded (and perverted) Holtzman's campaign against Ferraro subsequently promoted much discussion in the press about the appropriateness of expecting women to have higher standards than men, which voters *do* expect of women, irrespective of the fairness of that expectation. But this assumption requires women politicians and candidates to square an impossible circle, to be both morally superior to their male colleagues, but also to succeed in a highly dubious working environment—to be both as rough, tough, and aggressive as men, but to also make politics a more conciliatory and "nicer" process at the same time.

Elsewhere in the United States, the news media's differently gendered coverage of political candidates varies enormously from district to district, and it is determined by the volume of local media and the extent to which seats are marginal or safe. In Fox's (1997) study of the media's election coverage of the 1992 elections, he found that there were few differences between women and men candidates in terms of the amount of media coverage received but that women were more likely to be the focus of news reports if there was something different about them. Fifty per cent of party managers of women candidates interviewed for his study stated:

> Their candidate was covered in media stories focusing on the Year of the Woman. One female candidate was featured on *Nightline* in a special program on female candidates [and] another women received national attention because she had once been a single mother on welfare. (p. 129)

While some women party agents were less convinced by the hype of the Year of the Woman, they were nonetheless willing to concede that specific events, such as the Anita Hill-Clarence Thomas ruling, galvanized a latent interest in political activity among some women to take a more overt form (see, for example, Lake, DiVall, & Iyengar, 1997). However, by the time of the 1994 United States State elections, no party managers specifically mentioned the media's interest in women candidates. In the 2001 British general election, some media commentators themselves asked the question, "where are the women," since none of the Parties were pushing women in their campaigns. Fox (1997) argues that women candidates perceive negative media bias against them in greater proportions than men. When asked directly whether candidates felt that the media treated them fairly in the 1992 elections, 36 per cent of women challengers replied "yes" compared with 59 per cent of men (p. 132). Typical comments made by women candidates included, "I got little press, but when I was mentioned, it was often in reference to my family, particularly the amount of money my husband and I have . . . my identity was always associated with my husband" (cited in Fox, 1997, p. 133). The types of bias found in Fox's study included: non-reporting excessive coverage of male candidates, sex stereotyping, focus on physical attributes, and disparagement of candidates on gender lines. In other research focusing on women running for legislative office in Illinois, one candidate reported that the media concentrated on superficial aspects of themselves, such as: "stupid, little things such as clothes, hair, etc. which never comes up with men. They also use loaded adjectives to describe us such as feisty, perky, small and lively" (cited in Poole, 1993, pp. 6-7). When party managers in Fox's study were asked about the existence of media bias against their candidate, 64 per cent of managers of women candidates replied "yes," compared with 41 per cent of managers of male candidates. Typical comments from women managers included:

> I'll give you an example of gender bias. The press totally over-emphasized her divorce. She had a nasty divorce with child custody battles and the whole thing. The press was always bringing it up. I really don't believe a male divorcee candidate would have been sub-jected to as much focus on this personal issue . . . our [male] oppo-nent had a host of personal and family scandals and the press stayed away from them. (cited in Fox, 1997, p. 134)

Even when incumbent politicians are considered, their visibility as spokespeople for the government or the opposition is still minimal, as my own work on the British general election in 1997 has demonstrated (Ross, 1998b). In that study, one week of broadcast news was monitored during the election campaign period, and given the context of the study, it would be expected that politicians themselves, especially the party leaders, would feature significantly in news election coverage. Yet, the invisibility of women politicians from any party was highly disconcert-ing and echoed earlier work covering the previous election (University of Loughborough, 1992). Excluding appearances by the three main Party leaders, 135 Members of Parliament were featured during the monitoring period, and only 8 of these were women (6 per cent). The women politi-cians who did manage to attract a small spot of light were Margaret Beckett (Labour), twice—on Europe and on privatization; Diana Maddock (Liberal Democrat)—on Europe; Mo Mowlam (Labour Party)—on Labour Party policy on selection; Clare Short (Labour Party)—a very brief appearance on a women's health item; Edwina Currie and Theresa Gorman (both Conservative); and Margaret Ewing (Scottish National Party), all three on a panel discussing Europe. Interestingly, the "Europe" question was viewed by respondents in an Independent Television Commission's election study as being of little interest to voters in general; more than half the sample reported that they were either "not very interested" (35 per cent) or "not at all interested" (17 per cent) in the topic, with boredom thresholds lower for women—30 per cent of women said they were interested in the European Union com-pared with 48 per cent of men (Sancho-Aldridge, 1997, p. 25), although one must wonder if perhaps woman are just more honest? It is a hard irony, then, that five out of the paltry eight appearances of women politi-cians focused on an issue which did not appear to be an involving one for women voters, perhaps because they/we get exasperated by the con-structed and one-sided nature of so many political debates.

It is worth noting that women politicians received the same scant press attention during the 1997 general election campaign as has been noted in regard to other elelctions (see Ross & Sreberny-Mohammadi, 1997) and where they did feature, they were often trivialized. For example, five women candidates were contesting the Hampstead and Highgate constituency and were presented as the "Spice Girls" in the *Evening Standard*. Twin sisters Angela and Maria Eagle were both standing as Labour candidates and were featured in an item entitled "New Labour, New Crumpet" (McDougall, 1998a) and when 101 Labour women MPs were subsequently elected, they were immediately dubbed, "Blair's Babes." One of the key themes of the 1997 British General Election campaign was, arguably, that of "sleaze" and in particular, the controversy surrounding the standing of Neil Hamilton, an MP accused of corruption. His wife, Christine (who was either captioned simply as "Mrs. Neil Hamilton," or else given no credit at all) featured in five of the news items monitored, thereby achieving a level of visibility (albeit as adjunct rather than in her own right) only dreamt of by women politicians. Of the 26 appearances of politicians speaking "for the Government," none was a woman. Even when we looked at the separate category of local government politician (councilor), where a better gender balance actually exists, of the 12 local councilors who appeared in news items, none was a woman. Halfway through Tony Blair's first administration, in late 1999, internal polling among Labour Party members revealed a dissatisfaction with the way in which women MPs were progressing through the government, an impatience with the fact that competent and capable women did not appear to be achieving the office to which they were capable, and a disquiet over the way in which male-dominated politics still appeared to be the order of the day.

The way in which women candidates are covered by the news media finds obvious parallels with the way in which women and women's issues more generally are marginalised as legitimate topics of media interest. While a particularly "gendered" item might make the women's page in daily newspapers, it will rarely feature as a news item in the mainstream sections (Kahn & Goldenberg, 1997). Successive studies of the media's portrayal of women politicians and political candidates are unequivocal in their findings that the gender of politicians is an important factor in the differential coverage that women and men politicians receive at the hands of the media and that this differentiated coverage may have important effects on how candidates are evaluated by the electorate. Caroline Flint, one of the so-called "Blair's Babes" who was elected along with 100 other Labour women MPs in the 1997 British elections, is exasperated with a media discourse which is only interested in her views on women-oriented facilities in the House of Commons:

> [I am] ready to throttle the next journalist who asks me about toilets
> and crèches in the House of Commons . . . there are enough toilets
> for women MPs . . . and as for the crèche—there are very few
> women with children under five. They [the media] should focus on
> the diversity of women in Parliament. We are a mixed bunch and
> hopefully in many different ways represent the variety of women in
> Britain. (Flint cited in McDougall, 1998a, p. 79)

The media's persistent domestication of women Parliamentarians in this
way and their power to frame their female subjects as constantly in
thrall to their bodily functions sends out the clear message to the public
that this is indeed what preoccupies our women members. Is it any wonder then that stereotypes of the "weaker" sex continue to hold sway in
the collective public consciousness? If that's the discourse, then that's
the story. In Kahn's (1994a) comparative study of American Senate candidates during the 1982 and 1986 elections, she found that women generally received less media attention and that this could adversely affect
their chances because less information about candidates could mean that
intending voters had little to inform them about the specific policy positions of women candidates, and therefore voter recognition of women
candidates was weak. Kahn also found that the substance of media coverage was qualitatively different; for example, more time was devoted to
the "horse race" element of women candidates than to their policy positions and more time was spent discussing negative "horse race" elements than was the case with male candidates. This focus on competitive advantage (and especially disadvantage) can harm women's
chances since it suggests, in the minds of voters, that winning is itself an
issue for women candidates—regardless of whether or not they promote
a politics which voters believe in. In an interesting study comparing
media coverage of candidates from Northern Ireland who were standing
for the 1997 British general election and the local elections in Northern
Ireland (which were being held simultaneously), Whittaker (1999) suggests that women candidates for both elections were significantly and
consistently under-reported across the 22 newspapers which were monitored for the study, that women were virtually absent from leader comments, and that women candidates themselves were overwhelmingly
dissatisfied with their treatment at the hands of the media. Women tended to receive better coverage if they stood in both elections. Havick's
(1997) work on what influences media coverage of women candidates
found that political allegiance was one of two significant factors in determining the volume of media coverage given; the other salient feature
was whether women were running for the Senate or the House. Havick's
work also found that women from minority ethnic backgrounds
received less attention than white women

As far as identifying the extent to which elections are gendered in terms of women and men journalists covering these events, some work suggests that women are more willing than their male candidates to cover gender issues in their campaign reports although there are very few women journalists who work on elections. Kahn (1994a) suggests that women reporters are more likely to include discussions about so-called women's issues in their political campaign coverage than are their male colleagues, and this tendency becomes even more pronounced when the coverage focuses on women candidates. For Kahn and Gordon (1997), this concentration can have important and positive spin-offs for putative women politicians since

> media coverage affects the salience of issues for the public [and] voters exposed to races with female candidates may come to believe that female issues are important and these female issues, because they are more salient, may be used when voters evaluate the candidates. (p. 161)

The argument follows that if a particular issue is emphasized and this issue is seen as an area in which women do well, such as education, then women candidates may enjoy good press in the eyes of the electors. Overall, though, because of differences in volume, tone, and focus, Kahn's work concludes that the media act as a barrier against women's political aspirations and that women themselves could begin to reverse this trend if they were to take on interests and portfolios which defy the usual sex-stereotyped expectations, showing that they are as capable of economic policy development as they are when working on nursery education. However, the (relative) absence of women from political news reporting is a disappointing feature of the mediascape, and it corresponds with their lack of visibility in jobs which carry decision-making responsibilities. In work carried out by the British group Women in Journalism on gender and media employment in Britain, they found that, although women have begun to be appointed to senior roles (although below editor level), "leader writing [editorials] and political writing remain stubbornly male enclaves" (Christmas, 1997, p. 12). Women journalists who were interviewed for the report identify the political editor as a powerful figure in the newsroom because journalists consider that the reporting of politics helps define a newspaper's sense of self (and despite the increasing tabloidization of even the most respectable broadsheets, a definite political slant is still broadly apparent in news reporting), and during elections, political reporting becomes even more influential.

Those few women journalists who do cover elections often report a journalistic camaraderie which is "testosterone driven" and gender exclusive. Joanna Coles (1997), reporting for the *Guardian*, was one of the journalists on the 1997 campaign bus used by party apparatchniks to follow in their masters' [sic] wake and on which some of the media hitched a free ride. Coles likens these journeys to a minor stag party, with male colleagues leering at pornographic material previously downloaded from the internet, sharing cans of lager, and sniggering whenever a woman happened to wander down the aisle of the bus toward them. Coles was in the somewhat unenviable position of being both excluded from this spectacle of puerile masculinity by her sex—for example, when she approached the "porno" section of the bus, the computer in question had its screen discreetly lowered—but also included and expected to collude with her colleagues because of their shared professional "codes."

Yet, beliefs about the ability of political campaigns to change voting behaviour tend to depend on where one's vested interests lie, and many political communication scholars take their cues from the Columbia and Michigan models which suggest that such campaigns have minimal impact on change although they do have the effect of confirming and often entrenching existing political proclivities. Their point, then, is to perform a kind of ritualistic performance which is more symbolic than real, where predictable arguments are spun out and routine antagonisms televised, but where the electorate have already made up their minds some months or years before, based on personal beliefs and values which are usually more enduring than the politicians fronting the parties (Butler, 1989; Butler & Kavanagh, 1997; King, 1997). Political parties themselves, as well as pollsters, on the other hand, suggest a completely different effect: that even at the eleventh hour, a good campaign message can pull off a vital shift in voting beliefs and therefore in behaviour (Gould, 1998; Holmes & Holmes, 1998; Finkelstein, 1998): the real impact probably lies somewhere along the continuum of all–nothing. The relationship of political news coverage to voters is highly complex and not readily amenable to simplistic theories which frame the influence in absolute terms, and at least some election studies are developing analyses which go beyond that simple binary. In Norris, Curtice, Sanders, Scammell, and Semetko's (1999) study of the 1997 British general election, the authors suggest that claims of media influence, at least during the intensive six-week campaign period, were greatly exaggerated, and they also found that the agenda-setting powers of the media were considerably muted, especially regarding those issues which were already high on the public's agenda. For example, they argue persuasively that the news media's infatuation with the "Europe" question during the 1997 election campaign signally failed to capture public interest, demonstrating that the media's perspective is only one of several which individuals bring to bear when making their voting decisions and deciding on personal issue priorities. "In open-ended questions about the most important problems facing the country, the public continued to believe, no matter what the papers told them, that bread-and-butter issues were of far greater priority than Brussels" (Norris et al., 1998, p. 183). Ironically, this lesson was *not* learned for the 2001 British general election when, after another landslide victory of Labour, the Conservative Party leader stepped down, saying, among other things, that his campaign overstated "the Europe issue" (William Hague, MP, reported on the *Today* programme, BBC Radio 4, 8/6/01).

Where most studies of women candidates, media, and elections show largely negative findings, some exceptions are notable, and some of the research studies on the 1992 elections in the United States appear to demonstrate a different tone and style in portrayal, albeit for situationally specific reasons which might never again appear. For example, Walkosz and Kenski (1995) suggest that the combination of a large number of open seats for Congress, a large pool of talented women candidates, the legacy of the Anita Hill-Clarence Thomas hearings, resources available for women candidates, and a generally anti-incumbent mood in the country, opened up opportunities for women candidates to run and to succeed. They argue that their work on coverage shows that, while the print media continued to stereotype and marginalise women candidates in the usual way, television news was significantly different in several ways. Only Senate races which included women tended to be covered, women candidates were primed favorably as "viable" (often because the size of their campaign funds implied that others thought they had a chance), and hostility towards "politics as usual" advantaged women since they were seen as change-agents and thus different. This work sits awkwardly in the body of research on this particular election and others which more generally paint a much bleaker picture. Yet, it provides a timely corrective to the view that the media are always and everywhere reactionary and hostile to women's aspirations. However, as with any other proposition, one must ask the "right" question, and one can usually get the "right" answer. It *is* important to not always produce the easy, knee-jerk reaction to questions relating to women and media portrayal, just because they suit the politics and beliefs of the researcher. And, it is important to give as full attention to the exceptions as to the "norms." On the other hand, there are sufficient examples of dominant and one-way trends and patterns in the media's framing of political women to continue to give cause for concern, even as we celebrate those small chinks in the armor of the body journalistic which alert us to and give us hope for the possibilities of change.

As Khan's (1996) study argues, the way in which the media deliberately choose to frame the campaigns of women candidates in significantly different ways from those of male contenders can (and I would argue does) influence the potential of women's likelihood to achieve elected office. Not only is there a very clear skew in volume and slant in the way in which the media report on the political campaigns of women and men, but, as importantly, the way in which they "interpret" the reasons for success closes the loop in the agenda-setting circle. So, if the successful male candidate has stressed the importance of financial probity or has stood on an aggressive "zero tolerance" platform during his campaign, then the media is likely to report that the successful politician has accurately captured the public's anxiety with those issues as their priority concerns. Thus, the subsequent policy agenda following an election is likely to include legislation around precisely those areas which apparently "won" the election since politicians believe that those *were* the issues which carried the day. However, if the media had instead given equal weight to the policy priorities of women, then Khan (1996) argues that the electorate would come to view other issues, such as health and education, as equally important, and thus women politicians as equally important:

> Furthermore, since voters would be more concerned with these alternative issues, the election of women to the Senate who endorse these policy initiatives might lead elected officials to see these alternative issues as important, leading senators to demonstrate their commitment to these areas of public policy. (p. 134)

The hard fact is that the news media are simply not interested in discussing so-called women's issues or "soft" policy issues as a routine part of election campaign coverage, so a change of tactic among women aspirants is clearly needed, most obviously by grasping the nettle of so-called male concerns and perhaps putting a different spin on the issues. This could have at least two positive outcomes: it would demonstrate that women are as concerned with the economy, defense and taxation as their male counterparts, and it would encourage the media to provide more coverage of women's views, even if only for the novelty value:

> I took the treasury and finance portfolio because I didn't want to be pigeonholed into women's thinking, but I always feel that it was counter-balanced because on budget night in this country they'd have the treasurer and the shadow treasurer and then me and I was the only woman talking head and I'd go round the country and in airport lounges women would say to me, "god I got such a buzz to see your female head up there, talking all that economics stuff on budget night" so I was never marginalised . . . but that was by my choice of taking strategic portfolios. (Cheryl Kernot, Labor, Australia)

7

Conclusions

[The media] portray me as a right-wing shit bag. Careerist, shallow, you name it. I find it highly disturbing that women are judged like that and men aren't. I know men who got as much press coverage as I did, but they are not called careerists or media hussies. But because I'm a woman, because I'm young, it clearly means I'm ambitious. (Lorna Fitzsimmons MP (UK), cited in McDougall, 1998b, p. 77)

That there has been a significant change in the forms of news reporting over the past decade is now almost unquestioned among media scholars, and this paradigm shift is irrefutably bound up with the changing status of journalists—at least from their own point of view—from "reporter" to "interpreter." The traditional descriptive style of the journalistic craft has given way to an interpretative focus which empowers journalists, allowing them to enjoy an enhanced credibility and considerable control over programme content (Patterson, 1996). The concentration on negativity and a rampant, almost knee-jerk, cynicism towards the political process, which can only see government as the enemy of the people, promotes a similarly negative and cynical approach to be taken by the polity, making effective government more difficult and compromising the democratic imperative. Ironically, when journalists in an American study (see Weaver & Wilhoit, 1997) were asked to state their views on how well they felt their own organization performed in informing their audience, there were less favorable evaluations of news organizations by their own staff now than was the case a decade earlier, and any number of studies indicate the public persuasiveness of the media's construction of political news, even where individuals have first-hand (and often directly contradictory) knowledge of particular events, such as having attended speeches or rallies (Kendall, 1997).

While most studies argue strongly that the tabloidizing tendencies of the media, particularly in the United States, have had and continue to have a deleterious impact on democracy and an informed polity, some scholars have tended to take a more generous view (van Zoonen, 1998a). For example, Jamieson (1996) argues that the style of American political advertising has, in fact, made politics more—not less—meaningful to the public since their propensity to reduce everything to a personal level contributes to a more relevant sense-making process for voters. Similarly, Brants' (1997) work finds little evidence to support the claim that commercial television has marginalised political news. Yet, as with everything else, there will always be studies which support either the "media-is-bad-for-democracy" proposition or its opposite. One of the reasons it is so hard to measure the precise impact of an increasingly infotainment-centered news media on democracy—either its negative, positive or neutral affects—is the small-scale nature of most research datasets, coupled with the fact that many American studies make claims about effects based on experimental studies with groups of students or voters who live in a very discrete geographical area, or else they comprise short time-series analyses or limited samples of local print media. This is certainly not to discredit the utility of any of those research studies, but it is to argue that, while we can plot patterns and trends based on whatever our research reveals and pose explanatory theories to make sense of what we find, the very next study that asks a slightly different question of a slightly different cohort at a slightly different moment can produce very different and perhaps contradictory results. Part of the alleged virtue of doing quantitative research is that it can factor out precisely those human biases from the equation, but the findings of such studies are no better, in real terms, at revealing some hidden truth which can be held constant even in the short term because political culture, especially now in the 21st century, is such a volatile thing, susceptible to the vagaries of any number of external and internal factors which come (almost) from nowhere and which can knock over governments at a stroke. More importantly, the explosion in information sources—the world wide web, News24, cable, satellite and digital broadcasting—provide such a diverse range of information points and modes of communication (even if the processes of globalization mean that the content of these various bulletins are remarkably similar) that it is impossible to attempt to control for "all other" variables in order to more precisely measure the influence of this X on that Y.

My own experience as a media scholar for the past 15 years, as well as an avid news consumer and a feminist keen on identifying precisely the ways in which women's voices are rendered visible—both through their own articulated prose and speech as well as via the journalistic lens—leads me to a particular view of the media's role in the process of democracy. I would argue that the media *do* have a negative effect on the democratic process through their insistence on privileging their own perspectives above those of the political actors they purport to cover. In the specific instance of the gendered dimension of political reporting, the overwhelming majority of studies show clearly that women politicians, both incumbents and candidates, do not receive as much coverage as their male contenders, and when they do feature, they face the same problems of style-over-substance in the high-octane environment of elections as they do in the more mundane context of "ordinary" political discourse: their hairstyles always seem more newsworthy than their policy positions.

Despite the complacent cry of the media that they provide merely a looking-glass service to the public, mirroring back to us what we ourselves create and believe, such crass disingenuousness is less and less tenable in a media environment in which the sector actually relies on the public's knowledge of media manipulation, journalistic opportunism, and general mendacity for their success (see, for example, *Spin City*). The point is that the mass media do much more than the selfless act of reflection which they claim; they do more than hold up a mirror and breathe out our diverse and disparate selves and circumstances, our various hues and tones and varieties back to ourselves. Rather, they function simultaneously as both modern agenda-setter for the 21st century and orthodox gatekeeper of traditional social mores and values. Unfortunately, the end result of both impulses is the presentation of a world dominated by men and male concerns where women's voices and women's perspectives are marginal and peripheral to the main business of the day: history is made every day; *her*story struggles to make the back page. The media's largely stereotypical portrayal of the relationship between women and politics is merely symptomatic of this wider news malaise and, even when women politicians are treated relatively even-handedly, they are rarely considered outside the deeply conventional exclusionary frame of male-political-public vs. female-personal-private. Notwithstanding the generalized tendency of the news media to use their own interpretative lens though which to analyse politicians per se, male (rational) politicians receive coverage on what they say and what they believe, while women (emotional) politicians receive coverage on what they wear and what they feel in the gender-dependent articulation of style and substance politics.

Part of the answer to the "why does it matter?" question is that many women (and men) who could make an important contribution to the democratic project are put off from pursuing a career in politics because of how they think the political process works, and this perception is largely grounded in the media's coverage of politics and politicians. Women parliamentarians are particularly poorly treated by the news media and this harms democracy itself. Jeannie Ferris (Liberal, Australia) worked as a professional journalist for many years before entering politics, and she laments the direction which reporting has taken with regard to women:

> If you look at what has happened to some of the high profile women in the last five years, the media has been very very tough on them. I think that many professional women who see that think, "why should our families have to endure that scrutiny?" I don't find it hard to believe that women are reluctant to come forward for that reason. It must be difficult for younger women with children in primary or high school where they are vulnerable to peer contact.

When I first embarked on this research study, I expected to find a significant divergence of views across party political lines and possibly differences in experiences across the three specific geographical contexts. As far as general attitudes to the media are concerned, there was, instead, a surprisingly strong degree of agreement among women from all parties who were united in their condemnation of the media's coverage of politics and politicians. Women believe that the way in which the media report on and portray the political process has a damaging effect on the general public, distorting their understanding of politics and government, thus affecting the very foundations of democracy itself:

> The media are now players in the political process. Some of the people who are in the press gallery here have been here for 30 years . . . journalists are treated very cautiously by anybody who has been around this building for any length of time. First of all, they know that unless they go live on a programme, they could be edited, get half a sentence out which will come out as exactly the opposite of what they meant. Their words could be played down the line to someone else who might put a spin on it either from their side or another side and that could be the end of their career. That means that the public, the community, don't actually hear what they should hear, they hear a very cautious statement. (Jeannie Ferris, Liberal, Australia)

Less dramatically, women believe that other women are put off from thinking about a political career by the way in which the media frames politics in general and women politicians in particular. Women want to see different types of media opportunities presented to women politicians, ones which involve genuine discussions rather than slanging matches, arguing that women's contribution to more discursive and deliberative fora would be very positive. If more women were visible in the media, then the public would see their involvement in politics as routine, ordinary, valuable, and as relevant as that of their male colleagues. Equally, because women tend to have a more consensual style and are usually less aggressive—although there are obviously exceptions—their greater visibility in the media would encourage the electorate to take a more positive view of politics. They recognize that the media's denigration of women politicians also has a harmful impact on women's ability to continue to serve their countries because they get worn down by the media's relentless attacks:

> I think the woman who has been most poorly served by the media in this country is Carmen Lawrence. Now, I'm of a different political persuasion, but I think she's very bright, perhaps the most able of the women who have been built up, and she was destroyed by the media . . . she has been judged guilty. She has a huge amount to contribute to public life and I think the media has really cut short her ability. (Helen Coonan, Liberal, Australia)

Suzanne Vos (IFP, South Africa) suggests that women Parliamentarians have been saddened and frustrated at the media's almost total disregard for the work they have been doing in trying to make new policy more gender-friendly and to call to account inherited legislation which continues to discriminate against women: "It's in the make-up of women to want to feel that the work that they are doing has value, is a reflection of the values of the people you're working for and this has affected a lot of women MPs very badly. And it's deliberate." It is not that politicians believe that they should not be accountable to the polity or even to the media for their actions, but rather that the lack of balance in political reporting damages democracy. With continuing low levels of real political understanding, the media's role in constituting the primary source of information about the political process is pivotal:

> I regret the way they [the media] report on Parliament because I don't think they are doing democracy any favours by only reporting the sensational or the mistakes and the stupid and silly things without giving any balance. They [the electorate] seem to be flooded with stuff—newspapers, radio, television—and they are still quite uninformed. (Margaret Reid, Liberal, Australia)

While all the women in this study had negative views on the media and most had stories to relate about bad media experiences, they nonetheless acknowledge that they need the oxygen of publicity in order to get their views across, to represent their parties, to enable them to stand out from the crowd, and to give them credibility in the eyes of both their parties and their constituents, but they are all too well aware of the power of the media to determine what stands for "news," and most believe that the media—rather than politicians—are in the driving seat. The main areas of difference between women in this study centered on specifically women-oriented themes. For example, the Conservative and Liberal women were much more likely to say that their sex is largely irrelevant as far as being a politician is concerned, and that special pleading for women (quotas, all-women shortlists) is unfair, undemocratic, and a liability for women. Although they admit that the environment of parliamentary complexes could be made more woman-friendly, few believe that a macho atmosphere exists, although they did acknowledge sexism in the media. Their views on parliamentary disrespect and discrimination are in stark contrast to those of the great majority of Labor, Labour and ANC women, who cited numerous instances of personal sexism, both in their respective parliaments and in the media, but also in forms of institutional sexism which are part of the very fabric of democracy itself.

Despite women's acknowledgement of the media's preoccupation with their external appearance and private lives, few were willing to concede that their standing as politicians is undermined by the imagery and language which the media use when reporting on them. It is almost as if their view of themselves as professionals serves to override any threats to their ability to command respect as serious politicians. There was a strong refusal to believe that the media's strategies of trivializing women politicians—by their focus on outward appearance, hair, make-up, by the use of their first names, by photographing them in "feminine" environments rather than in front of a parliamentary building—function to undermine women's credibility. The suggestion that these frames might domesticate and therefore make safe any potential threat that political women might pose to the status quo was keenly resisted.

Even as the women in this study reported their irritation with the media's preoccupation with their appearance, few believed that they were especially trivialized by the media's treatment of them, or at least they did not believe that the media's construction of them would be harmful at the ballot box. For example, the press strategy of using women politicians' first names was often seen as a positive construct, in that it made them seem much more accessible to their constituents and the public more generally, than their male counterparts. Few women believe that this personalizing form of address might have the effect of undermining their credibility.

At a deep and significant level, there was a marked antipathy to the implied suggestion that their sex might be their political undoing, even while women accepted that the media do operate a gendered reporting practice which can undermine their credibility as serious politicians. While they could accept, at an abstract and once-removed level, the possibility of trivializing "political woman," it was some *other* woman who would be the casualty of this media mugging, not the respondents themselves. Many believe that, while the media's attention on their clothes and hairstyle might be annoying, it is better than not being reported on at all, and that there are still sufficiently few women politicians for them to be seen genuinely as a novelties and therefore of more interest to the media than their backbench male colleagues. In other words, no publicity is bad publicity, although some of the more astute politicians could see the dangers in adverse publicity, particularly that which undermined the authority of women's political voice. While Robinson and Saint-Jean (1996) point to discernible shifts over the past three decades in the way in which the media choose to report on women politicians, they suggest that old stereotypes are simply being replaced with new ones. And, the antifeminist drive which characterized much of the 1990s largely negated any positive gains which women have achieved in their media coverage and there seems to be little deviation in the media's preoccupation with women politician's sartorial style over the substance of their speeches.

The kinds of stories, perspectives, and interests we see and read in the media are irresistibly bound up in the socioeconomic relations which exist in news organizations themselves, as sites of news production. In an industry which is dominated by men at the top, who make key decisions while visiting the urinals or trading shots across the fairway, it is small wonder that the major decision that women who present the news have to make is whether to wear the diamonds or the pearls today. The political economy of the newsroom provides a strongly gendered context in which the traditional power of patriarchal relations—men on top and women underneath—are played out in abidingly conventional (read "sex-stereotyped") ways. Women recognize that most media professionals and certainly all the owners and controllers of media institutions are men and that the way in which politics is reported is determined, to a large extent, by a male-oriented agenda which privileges the practice of politics as an essential male pursuit. The journalist Joanna Coles (1997) suggests that the atmosphere at a typical press conference resembles that of a boys' public school, where a few clever girls have been allowed into the sixth form. The men on the platform address the journalists in their midst by their first names: "Yes, Michael, do you have a question? Richard? Andrew?" The few women in the press corps are not similarly addressed, still less invited to put their questions. It seems clear that the ways in which women are represented in the media are inextricably linked with who produces those media outputs, which in turn is linked with who (or what) owns those means of production.

As Carter, Branston, and Allan (1998) point out, "feminist and gender-sensitive studies of journalism are becoming increasingly concerned with the changing patterns of news media ownership [especially] within local, national and global contexts" (p. 3). Although space does not permit a fuller discussion of the implications of the increasing convergence and concentration of myriad small media organizations in the hands of a few "big" players, that one big global problem of conglomeratization provides the contextualising backcloth to the discussion on gender, space, place, and portrayal which I have sketched out here. Sex, politics, and money have always enjoyed intimate relations, and the media's involvement in that triumvirate merely adds another player to the field. It will take a concerted effort of will to unravel the vested interests which are deeply embedded in that particular nexus, and the hope is that as more women do succeed to positions of influence and authority, they will open out spaces for different voices and different perspectives to emerge and speak in all their varied tongues.

The image and language of mediated politics, therefore, supports the status quo (male as norm) and regards women politicians as novelties, viewing strategies which encourage even more members on the distaff side into power as absolute anathema. Male paranoia and fear lie at the root of much women-bashing copy, displays of orthodox male chauvinism dressed up in new clothes. As all the old certainties about women's roles and men's roles are increasingly brought into question, the privileged position of white, middle-class men is being challenged, and the fear is that they might be found wanting. Within this uncertain and changing landscape is an acute anxiety, that once they achieve power, women will do to men what men have done to women through the ages, but more skillfully and with more devastating results. And it is the male-dominated media's neatest trick to use their women journalists to do their dirty work.

The current chilly climate for politicians may well encourage, perversely, an upturn in the fortunes of women politicians, as the media's continuing fascination with sex and scandal routinely fixes a male subject in their lens, enabling women to claim the moral high ground (by proxy in the eyes of the voters, if not by virtue of their own articulations). Yet, women need to make much more concerted efforts to get their messages across, and using the media for these activities would seem to be a fairly crucial part of any strategy to win votes, especially when conservatism among voters still seems to be the default position.

More than 10 years ago, Hewitt and Mattinson's (1989) study of British voters asked participants, who were shown pictures of men and women of different ages, with different styles and in different settings, which ones were the politicians. The authors report that most of the participants chose the well-dressed older men. A growing body of more recent work in the United States suggests that the ways in which the media favor male politicians and political candidates in their reporting may seriously disadvantage women politicians' status and career aspirations (see, for example, Kahn, 1994b; Goodman, 1999). Media image and media language commodify women in very specific ways (see Women in Journalism, 1999; Ross & Sreberny, 2000), and as women politicians are sexualized to the same degree as any other women, they become somewhat *less* than the sum of their body parts. Similarly, Herzog's (1998) study of press coverage of women involved in Israeli politics at the local level argues that gender binaries are reinforced by the media's insistence on framing their discussion of women politicians within an exclusionary structure which pitches a male-public-political rhetoric against a female-private-apolitical one. The constituent components of that structure include the media's use of linguistic and ideological strategies, such as "compartmentalization, protective chivalry and framing women in traditional women's roles" (p. 26). Even if we take the most generous view of the media's role in the persistent articulation of a normative social world order which privileges men and male concerns over those of women—that is, as unconscious agent of control—it is nonetheless irresistible to contend that there must be some element of complicity, some sense of collusion with the circulation of normative renditions of what it is to be female and male in contemporary society. And, it is precisely the "packaging" of politics (following Franklin, 1994), and in the current context, the "packaging" of women politicians, which is important to map out and understand. If news is a commodity and we are all consumers, then how women politicians are "sold" to us in qualitative terms is as important as how often they appear: volume matters, but context matters more. Commenting on the way in which women Members of the Scottish Parliament have very quickly begun to change the political agenda since their election in May 1999, the Fawcett Society (1999) argues that the media have nevertheless ignored that shift:

> The lobby correspondents are predominantly men who have developed a particular style of reporting . . . sections of the media simply ignore certain stories. For example, in a debate on domestic violence—an issue which affects one in five women in their lifetimes and as many as 100,000 children in Scotland alone—the press gallery was virtually empty. (p. 24)

If lobby and other political journalists persistently fail to report those issues with which women politicians are specifically involved and on which they have campaigned vigorously, then perhaps it is not that surprising that the electorate at large believes that our women politicians are no different from their male colleagues, that is, they do very little to earn their salary. However, there is some positive evidence to suggest that the media are not always and everywhere hostile to women politicians and that some journalists, women and men, are attempting to shift the agenda through their own reporting of a different range of stories. Braden (1996) argues that greater numbers of women in Congress after the 1992 elections has meant not only a shift in the policy agenda, but also has encouraged the media to cover those changes, and she argues that the ways in which the media chronicled stories about women's first few months in office were far more persuasive than the hype which surrounded the Year of the Woman: "Stories were frequently patterned on the traditional formula of David vs. Goliath or the new kid on the block taking on the bully" (p. 131). Braden cites a particularly poignant example which perfectly captures the patronizing tone by which women politicians have become accustomed to being addressed by male colleagues and the assured response which quickly dispels both the casual put-down but also public unease with the competencies of women politicians. In an exchange on firearms control, Senator Dianne Feinstein was accused by a male Republican Senator of being a "gentlelady" who needed to do her homework on the power of guns. Feinstein's response was personal and deadly:

> I became mayor as a product of assassination. . . . I proposed gun control legislation in San Francisco. I went through a recall on the basis of it. I was trained in the shooting of a firearm when I had terrorist attacks, with a bomb at my house, when my husband was dying, when I had windows shot out. Senator, I know something about what firearms can do. (cited in Braden, 1994, p. 4)

Press reporting of such exchanges has encouraged a better understanding of the kinds of experiences which women politicians in male-dominated parliaments must endure and the robustness of their responses when their credibility is challenged. In a *Washington Post* article, the African-American journalist Kevin Merida quoted the feelings of intimidation reported by a white, middle-aged Republican Senator (Henry J. Hyde), on being verbally "attacked" by a group of African-American women Senators because of his use of racially offensive and paternalistic language in a debate over funding abortions for working-class women, giving the last word to the women protagonists: "We're shaking up the place . . . If one of the godfathers says you can't do this, my next question is, why not? And who are you to say we can't?" (*Washington Post* 2.8.2000). The commitment, by some sections of the media, to covering stories involving women politicians which show women as capable, competent, and professional goes some way in providing a corrective to the more routine, sensational, and trivializing proclivities which push so many journalists to portray women politicians negatively. And, if back-benchers—and most women politicians are in this category—find it hard to achieve prominence in the national media because of newsroom pressures to deliver to increasingly tight deadlines and therefore less time to obtain quotes from other than the usual suspects, then local media at least offers far more opportunities for publicity and self-promotion. As the MP Tony Wright (1998) argues, "when backbench politicians perform in Parliament, their real eye is frequently on their local media" (p. 21). An intervention from the floor—be it a prepared speech, the introduction of an amendment or a new policy intention, or an impromptu point—can all be quickly (re)packaged and delivered to a news hungry local news desk as a press release: "local MP challenges . . ." and so on.

Women in politics, as in many other competitive, male-dominated professions, tend to work longer hours (on average, 10 hours more per week) and spend more time on the less "glamorous" side of politics, that is, constituency work, than their male colleagues (Norris, 1996). With a growing critical mass of women in many Western parliaments as we move through the early years of the new millennium, the blatantly gendered reporting of politics might become a more mundane trashing of women politicians because they are politicians rather than because they are women. It's progress of sorts, but only in the context of a pervasive and creeping cynicism which manifests itself in increasingly poor voter turnouts and a belief that it really does not matter which party gets in because, at base, they are all the same. Some women are making a difference, but the media seem disinterested in reporting on their achievements. In Britain, the achievements of women Parliamentarians, documented in Fiona Mactaggart's (2000) report on the first 1,000 days of the Blair administration, are little understood by the woman (or man) in the street, because their meaning, while important in real terms to the lives of real women and men, does not seem to be important to those who give us our daily news fix. Perhaps it's time to change the pusher?

> One of my old ladies, I call her a lady because she's about 75, well she said to me once that the House of Commons is like a long-stay mental institution where the doors are always open but nobody wants to leave. I think that was a terribly wise thing to say, and the media is part of all that. (Margaret Hodge, Labour, UK)

McNair (1995) suggests that the contradictory responses to political communication—all/no effect—can be seen in terms of "romantic pessimists" on the one hand and "pragmatic optimists" on the other. The former supports the view that democracy is undermined by the incursion of the "persuasive arts" into public, political discourse; performance politics lacks substance and drives voter hostility and apathy, operating merely as self-promotion instead of as information-giving. The latter takes the opposite view, arguing that the more user-friendly advertising strategies, the more interactive public spheres opened up by "town hall" democracy, on-line discussions and phone-ins (see Coleman, 1999), all make politics more popular and intelligible and, importantly, strengthen democracy because they make politics relevant and real. Both positions are plausible, and the extent to which either is an accurate or fair description of mediated politics is entirely moot. However, what does seem clear is that if political communication research continues to ignore the salience of gender (and all those other cross-cutting variables which speak to our individuality and not our mass) in their analyses, we will continue to misunderstand what politics and society actually means for women and men, and we will be significantly "off message" in our efforts to measure communication strategies and media effects. If voters around the globe are fed up with "politics as usual," perhaps it's time to give the women a chance? Perhaps they will prove to be as dishonest, intolerant, and self-serving as their male colleagues, but somehow, I don't think so.

X marks the spot. How appropriate.

Appendix 1

Notes From the Field—Women and Politics in South Africa's Rainbow Nation

BACKGROUND

As part of this study on women, politics and media, I am going to visit South Africa to interview women parliamentarians in their election year (1999), only their second democratic elections in a painful history bloodied by apartheid. The elections are likely to take place in May, and having contacted the Parliament's media officer, I realize that the last few weeks in which both Houses (the National Assembly and the Provincial Parliament) will be sitting will be in March before they go into recess and the politicians begin campaigning in earnest. I wait until October 1998 to send out a round-robin letter to women parliamentarians in both parliaments—117 in all. By December 1998, only 6 women have agreed to be interviewed. As Parliament is now in recess, I wait until late January 1999 to write again. By the time I leave for Cape Town, 15 women have agreed, so on arrival in the beautiful Cape, I set about the task of trying to make firm appointments with them. Most of my putative interviewees wanted me to contact them once I had arrived in Cape Town since the parliamentary schedule is posted quite late and they didn't want to confirm anything in case it had to be changed. I could do nothing but agree, although five women did give me a firm date and time before I left, for which I was grateful. When I lamented my somewhat frustrated progress, my colleague at the University of Cape Town simply said, phlegmatically, "Welcome to Africa."

THE FIELD

Within 24 hours of arriving, I have my first interview, having been faxed the previous Thursday to be told that I had an audience with Minister Shandu (Inkatha Freedom Party) at 10 o'clock sharp at the Good Hope Building at Parliament. While Mrs. Shandu had been on my circulation list, as she was Deputy Minister for Public Works, she had since moved on to become Education Minister in the Province of Kwa-Zulu Natal. She is not, therefore, a national politician, but it seemed ridiculous not to interview her so I find the building—the Cape Town HQ for the IFP—and ask to see her. Security is very, very tight at Parliament and I am kept in the very small lobby area while the security police try to understand my accent and the name of the person I wish to see. No, there is no Shandu listed, I must have made a mistake. I explain that she had recently moved to the Provincial Government in Kwa-Zulu Natal but had arranged to meet me here in Cape Town. I suggest they ring the IFP offices for confirmation. Eventually, aware that I was getting later and later for the appointment, I am allowed through the security cordon and directed to the IFP offices. I explain my story once more, and the woman with whom I am speaking looks at me pityingly and reports that Mrs. Shandu is in Kwa-Zulu Natal but will be flying down to Cape Town later in the day. Could I come back at 1:30 p.m.? I say "of course." I walk back through the security gate and hand in my pass at reception. The two guards look at me with raised eyebrows, as if I had tried to perpetrate some kind of con and it had backfired. I say I will be returning at 1:30 p.m. and they give me a "yeah, yeah" kind of look. I leave the building, walking into a warm, sultry day.

I now have to do some fast thinking. My Natal University host has arranged for me to meet an old friend who is now Professor of Sociology at the University of Cape Town so that I can obtain temporary visiting rights there to use the library. Trouble is, I am supposed to be taking tea with him a 2 p.m. I try to contact him but can't seem to get the dialing code right, no matter how many permutations I try. I decide to be bold and take a taxi to the campus and hope he can see me early. In the end, that part of the jigsaw slots together perfectly and I manage to see Ken Jubber, receive my letter of authorization, and get back to Parliament in good time. I show up at the Good Hope Building for the second time that day, only to find that the security guards have changed shift, and I have to go through the whole story again. Once more, I am directed through security and on to the IFP offices with which, at least this time, I am familiar. But still no sign of Mrs. Shandu. Or, in fact, anyone. After a couple of minutes, a man appears in the corridor and he seems familiar—he is Chief Buthelezi! He takes pity on me, explaining the Mrs. Shandu *would* soon be arriving and perhaps I would like to wait in the library and he would arrange tea. Forty-five minutes later, Mrs. Shandu arrives, saying that her office had tried to contact me on Friday to change the plan. Anyway, now she has to go immediately to the Chamber to listen to the debate on education. Could I come back at say, 3:30 p.m.? Of course I could. During that frustrating first day and subsequently, I get to know all the cafes and bars in the immediate vicinity but, having conducted much previous work with parliamentarians in other parts of the world, working on the hoof, changing plans, and being flexible all goes with the territory.

I contact most of the women on my list that first Monday, but by the end of the day, no one has rung back. Strange. I contact on MP at her home, having been given that number by a novice secretary who should not have really parted with it. However, she is nice and friendly and says that she has, in fact, tried to ring me back on my mobile but all she got was the engaged tone. From my end, the phone has remained sullenly silent all day. I chat this conundrum over with my guesthouse host and he says, no, I need to put the international code in front of the number as the call would have to go to the U.K. first and then back to South Africa. Well, that explains it.

Back again at the Good Hope Building at 3:30 p.m.—same frustration with the security guards since one was a new face and the other had not, apparently, witnessed my meeting with Mrs. Shandu (although we had been speaking together in front of the desk scarcely an hour before). Go back to the IFP library. At 4 p.m., Mrs. Shandu arrives a little breathless. She tells me she can give me 20 minutes and shall we take tea in the Members' Tea Room? Yes, please. She sits herself in front of the T.V. which is broadcasting the debate in the Chamber. It is important that she follows the debate as she will be returning to the Chamber after our interview, but I want to tape record the interview and wonder how the microphone will be able to compete with the television. She compromises by sitting two tables away, and in between sips of tea and mouthfuls of cake, she answers my questions. She is still in full flow when the tape clicks off, and she realizes that she has been talking for 60 minutes. She asks me if I would like to accompany her to the Chamber to listen to the rest of the debate. Of course I would! We hurry down the cobbled pathway to the main Parliamentary building, and she bids an aide to get me a pass while I'm loitering in yet another lobby. The aide eventually arrives with the pass, and I'm checked through security. The aide takes me to the Strangers' Gallery and sits me next to Mrs. Shandu, who takes my hand and squeezes it in acknowledgement before turning back to observe the proceedings below. She keeps up a running commentary of gossip and invective alternately as each parliamentarian comes to the rostrum to speak. The Chamber is even emptier than an ordinary sitting in the British commons, which comes as a great surprise so near to the election and given the nature of the debate, where education for non-whites is an extremely hot issue. When the debate concludes, she collects her various papers, bags, cell phone and other accoutrements, and we leave together. She bids me farewell at the door and wishes me well for my work. A curate's egg kind of day but one which brought its own unexpected rewards; it also set the tone, inevitably, for the rest of my time in Cape Town with its mix of strangeness, frustration, and joy.

My second day is more of the same, trying again to make contact with the women on my list to arrange appointments. Conscious of the cost of telephoning back and forth, on one of my sallies down Parliament Lane I spot the British High Commission. I ask if I can use the phone to make some calls to Parliament. The staff there are very obliging and usher me into the front office, give me a chair, a cup of tea, and a telephone. I begin again. The process is about 75 per cent successful. I have three interviews today, starting with Melanie Verwoerd. She immediately dispels my preconceptions about what an ANC (and therefore government) MP is like: she is young, lively, and white. She is candid and charming and makes a number of suggestions of other people I should contact, including the head of the South African Broadcasting Corporation team at Parliament and the head of the parliamentary team at Independent Newspapers—both are women. Dropping Melanie's name with both these women the following day when I make contact opens the door to an interview with the latter and a "Sorry, but I'm out of town," from the former. Thank you, Melanie. Throughout the interview (and in subsequent ones), the brief history of democratic South Africa in the post-1994 period of transformation is brought alive for me in a way that is otherwise impossible to know, when all the information we receive in the West is the partial perspective afforded us by the media. Issues of race, class, and gender continuously cross-cut and inform Verwoerd's narrative, making complex what is seen as the simple process of Mandela's release, the dismantling of apartheid, and the dawn of a new South Africa. It *is* all that, of course, but also so much more, and the gender dimension, which is the aspect in which I am especially interested, insinuates through the agenda.

At lunchtime, I interview Koko Mokgalong, a backbench ANC MP who has plenty to say about cultural politics and the role of women in the democratic process. I notice that my tape recorder clicks off somewhat before 45 minutes have gone by, but turn the tape over anyway and continue with the interview. Between appointments, I check the tape and find that the second side is blank and the first side stops peremptorily mid-way along. Damn. That's most of the interview. I curse the tape and the street vendor who sold it to me. I have barely 10 minutes to find somewhere else that sells tapes, now anxious for the viability of the rest of the tapes in my bag. I see a video shop and buy one 90-minute tape. This one will be OK. I unwrap it as I walk along and shove it in the machine. I press record and start and nothing happens. I fast forward it a little and try again. It won't budge. I take the tape out and examine it. It looks OK. I then notice that the tabs on the top are missing. Damn again. I approach another street vendor selling perfect-looking, wrapped TDK90s. They are 40p each. I buy one and stand at the stall unwrapping it and putting it in the machine. It records perfectly. I have five minutes to get to my last appointment. There is a god, and she is smiling on me. My last appointment is with Mrs. Kgositsile, the Deputy Speaker of the House, and the most senior woman so far on my list. I am asked by her assistant, Ina, to be aware that Mrs. Kgositsile has another appointment at 3:15 (my interview is for 2:30 p.m.) so it might be a bit rushed. Ina arranges tea and newspapers while I wait. "The Deputy Speaker is still in the Chamber but will be out any minute," says Ina. The clock ticks on, and I follow the debate from the comfort of an armchair in the Deputy Speaker's plush office. It gets to 3 p.m. Ina, in the meantime, has kept me abreast of what's happening, but even she is looking a little concerned—this is going to be a very short interview indeed. It gets to 3:10 p.m., and I can see that this interview is not going to happen. Ina checks Mrs. Kgositsile's diary and looks glum—no space in the next 10 days. I say that I will, in fact, be back in Cape Town over Easter to take some holiday time at the end of the fellowship. She brightens considerably, and we pencil in another time and date, although Ina is a bit worried that she'll be on holiday herself then, and she's not sure she can trust her replacement to do the necessary juggling. I say that I'll take a chance. It is now 3:25 p.m. Ina escorts me down to the exit, and we chat on the way. She is still feeling guilty about my wasted trip although I keep saying that this is not unusual, and it's a recognized part of the process when your subjects are parliamentarians who have to stay in the Chamber or leave to vote or have impromptu meetings thrust upon them at very short notice. As these are the closing weeks of this session before the general elections, I am thankful that I can get anyone to talk to me. Ina seems little consoled and rashly suggests we have dinner together as she lives very near where I'm staying. I say, yes, of course, but I'm not sure that the dinner will materialize. I hope it does because, apart from making a change from eating alone with just the company of a book, it would be nice to talk to someone who could give me some insider insights.

Wednesday dawns and I have four interviews set up for the day, with another six in the bag and only four outstanding appointments yet to make. Having now been backwards and forwards to Parliament a number of times over the past two days, it continues to surprise me that the guards do not know the names of their own parliamentarians, even Ministers. Each time I arrive for an appointment, I have to show them my now dog-eared matrix of names and contact numbers, and even then, they seem reluctant to look up names in their internal phone directory, and they prefer that I tell them the appropriate extension (which I rarely know). Even when I show them the correct spelling of a parliamentarian's name, they read it as if for the first time, blankly and with incredulity. At first, I decide it is simply a problem of pronunciation and my inability to get my tongue around the unfamiliar Xhosa names, but the same thing happens when I ask for a parliamentarian with an "easy" name like Gill Marcus. Each time (and this feeling never left me), I feel like I'm trying to con my way into the hallowed space, but once I have been verified and checked through security, I am free to wander wherever I please, with no accompanying officer. It feels at once open and dangerous, as if they've got the first part about security right, but then there's no follow-through.

The first interview today is with Mrs. Botha (Democratic Party) who collects me in person, takes me up to her room, and asks if I'd like the air conditioning switched on. It is only 9 a.m., but already I am soggy and tired. We are constantly interrupted while she orders tea, answers her phones (desk and cell), and entertains visitors. She apologizes profusely for each interruption, throwing up her hands in horror at the "lot of the politician" and eventually takes a few minutes to work out how to turn the ringer off on her mobile. We have a few minutes of clear interview time before I realize that it is now 10 a.m., and I have another interview. She also needs to go to a meeting, and as we are saying our goodbyes, her secretary arrives with the long-awaited tea. She gives me an accusatory look when I say that I must leave, and Mrs. Botha gives her a mean "eye" back.

My next interviewee is Tersia King, who I had seen in full flow on Monday during the education debate. As I am waiting to be checked by security—all the opposition MPs are housed together in a building on the opposite side of the Chamber—I spot Dr. King rushing through the security arch. As she goes through, she mutters something about a meeting, and I call out to her that it is probably with me. She turns and asks, "Dr. Ross?" and I say, "yes." The security guard quickly takes my bag off the conveyor without it being camera-checked and whisks me through. I run to keep up with her and am practically panting as we get to her door. She unlocks it and flops down inside, having been summoned by her secretary at 8 a.m. that morning to attend a meeting about which she had had no knowledge. I ask if she would like me to wait a few minutes before starting, but she brushes my concern aside and seems eager to talk. She is the first National Party MP I have interviewed, and as soon as I ask the preliminary question about being a woman in Parliament, she launches into a potted history of her career (parliamentary and otherwise), including her divorce and the difficulties of running two households and having to remember to buy the toilet paper "for *all* the bathrooms," as she doesn't even have a servant. She is, unsurprisingly, scathing about the government and displays the same kind of sullen disrespect which I witnessed in the Chamber earlier. She doesn't believe in quotas—the ANC has a quota of 30 percent women throughout the party structure, including for elected members—and feels that many (women) parliamentarians are there as "voting fodder." She talks fondly about the early days and insists that she is proud to be a woman—she is wearing a shocking pink Chanel style two piece with gold jewelry—and is pleased when her male colleagues tell her that she's looking especially nice. As I listen to her talk, I am already mentally putting her remarks in appropriate "theme" folders for later use— although I hate her politics, I know this is a very good interview.

I have a lunchtime appointment next with Dr. Tshabala-Msimang, Deputy Minister for Justice, and when I arrive, her assistant is looking apologetic. She explains that the afternoon debate has been brought forward, and the Minister is no longer able to keep the appointment. However, the Minister would like to tell me this sad news herself, and I am ushered in to her office. She greets me warmly and wastes no time telling me that her husband was, until recently, the High Commissioner in London, and that she knows Britain well. However, the meeting is now impossible and perhaps I could kindly try to rearrange with her secretary. I go back to her assistant, Zethu, and we check our diaries. The Minister's one is impossibly full, but she could probably fit me in next Tuesday at 11:30 a.m. I check mine, and I see that I'm down for an interview at 12 noon. Zethu suggests that I simply rearrange my 12 noon appointment, but I am loathe to do so as it is with Jenny Malan, the only other National Party MP who I am due to interview. We nonetheless agree to the 11:30 time, and I say that it will simply be a short interview. Although this new appointment is in both our diaries, Zethu cautions that things might change again, so I decide not to try and change the 12 noon meeting after all: a good decision, as it turns out.

As I now have several hours to spare before the next interview, I go off in search of an internet cafe where I can check my email, drink mango juice, and "chat" with colleagues back home. I find the cafe recommended by the Lonely Planet guide, and it's the perfect blend of high technology, psychedelic wallpaper, and laid back "waitrons." My last interview is with Gill Marcus, Deputy Minister of Finance, who turns up bang on time and invites me into her office. Despite us wearing hers'n'hers AIDS ribbons, I immediately sense a restrained hostility, and she takes a somewhat combative stance to my questioning. However, we speak for 45 minutes until the tape clicks off, and by the end, I think she's warmed to me a bit and offers me an excellent quote on the media's portrayal of her colleague, Nkokosama Zuma, which instantly redeems her in my eyes.

I have no appointments on Thursday, so I take the bus to the University and spend several pleasant hours in the African Studies library being helped by courteous, efficient, and knowledgeable staff, none of whom asks for my letter of introduction. I get frustrated by being told that I am not allowed to print out from the machine I'm using as it's very expensive, and I sink at the prospect of having to summarize web-based articles from the *Cape Times*, but then I hit on the possibility of mailing the pages to my hotmail address, which I do, and I hope it works. It does. There are signs up everywhere asking users *not* to use the machines for emailing so I suppress the urgent desire to check my email and wait to use the internet cafe later that night. Even though everyone else seems to be emailing to their hearts' content, I do not feel bold enough to flout the rules on my first day. I also continue to try to contact the four women remaining on my list, but I luck out. I spend an hour or two wading through two months' worth of the *Cape Times* and ask if I can do some photocopying. I am directed two blocks over to buy a copying card, and I still can't get used to how cheap everything is: £1 for 40 copies. I have an exciting bus ride back down to the city: Table Mountain has been on fire for the past two days, and as we approach a bend in the road, we are met with dense smoke in front of us. Everyone rushes over to one side to close the windows, and we are almost choking inside. Thankfully, the driver slows down a bit, and we proceed at a still dangerous speed for another 200 metres before hitting a road block. Traffic police have blocked motorists from taking the road up which we have just come down, and there is palpable relief when we realize that ours is probably the last bus allowed to leave campus.

I am beginning to get some sense of Cape Town now, especially after the excitement of yesterday, and even though I have a disjointed day on Friday, with one interview scheduled for 8 a.m. and a second for 1 p.m. I am feeling very upbeat. I have done six interviews with two cancellations and two more today, so I am nearly half way through, and my progress is pretty much as I would have expected. Val Viljoen (ANC) collects me herself at the visitor's entrance at 8 a.m. sharp, apologizing that we can't have a drink as the restaurant is not yet open. We do a good interview, but she is not that forthcoming although she is very eager to please. I am pleased, perversely, when the tape clicks off, and I head back to my guesthouse for a late breakfast. I decide that today is the last day that I will try to contact the remaining women on my list. I try again. Eureka! I manage to get through to two of them by telephone and set up appointments. I am absurdly pleased with my success. I also manage to speak to the assistant of another woman MP who is not on my list but who, according to my new friend Ina, has been very much involved with gender issues. I don't really like cold calling, but I drop Ina's name into the conversation, and this seems to do the trick. The assistant, Imogen, asks me to ring back on Tuesday when she hopes to have a firm appointment for me. It never happens, but that's how it is sometimes.

I return to Parliament for my lunchtime interview with Gertrude Fester (ANC). When I speak to her from the lobby phone, she expresses surprise that I am there, saying that she had me down in her diary, but as I hadn't confirmed, she had gone ahead and made another appointment. I know that I did confirm, but I'm not about to argue. She suggests we meet for lunch anyway as her other visitors have not yet arrived. We meet in the parliamentary restaurant and conduct an impromptu interview although she is a little anxious about being taped, but eventually she agrees. Ten minutes into lunch/interview, her visitors arrive. They are from a women's project, and she has commissioned them to do some research on women political prisoners. As she talks, it becomes clear that her interest is not purely academic because she talks about her own life as an exile and prisoner. We have an interesting lunch, and she then takes me back to her office to do the interview proper. As we talk, the reason for her caution about being taped becomes apparent: she is a little critical of the ANC's commitment to follow through on their pledge of empowering women within the political structure. I reassure her that I will let her have a copy of the transcript and that she can identify which of her comments should be anonymized. The interview goes well. As I'm leaving, Ms. Fester suddenly remembers that the Commission on Gender Equality is launching its Annual Report the following week and rushes off to photocopy the programme for me. I check my diary and see that I can attend. But the invitation is for MPs, and I'm not sure how "public" it is. She assures me that I simply need to wave the invitation at the security guards, say that I'm there by her personal invitation, and I'll be let in. All my previous dealings with the parliamentary guards would suggest that this might not be as straightforward as Ms Fester seems to think, but I'm going to try my luck anyway.

I discover another internet cafe around the corner from Parliament and check my email. I find that two more MPs have agreed to be interviewed, and I email them back straightaway with promises to contact them on Monday. I might yet achieve my goal of 20 interviews after all. At the end of my first week, I'm happy with the way in which the research is going, and I'm looking forward to spending the weekend eating and shopping and not feeling guilty because I haven't made a start on all the work I've brought with me in case I got bored. I have seven confirmed appointments next week with the possibility of a further four. This life is not so bad.

SECOND HALF

I think the previous paragraphs will have provided some insights into the process of doing research in Parliamentary contexts, and the second week in Cape Town was pretty much the same. Monday was a "thin" day, with only one scheduled interview, with Suzanne Vos, an unexpectedly white South African member of the Inkatha Freedom Party. Because of the Western media's simplistic presentation of South African politics, my expectation is that Vos will be black since the IFP is portrayed as an avowedly black party. But no, here is Vos reporting that her involvement with the IFP goes back 30 years, and that for her, their non-violent agenda and commitment to a truly multicultural South Africa means that they are the only party to which she feels comfortable belonging. I am supposed to meet Vos in her office, but before I can even contemplate the usual battle to be done with the security guards, I am handed a note from her. My heart sinks. However, the note directs me to another building on the Parliament site where she's attending a meeting in which she thinks that I, too, might be interested. The Joint Standing Committee on the Quality of Life and the Status of Women is meeting to ask the Office on the Status of Women to report on its progress on engendering the political agenda. Yes, I *am* interested, so I turn up at the relevant security lobby, show my "invitation," and I am quickly whisked through and escorted to the meeting room. The committee has only just started, and I sit taking notes, although most of the presentation is about what is yet to be done rather than achievements chalked up. Sometimes it feels like gender issues are always on the brink of becoming important, only to slide down the agenda because something bigger takes center stage. As I arrive, I survey the sea of faces expectantly, hoping that my interviewee will realise who this late interloper is and make some kind of signal. Thankfully, she does and mouths "lunch" to me with a questioning look. I nod my assent. My lunch appointment cancelled late on Friday night, so the day is all for Vos.

After the meeting, she takes me to the dining room in the Marks Building, which is where most of the opposition parties are sited. The room has a very different air to its sister in the National Assembly, not least because it is much bigger, which seems rather anomalous given the relatively tiny size of the opposition parties compared to the ANC's numbers. But the buzz is also different, more friendly and laid back, and the tables and the furnishings are somehow more elegant, more luscious. And the food is certainly better. It's almost as if, although defeated politically, the main opposition parties, that is the "white"parties, are determined to dine at least in the style to which they have become accustomed. At the start of lunch, I set up my tape recorder on Vos' side plate and we have a very pleasant lunch and a good interview. On my return to the guesthouse, I find that two women have cancelled because of unexpected commitments, but I do manage to contact one of the two MPs who had emailed on Friday, and I set up a meeting later on in the week. I also ring another one who had contacted my office the previous Friday wondering why I had not been in touch with her about an interview. I had sent her the same two letters which all the MPs had received and she had not replied, so, of course, I had not made further contact. I speak to her cell phone answering service and leave a message, and later on Monday evening, she rings me and speaks to me warmly, suggesting lunch on Thursday. I imagine yet another tape recording with high levels of background noise punctuated by instructions about glasses of water and vegetable side dishes.

Tuesday dawns with yet another impossibly blue-sky sunny day, and I have an early breakfast with the prospect of four interviews to undertake, including one with Zubeida Jaffer, head of parliamentary reporting for the Independent Newspaper group. However, in the end, not a good day. My first interviewee has been called away suddenly to Johannesburg and a rescheduled appointment is not possible at this time as she likes to make her own appointments and her diary is unavailable for comment. My second appointment is already one postponed from last week. The woman in question, Minister Shabalala, breezes in at the appointed hour, but not to see me—her secretary had made the appointment in the office diary, but apparently it had not made its way onto the Minister's schedule for the day. The Minister is apologetic but really has too much to do today. Of *course* I understand. My third appointment does materialize, with Jenny Malan (National Party), who is lively and engaging, even though she insists that "banging on" about gender and feminism is a load of nonsense. She speaks with an arrogance borne of centuries of domination and is unashamedly unreconstructed, reveling in the un-PC-ness of her narrative.

After lunch, I am approaching Parliament for my fourth and final interview of the day when my phone rings. It is the assistant of Zubeida Jaffer, at 2:55 p.m., saying that Zubeida is unfortunately tied up and can't now make our 3 p.m. meeting. She hurriedly suggests an alternative time, and I struggle to get my diary out of my bag, cradle the phone, and avoid other pedestrians as I dither on the pavement. My instinct tells me that this new time is not going to work out either, but we'll see. I walk back to my lodgings feeling thoroughly disgruntled and treat myself to an excellent (and cheap) supper and an evening of mindless TV. At least there were two messages for me suggesting interviews for Thursday and Friday (both of which I can make) which is compensation for the no shows today. Tomorrow, I have three interviews scheduled, and if two pan out, after today, I'll be happy.

If I were of a more pessimistic nature, I would have written this week off and myself with it. As it is, I am an experienced researcher who has worked in the field of political research for some years, so the fact that today started off with yet another MP not turning up is just more grist to my mill. This time, though, there wasn't even the excuse that she had been called away urgently—she just simply did not show up. I hang around in her office for 30 minutes and then cut my losses and arrive early for my next meeting which happens to be the launch of the Commission for Gender Equality's Gender Audit of current legislation. It is an interesting meeting, chaired by Pregs Govender, whom I have been trying to interview ever since I arrived in Cape Town. As the meeting starts a little late, I take the opportunity to introduce myself. Pregs Govender looks embarrassed, as if meeting me in the flesh and seeing that I'm attending the meeting makes her realize that I am committed to the work and that perhaps she can find the time for an interview after all. I give her my contact details, and she promises to see if there is a window in her diary on Friday.

I get a call from Imogen who says that if I want to see her boss, Mrs. Mapisa (who had been called away to Johannesburg unexpectedly on Monday and so couldn't make our meeting), the only possible time is this afternoon if I accompany Mrs. Mapisa to the airport in her shuttle car. The car is supposed to be leaving at 3:30 p.m., and I explain that, unfortunately, I won't be able to do the interview on the run as I have another interview at 5 p.m. Imogen assures me that I will be back in time, but my instinct is that the car will not leave on time and that I will not get back for 5 p.m. I say, sorry, but maybe next time. Imogen then suggests that perhaps I could come to the office at, say, 3:15 p.m. and speak to Mrs. Mapisa very quickly. I am reluctant to do this, but eventually agree although, as it turns out, Mrs. Mapisa is too distracted to talk to me properly. She asks me when I will be back in Cape Town, and I say that I am flying to Pietermaritzburg on Saturday and returning the following Saturday. She suggests that perhaps we could have coffee together on Saturday afternoon and gives me her cell phone number so that I can ring her to see if this is possible nearer the time. I agree, but have no expectation at all that this third attempt will fare any better than the other two. It doesn't.

My 5 p.m. appointment with Sheila Camerer (National Party) lasts 20 minutes as she has been asked to deputize for a colleague and give an impromptu address at a Rotary dinner later on in the evening, so she too is not at her best, although she does give a good interview. My next and last appointment is with Patricia de Lille, the only female MP in the Pan African Congress Party and, allegedly, notorious for taking the government to court over their treatment of her—they attempted to discipline her for abusing Parliamentary privilege when she rose to their challenge to name members of the ANC whom she claimed had collaborated with de Klerk's government. Security has suddenly tightened up over the last 24 hours, and I am stopped from using my "usual" entrance into the parliamentary complex today because I don't have a permit, which hasn't been a problem on any of the previous eight days. However, now it's all changed, and this morning, I have to go the long way around, have my bag checked through one security point, and then into Government Lane, and back through another security check. I don't mind, really, but then this afternoon, suddenly, not only do I have to go through this new procedure, but I also have my name entered onto a security computer and have my photograph taken. It gets a bit wearing after a while.

Patricia de Lille greets me warmly even though I am 20 minutes early, and I settle myself at a table in her room and read the papers until she finishes what she's doing and joins me. We do a good interview and, although she doesn't know it, she has saved the day for me; it has not been as successful a week as I had hoped. I like her very much, even though the PAC is seen in many quarters as an extremist party, but she gives me a good interview, open and honest. I return to the guesthouse and see the portentous message slip dangling by my key—no doubt a message from a prospective interviewee canceling a meeting at 24 hours' notice. Well, not quite, but Inka Mars (IFP) asking for a readjustment: can we bring our lunch meeting tomorrow forward to 8 a.m.? I phone her on her mobile saying "Of course, no problem." I plan an early night.

The day does not start well. I walk briskly down to Parliament for the early morning meeting, only to be told that Inka Mars has been delayed. I am made to stand in the very small lobby area until her assistant arrives to take me down to the library to wait for the tardy Mrs. Mars. I say "Yes, tea would be lovely." Even when I finish the interview with Mars—who arrived not too late and did a good interview—the tea had still not arrived. I ask Mrs. Mars if I could have a copy of the IFP manifesto, and she digs around in her bag and pulls out a tiny but perfect fold-away booklet which details what the IFP would do if it managed to achieve majority party status. She tells me that she will collect some other material for me, and perhaps I could "pop in" to her house in Durban on my way back from Pietermaritzburg next week? I say "Of course." I rush off to my next interview at 9 a.m. with Janet Love (ANC)—yet another white MP—who, despite her rather terse personal style, has some extremely pertinent things to say about gender discrimination. Two out of two so far is pretty good—I feel that today I might get to achieve the full complement of interviews. After lunch, I interview Mary Turok (ANC)—yet another white MP—who is refreshingly, amazingly candid about her experiences and the attitudes which still prevail around women in politics and especially the ANC's *real politik* when it comes to a serious commitment to gender. The reason for her forthcoming attitude soon becomes apparent—she is standing down at the coming elections and abandoning formal politics for a career outside, having had more than enough of "trying to struggle from within."

My last interview is with Zubeida Jaffer, the head of parliamentary reporting for the Independent Newspaper group. This interview is a rescheduled one, since Zubeida had cancelled our first appointment earlier in the week. On our way to the press gallery tea room, she confides that she had nearly cancelled this one as well, but had decided that she would prioritize our meeting as I had traveled so far. When we arrive at the tea room, we are told by a surly white Afrikaans man that we can't sit in the tea room since he will need to prepare the tables for a function later in the day. Zubeida ignores him and, having settled me at a far table, goes off in search of tea. Minutes later, she returns with a large wooden tray, tea in a silver pot, and beautiful bone china cups. The interview is excellent, with Zubeida speaking matter-of-factly about her regular (and horrendous) experiences of being a black woman in a white male world and of being a black woman journalist in Parliament. She is open and honest about the difficulties she has resolutely overcome, but which, in small but insidious ways, continue to dog her work. It is clear that, if South Africa is addressing racial and ethnic inequalities with some force, the attendant issues of gender discrimination have been tackled with rather less alacrity. As she points out, equalizing race has meant encouraging black men, and equalizing gender has meant getting more white women into work. For black women, then, real political progress has lagged and is still lagging a long way behind. During the interview, we notice that several white male journalists enter the tea room and are having noisy conversations at the bar, the surly attendant joining in. I am pleased that Jaffer had made her very obvious point of having the meeting here, and she says, as we leave, that the incident is typical of the ways in which black women—she is one of only two black women journalists in the press gallery in Parliament—and women more generally—are treated. Given that she is the most senior journalist for the whole of the independent press sector in Parliament and is therefore known to the barman, his rude manner is clearly a deliberate strategy to denigrate her position. She cares, but she doesn't show it, and it is in the winning of these very small but important battles that gender and race politics are played out in the real world.

My last day of interviews: I am due to interview Pregs Govender, and I hope that this interview really will materialize since her pivotal role in the placing of gender on the political agenda means that her insights will be incredibly valuable to the debate which I intend to develop in my work. But we are not meeting until 11 a.m. so I plan a leisurely breakfast. I am writing up my journal in my room when the assistant to Dene Smuts from the Democratic Party rings, saying that she can see me at 10 a.m. if I can make it. I have been trying to arrange this interview since I arrived in Cape Town since no one else in the DP has agreed to take part in the study. It is 8:45 a.m., so I hurry breakfast and make the meeting. She is an engaging interviewee who, because of her background in magazine journalism, is forthright and forthcoming on the topic of women, politics, and the media. She begins the interview by telling me that, in the past hour, she has been told she needs to attend an important meeting, so we will have to do a very short interview. I agree, of course. Forty-five minutes later, she is still in full flow, but I need to leave for my next and final interview of the day. We part on friendly terms, with me promising to send her a copy of the book when it's published.

At last I get to see Pregs Govender: when I get to her building, security try and ring her, but there's no answer. I am told that she is in the Chamber, and I am directed to write a note and ask one of the ushers to give it to her as she has obviously forgotten that she has an appointment with me. I tell the guard that I don't think that she is in the Chamber since I spoke to her secretary only this morning. No, he insists that as Parliament is now sitting; she must be there. I agree to do as I am told and go through the security gate. But I remember seeing her on the 5th floor when I met one of the other MPs, so I make my way to her assistant's office and announce my arrival. Kim is expecting me and takes me along to Ms Govender's office. I am pleased at my enterprise. In the two weeks that I've been here, I have begun to get the measure of the place, and in a perverse way I feel sorry that my time here has been so short. I do a good interview although the MP speaks so softly, that I am afraid that the tape won't pick up her voice. Happily, though, when I play it back, it sounds fine.

POST-HOC REFLECTION–THEORY AND PRACTICE AND THE GAPS BETWEEN

The work that I have undertaken with women politicians has been fascinating, amazing, insightful, and (mostly) sisterly. I am privileged to have had the opportunity to talk to so many good women, and the work that comes out of this project will, I am sure, push forward our thinking about the gendered nature of formal politics, the expectations (reasonable or otherwise) we might have, as feminists, of women in decision-making positions, and the relationship which elected women representatives have with other women. While I am not so naive to imagine that everything my interviewees chose to tell me was always entirely accurate—professional rhetors are especially difficult to interview because of their special skills in persuasion and artifice—but then nor do I believe women politicians have the same motivations as their male colleagues in agreeing to do academic interviews. Although I believe that Williams (1980) errs a little on the side of generosity when he says, of the veracity of political rhetoric that "one might begin with the simple and charitable assumption that on the whole people will seek to tell you the truth," since many of us have very direct experience of politicians being rather economical with the truth, I nonetheless believe that the motivations for women politicians to agree to take part in this study were other than simply to have the opportunity to talk about themselves for their own purposes.

In some fundamental ways, I was surprised by the narratives of some of my interviewees, surprised by the claiming of a "feminist" identity among some of the Liberal women, and by the insistence of having never experienced gender discrimination by some of the socialist women. Given that I was interviewing women who had *agreed* to be interviewed and knew the context in which the discussion was taking place, I was surprised by the hostile response to some of my questions by some of my interviewees, particularly those relating to women's experience of a male-ordered environment such as Parliament. It sometimes seemed that women needed to make a vigorous denial of gender discrimination in case it sounded either like special pleading or else that they were being disloyal to their male colleagues. Perhaps they genuinely did believe that they had never been the target of discriminatory behaviour or practice, but the testimonies of others of their women colleagues tended to give the lie to that suggestion, most of whom insisted that Parliament (in each of Britain, Australia, and South Africa) remains a seat of sexist male behaviour and, with relatively small numbers of women parliamentarians (many of whom only "last" one term anyway), they are likely to remain so in the near future. Many women felt empathy for others of their sex, but not of their political persuasion, who had suffered at the hands of male colleagues and the male-dominated media. They could easily relate to the injustice of media coverage of a female (opposition) colleague which centered on her sex rather than her policy position while at the same time, distancing themselves from her politics. In some ways, this was also my position, I mostly liked the women, but sometimes I hated their politics.

Appendix 2

Women Politicians Interviewed, 1995-2000

BRITISH INTERVIEWEES–1995

Alice Mahon, Labour
Angela Eagle, Labour
Ann Taylor, Labour
Rt. Hon. Ann Widdecombe, Cons
Anne Clwyd, Labour
Clare Short, Labour
Dawn Primarolo, Labour
Elizabeth Peacock, Cons
Glenda Jackson, Labour
Gwyneth Dunwoody, Labour
Hilary Armstrong, Labour
Jean Corston, Labour
Joan Walley, Labour
Joyce Quin, Labour
Judith Church, Labour
Llin Golding, Labour
Lynne Jones, Labour
Margaret Hodge, Labour
Marion Roe, Cons
Dame Peggy Fenner, Cons
Rachel Squire, Labour

Completed Postal Questionnaire

Dame Angela Rumbold, Cons
Anne Coffey, Labour
Estelle Morris, Labour
Helen Liddell, Labour
Joan Lestor, Labour
Maria Fyfe, Labour
Teresa Gorman, Cons

21/63 (33 per cent)

BRITISH INTERVIEWEES-2000

Fiona Mactaggart, Labour
Rt. Hon. Harriet Harman, Labour
Rt. Hon. Joan Ruddock, Labour

AUSTRALIAN INTERVIEWEES-1998

Hon. Amanda Vanstone, Minister for Justice, Liberal
Dr. Carmen Lawrence, Labor
Cheryl Kernot, former Leader of the Australian
    Democrats
De-Anne Kelly, National Party
Dee Margetts, Greens
Elizabeth Grace, Liberal
Fran Bailey, Liberal
Helen Coonan, Liberal
Hon. Judi Moylan, Minister for Women, Liberal
Hon. Judith Troeth, Liberal
Jeannie Ferris, Liberal
Jenny Macklin, Labor
Kathy Sullivan, Liberal
Lyn Allison, Australian Democrats
Margaret Reid, President of the Senate, Liberal
Hon. Margaret Reynolds, Labor
Meg Lees, Leader of the Australian Democrats
Natasha Stott Despoja, Deputy Leader, Australian
    Democrats
Sue Mackay, Labor
Sue West, Deputy President, Labor
Trish Crossin, Labor

21/148 (14 per cent)

SOUTH AFRICAN INTERVIEWEES-1999

Dene Smuts, Democratic Party
Mrs. E. Shandu, former Deputy Minister for Public
    Works, ANC
Geraldine Fester, ANC
Gill Marcus, Deputy Finance Minister, ANC
Inka Mars, Inkatha Freedom Party
Janet Love, ANC
Jenny Malan, NP
Koko Mokgolong, ANC
Mary Turok, ANC
Melanie Verwoerd, ANC
Ntombazana Botha, National Party
Patricia de Lille, Pan Africanist Congress
Pregs Govender, Chair, Joint Standing Committee,
    Quality of Life and Improving the Status of Women,
    ANC
Sheila Camerer, National Party
Suzanne Vos, Inkatha Freedom Party
Tersia King, National Party
Val Viljoen, ANC

16/117 (13 per cent)

References

American Society of Newspaper Editors. (1998). *ASNE Journalism Credibility Project*. [On-line]. Available: http://www.asne.org/works/jcp/jcp-main.htm.

Ansolabehere, S., Behr, R., & Iyengar, S. (1991). Mass media and elections: An overview. *American Politics Quarterly, 19*, 109-139.

Ansolabehere, S., & Iyengar, S. (1997). *Going negative*. New York: Free Press.

Ansolabehere, S., Iyengar, S., & Simon, A. (1997). Shifting perspectives on the effects of campaign communication. In S. Iyengar & R. Reeves (Eds.), *Do the media govern? Politicians, voters and reporters in America* (pp. 149-155). Thousand Oaks, CA: Sage.

Baistow, T. (1985). *Fourth-rate estate: An anatomy of Fleet Street*. London: Comedia.

Ballington, J. (1998). Women's parliamentary representation: The effects of list PR. *Politikon, 25*(2), 77-93.

Ballington, J. (1999). *The representation of women*. Electoral Institute of South Africa Election Update 99: 15. Auckland Park, South Africa.

Barnhurst, K. G. (1998). Politics in the fine meshes: Young citizens, power and media. *Media, Culture and Society, 20*(2), 201-218.

Barnhurst, K. G., & Mutz, D. (1997). American journalism and the decline in event-centered reporting. *Journal of Communication, 47*(4), 27-53.

Barrett, E. J. (1995). The policy priorities of African American women in state legislatures. *Legislative Studies Quarterly, 20*, 223-248.

Bartels, L., & Wilson, W. (1996, August). *Politicians and the press: Who leads, who follows?* Paper presented at the meeting of the American Political Science Association, San Francisco, CA.

Baudrillard, J. (1992). Transpolitics, transexuality, transaesthetics. In W. Stearns & W. Chaloupka (Eds.), *The disappearance of art and politics* (pp. 20-22). New York: St. Martin's Press.

Bavelas, J. B., Black, A., Bryson, L., & Mussell, J. (1988). Political equivocation: A situational explanation. *Journal of Language of Social Psychology, 7,* 137-145.

Beattie, G. W. (1982). Turn-taking and interruptions in political interviews—Margaret Thatcher and Jim Callaghan compared and contrasted. *Semiotics, 39,* 93-114.

Becker, L. B., & Dunwoody, S. (1982). Media use, public affairs knowledge and voting in a local election. *Journalism Quarterly, 67,* 708-722.

Behr, R. L., & Iyengar, S. (1985). Television news, real-world cues and changes in the public agenda. *Public Opinion Quarterly, 49,* 38-57.

Benhabib, S. (1992). *Situating the self: Gender, community and postmodernism in contemporary ethics.* Cambridge, UK: Polity Press.

Bennett, S. E., Flickinger, R. S., Baker, J. R., Rhine, S. L., & Bennett, L. L. M. (1996). Citizens' knowledge of foreign affairs. *Press/Politics, 1*(2), 10-29.

Bennett, W. L. (1996a). An introduction to journalism norms and representations of politics. *Political Communication, 3*(4), 373-384.

Bennett, W. L. (1996b). *News: The politics of illusion.* White Plains, NY: Longman.

Bennett, W. L. (1997). Cracking the news code: Some rules that journalists live by. In S. Iyengar & R. Reeves (Eds.), *Do the media govern? Politicians, voters and reporters in America* (pp. 103-117). Thousand Oaks, CA: Sage.

Berkman, M. B., & O'Connor, R. E. (1993). Do women legislators matter? Female legislators and state abortion policy. *American Politics Quarterly, 21,* 102-124.

Bhavnani, K. K., & Phoenix, A. (1994). Shifting identities shifting racisms: An introduction. In K. K. Bhavnani & A. Phoenix (Eds.), *Shifting identities shifting racisms* (pp. 5-18). London: Sage.

Bird, S. E. (1998). News we can use: An audience perspective on the tabloidisation of news in the United States. *Javnost (the Public), 5,* 33-49.

Blankenship, J., & Robson, D.C. (1995). A "feminine style" in women's political discourse: An exploratory essay. *Communication Quarterly, 43*(3), 353-366.

Blumler, J., & Gurevitch, M. (1995). *The crisis of public communication.* London: Routledge.

Boles, J. K. (1991). Advancing the women's agenda within local legislatures: The role of female elected officials. In D. L. Dodson (Ed.), *Gender and policy-making: Studies of women in office* (pp. 39-48). New Brunswick: Center for the American Woman and Politics, Eagleton Institute, Rutgers University.

Box-Steffensmeier, J. M., DeBoef, S., & Lin, T. M. (1997, August). *Macroideology, macropartisanship and the gender gap.* Paper presented at the meeting of the American Political Science Association, Washington, DC.

Braden, M. (1996). *Women politicians and the media.* Lexington: University of Kentucky Press.

Braidotti, R. (1991). *Patterns of dissonance.* Cambridge, UK: Polity Press.

Brants, K. (1997). *Who is afraid of infotainment?* Paper presented at the Images of Politics conference, Netherlands Audiovisual Archives, Amsterdam.

Broughton, D. (1995). *Public opinion polling and politics in Britain.* Hemel Hempstead: Harvester Wheatsheaf.

Bryman, V. (1992). *Feminist political theory: An introduction.* Basingstoke, UK: Macmillan.

Buchanan, B. (1991). *Electing a president: The Markle Commission's report on campaign '88.* Austin: University of Texas Press.

Bull, P. E., & Mayer, K. (1988). Interruptions in political interviews: A study of Margaret Thatcher and Nil Kinnock. *Journal of Language of Social Psychology, 7,* 35-45.

Burns, T. (1997, September). *The impact of the national press on voters in 1997.* Paper presented to the Political Studies Association Specialist Conference on Elections, Public Opinion and Parties, Essex.

Burrell, B. (1994). *A woman's place is in the house.* Ann Arbor: University of Michigan Press.

Butler, D. (1989). *British general elections since 1945.* Oxford: Basil Blackwell.

Butler, D., & Kavanagh, K. (1997). *The British general election of 1997.* London: Macmillan.

Butler, D., & Stokes, D. E. (1974). *Political change in Britain: The evolution of political choice.* London: Macmillan.

Buxton, F. (2000). *Equal balance: Electing more women MPs for the conservative party.* London: The Bow Group.

Cabinet Office. (1999). *Voices: Turning listening into action.* London: Women's Unit.

Callaghan, S. (1991). Does gender make a difference in moral decision making? *Second Opinion, 17*(2), 67-77.

Cappella, J. N., & Jamieson, K. H. (1997). *Spiral of cynicism: The press and the public good.* New York: Oxford University Press.

Carroll, S., Dodson, D. L., & Mandel, R. B. (1991). *The impact of women in public office: An overview.* New Brunswick: Centre for the American Woman and Politics, Eagleton Institute of Politics, Rutgers University.

Carter, A. (1988). *The politics of women's rights.* London: Longman.

Carter, C. (1998). When the "extraordinary" becomes "ordinary": Everyday news of sexual violence. In C. Carter, G. Branston, & S. Allan (Eds.), *News, gender and power* (pp. 219-232). London: Routledge.

Carter, C., Branston, G., & Allan, S. (Eds.). (1998). *News, gender and power.* London: Routledge.

Cavanagh, M., McGarvey, N., & Shephard, M. (2000, April). *New Scottish Parliament, New Scottish Parliamentarians?* Paper presented at the annual conference of the Political Studies Association, London.

Center for American Women and Politics. (1995). *Voices, views and votes: The impact of women in the 103rd Congress.* New Brunswick: Center for American Women in Politics, Eagleton Institute of Politics, Rutgers University.

Center for the American Women and Politics. (1993). *Fact Sheet.* New Brunswick: Center for American Women in Politics, Rutgers University.

Chaney, C., & Sinclair, B. (1994). Women and the 1992 House elections. In E. A. Cook, S. Thomas, & C. Wilcox (Eds.), *The year of the woman* (pp. 123-139). Boulder, CO: Westview.

Chaney, C. R., Alvarez, M., & Nagler, J. (1998). Explaining the gender gap in the U.S. presidential elections 1980-1992. *Political Research Quarterly, 51*(2), 311-340.

Christmas, L. (1996). *Women in the news: Does sex change the way a newspaper thinks?* London: Women in Journalism.

Cirksena, M. K. (1996). Sources of access and competence in women's political persuading 1964-1984. *Communication Quarterly, 44*(4), 227-245.

Cole, M., & Howe, J. (1994). Women and politics. *Politics Review, 4*(2), 16-18.

Coleman, S. (1999). *Electronic media, parliament and the people: Making democracy visible.* London: Hansard Society.

Coles, J. (1997, April 28). Boy zone story. *Guardian,* p. 12.

Connell, I. (1998). Mistaken identities: Tabloid and broadsheet news discourse. *Javnost (the Public), 5*(3), 11-32.

Conover, P. J. (1988). Feminists and the gender gap. *Journal of Politics, 50*(2), 985-1010.

Conway, M. M., Steuernagel, G. A., & Ahern, D. W. (1997). *Women and political participation.* Washington, DC: CQ Press.

Cook, T. E. (1996). Political values and production values. *Political Communication, 3*(4), 469-481.

Cook, T. E. (1998). *Governing with the news: The news media as a political institution.* Chicago: University of Chicago Press.

Coote, A. (1999, May 11). It's lads on top at Number Ten. *Guardian,* p. 10.

Creedon, P. J. (1993). The challenge of re-visioning gender values. In P. Creedon (Ed.), *Women in mass communication* (2nd ed., pp. 3-23). Newbury Park: Sage.

Critchley, J. (1994). *A bag of boiled sweets.* London: Faber and Faber.

Danielian, N. R. (1939). *The AT&T.* New York: Vanguard.

Darcy, R., & Schramm, S. (1977). When women run against men. *Public Opinion Quarterly, 41,* 1-12.

Darcy, R., Welch, S., & Clark, J. (1994). *Women, elections and representation.* Lincoln: University of Nebraska Press.

Daughton, S. M. (1994). Women's issues, women's place: Gender-related problems in presidential campaigns. *Communication Quarterly, 42*(2), 106-119.

Davies, J. A., & Smith, T. W. (1993). *General social surveys, 1992-1993.* Chicago: National Opinion Research Center.

Day, R. (1989). Interviewing politicians. In I. Crewe & M. Harrop (Eds.), *Political communication: The general election campaign of 1987* (pp. 126-136). Cambridge, UK: Cambridge University Press.

Day, R. (1993). *But with respect, Sir.* London: Weidenfeld and Nicolson.

Delli Carpini, M. X., & Keeter, S. (1991). Stability and change in the U.S. public's knowledge of politics. *Public Opinion Quarterly, 55,* 583-612.

Dines, G., & Humez, J. M. (Eds.). (1995). *Gender, race and class in media.* Thousand Oaks, CA: Sage.

Di Stefano, C. (1990). Dilemmas of difference. In L. Nicholson (Ed.), *Feminism/postmodernism* (pp. 63-83). New York: Routledge.

Dolan, K. (1998). Voting for women in the "Year of the woman". *American Journal of Political Science, 42*(1), 272-293.

Downing, J. D. H. (1990). The political economy of U.S. television. *Monthly Review, 42*(1), 30-41.

DuBois, E. C. (1978). *Feminism and suffrage: The emergence of an independent women's movement in America 1848-1869.* Ithaca, NY: Cornell University Press.

Duverger, M. (1954). *Political parties: Their organization and activity in the modern state.* London: Methuen.

Economou, K. (1997). Representing politics—politicising journalism: Exploring communicative dilemmas in the collegial relationship between Swedish journalists and politicians. *Javnost (the Public), 4*(2), 91-102.

Eisenstein, Z. (1989). *The female body and the law.* Berkeley: University of California Press.

Eldridge, J. (Ed.). (1995). *News content, language and visuals.* Glasgow Media Group Reader, vol. 1. London: Routledge.

Entman, R. M. (1989). How the media affect what people think: An information processing approach. *Journal of Politics, 51*, 347-370.

Epstein, L. (1967). *Political parties in western democracies.* New York: Praeger.

Faludi, S. (1991). *Backlash: The undeclared war against American women.* New York: Crown.

Fawcett, M. (1918). Speech to the Labour Party annual conference 1918 for the National Federation of Women Workers. *Labour Party Report 1918.* London: Labour Party.

Fawcett Society. (1996). *Winning women's votes: The gender gap in voting patterns and priorities.* London: Fawcett Society.

Fawcett Society. (1997). *Fawcett survey of women MPs.* London: Fawcett Society.

Fawcett Society. (1999). *Winning women: Lessons from Scotland and Wales.* London: Fawcett Society.

Ferguson, K. (1984). *The feminist case against bureaucracy.* Philadelphia: Temple University Press.

Figes, K. (1994). *Because of her sex: The myth of equality for women in Britain.* London: MacMillan.

Finkelstein, D. (1998). Why the conservatives lost. In I. Crewe et al. (Eds.), *Political communication: Why Labour won the general election of 1997.* London: Frank Cass.

Finnegan, M. (1999). *Selling suffrage: Consumer culture and votes for women.* New York: Columbia University Press.

Fiske, J. (1987). *Television culture.* London: Routledge.

Fiske, J. (1990). *Introduction to communication studies.* London: Routledge.

Flammang, J. A. (1997). *Women's political voice: How women are transforming the practice and study of politics.* Philadelphia: Temple University Press.

Fletcher, F. J. (1996). Polling and political communication. In D. Paletz (Ed.), *Political communication in action* (pp. 299-316). Cresskill, NJ: Hampton Press.

Flexner, E. (1975). *Century of struggle: The women's rights movement in the United States* (rev. ed.). Cambridge, MA: Belknap Press.

Fowler, J. (1995). *Women in politics: A fair press?* Unpublished master's thesis. University of Sheffield, England.

Fowler, R. (1991). *Language in the news: Discourse and ideology in the press*. London: Routledge.

Fox, R. L. (1997), *Gender dynamics in congressional elections*. Thousand Oaks, CA: Sage.

Fox, R. L., & Smith, E. R. A. N. (1998). The role of candidate sex in voter decision-making. *Political Psychology, 19*(2), 405-419.

Francovic, K. (1982). Sex and politics—new alignments, old issues. *Political Science and Politics, 15*, 439-448.

Franklin, B. (1994). *Packaging politics: Political communication in Britain's media democracy*. London: Edward Arnold.

Franklin, B. (1997). *Newszak and news media*. London: Arnold.

Franklin, B., & Murphy, D. (Eds.). (1998). *Making the local news: Local journalism in context*. London: Routledge.

Fraser, N. (1989). *Unruly practices: Power, discourse and gender in contemporary social theory*. Minneapolis: University of Minnesota Press.

Fraser, N. (1992). Sex, lies and the public sphere: A contribution to the critique of actually existing democracy. *Social Text, 25/26*, 56-80.

Freeman, J. (1975). *The politics of women's liberation: A case study of an emerging social movement and its relation to the policy process*. New York: McKay.

Gelb, J., & Palley, M. (1987). *Women and public policies*. Princeton: Princeton University Press.

Gertzog, I. N. (1984). *Congressional women: Their recruitment, treatment and behavior*. New York: Praeger.

Gilbert, S. M., & Gubar, S. (1979). *The madwoman in the attic: The woman writer and the nineteenth-century literary imagination*. New Haven, CT: Yale University Press.

Gilens, M. (1988). Gender and support for Reagan: A comprehensive model of presidential approval. *American Journal of Political Science, 32*, 19-49.

Gilligan, C. (1982). *In a different voice: Psychological theory and women's development*. Cambridge, MA: Harvard University Press.

Gitlin, T. (1990). *The whole world is watching: Mass media in the making and unmaking of the new left*. Berkeley: University of California Press.

Glasgow University Media Group. (1976). *Bad news*. London: Routledge and Kegan Paul.

Glasgow University Media Group. (1980). *More bad news*. London: Routledge and Kegan Paul.

Glasgow University Media Group. (1985). *War and peace news*. Milton Keynes, UK: Open University Press.

Goldenberg, E. N., & Traugott, M. W. (1987). Mass media effects in recognizing and rating candidates in U.S. Senate elections. In J. Vermeer (Ed.), *Campaigns in the news: Mass media and congressional elections* (pp. 109-131). New York: Greenwood Press.

Goodman, J. R. (1999, May). *Imaging influential wives: A comparative study of presidential candidates wives' photographic representations in* Time Magazine. Paper presented at the meeting of the International Communication Association, San Francisco.

Gould, P. (1998). Why Labour won. In I. Crewe et al. (Eds.), *Political communication: Why Labour won the general elelction of 1997.* London: Frank Cass.

Graves, P. (1994). *Labour women: Women in British working-class politics 1918-1939.* Cambridge, UK: Cambridge University Press.

Greatbatch, D. (1986). Aspects of topical organization in news interviews: The use of agenda-shifting procedures by interviewees. In R. Collins, J. Curran, N. Garnham, P. Scannell, P. Schlesinger, & C. Sparks (Eds.), *Media, culture and society* (pp. 112-134). Beverly Hills, CA: Sage.

Greatbatch, D. (1988). A turn-taking system for British news interviews. *Language in Society, 17,* 401-430.

Gurevitch, M., & Blumler, J. (1990). Comparative research: The extending frontiers. In D. Swanson & D. Nimmo (Eds.), *New directions in political communication.* Newbury Park, CA: Sage.

Habermas, J. (1989). *The structural transformation of the public sphere: An inquiry into a category of bourgeois society* (T. Burger & F. Lawrence, Trans.). Cambridge, MA: MIT Press.

Hallin, D. (1997). Sound bite news. In S. Iyengar & R. Reeves (Eds.), *Do the media govern? Politicians, voters and reporters in America* (pp. 57-65). Thousand Oaks, CA: Sage.

Hallin, D. (1998). A fall from grace? *Media Studies Journal, 2*(2), 42-49.

Hallin, D. (1996). Commercialism and professionalism in the American news media. In J. Curran & M. Gurevitch (Eds.), *Mass media and society* (pp. 243-264). London: Edward Arnold.

Hamilton, L. H. (1998). What makes a journalist fair? Not just asking questions but listening to answers. *Media Studies Journal, 2*(2), 86-91.

Harman, H. (2000, January 18). Speech to Labour Renewal Network Seminar. London, England.

Harrison, M. (1992). Politics on the air. In D. Butler & A. King (Eds.), *The British general election of 1992* (pp. 155-179). London: Macmillan.

Hart, R. (1987). *The sound of leadership: Presidential communication in the modern age.* Chicago: University of Chicago Press.

Havick, J. (1997). Determinants of national media attention. *Journal of Communication, 47*(2), 97-111.

Hayes, B., & Makkai, T. (1996). Politics and the mass media: The differential impact of gender. *Women and Politics, 16*(4), 45-74.

Hencke, D. (1996, August 8). Short flays Blair's "dark men." *Guardian.*

Herman, E. S., & Chomsky, N. (1988). *Manufacturing consent: The political economy of the mass media.* New York: Pantheon.

Hershey, M. (1977). The politics of androgyny: Sex roles and attitudes toward women in politics. *American Politics Quarterly, 3,* 261-287.

Herzog, H. (1998). More than a looking glass: Women in Israeli local politics and the media. *Press/Politics, 3*(1), 26-47.

Hewitt, P., & Mattinson, D. (1989). *Women's votes: The key to winning.* Fabian Research Series No. 353. London: Fabian Society.

Hitchon, J. C., & Chang, C. (1995). Effects of gender schematic processing on the reception of political commercials for men and women candidates. *Communication Research, 22*(4), 430-458.

Holland, P. (1987). When a woman reads the news. In H. Baehr & G. Dyer (Eds.), *Boxed in: Women and television* (pp. 133-149). New York: Pandora.

Holland, P. (1998). The politics of the smile: Soft news and the sexualisation of the popular press. In C. Carter, G. Branston, & S. Allan (Eds.), *News, gender and power* (pp. 17-32). London: Routledge.

Holmes, R., & Holmes, A., (1998). Sausages or policemen? The role of the liberal democrats in the 1997 general election campaign. In I. Crewe et al. (Eds.), *Political communication: Why Labour won the general election of 1997.* London: Frank Cass.

hooks, b. (1984). *Feminist theory: From margin to center.* Boston: South End Press.

hooks, b. (1989). *Talking back: Thinking feminist, thinking black.* London: Sheba Feminist Publishers.

hooks, b. (1991). *Yearning: Race, gender and cultural politics.* London: Turnaround.

Horton, N. H. (1999). Uncovering the dimensionality of gender voting in Congress. *Legislative Studies Quarterly, 24*(1), 65-86.

Huddy, L., & Terkildsen, N. (1993). Gender stereotypes and the perception of male and female candidates. *American Journal of Political Science, 37*(1), 119-148.

Hunter, A. A., & Denton, M.A. (1984). Do female candidates lose votes? The experience of female candidates in the 1979 and 1980 Canadian general elections. *Canadian Review of Sociology and Anthropology, 21,* 395-406.

Iyengar, S. (1987). Television news and citizens: Explanations of national affairs. *American Political Science Review, 81,* 815-831.

Iyengar, S. (1991). *Is anyone responsible? How television news frames public issues.* Chicago: University of Chicago Press.

Iyengar, S., & Kinder, D. (1987). *News that matters: Television and American opinion.* Chicago: University of Chicago Press.

Iyengar, S., & Reeves, R. (Eds.). (1997). *Do the media govern? Politicians, voters and reporters in America.* Newbury Park, CA: Sage.

Iyengar, S., & Simon, A. (1997). News coverage of the Gulf Crisis and public opinion: A study of agenda setting, priming and framing. In S. Iyengar & R. Reeves (Eds.), *Do the media govern? Politicians, voters and reporters in America* (pp. 248-257). Thousand Oaks, CA: Sage.

Iyengar, S., Valentino, N. A., Ansolabehere, S., & Simon, A. F. (1997). Running as a woman: Gender stereotyping in women's campaigns. In P. Norris (Ed.), *Women, media and politics* (pp. 77-98). Oxford: Oxford University Press.

Jacobson, G. C. (1992). *The politics of congressional elections.* San Diego: Harper Collins.

James, S. (1992). The good-enough citizen: Citizenship and independence. In G. Bock & S. James (Eds.), *Beyond equality and difference: Citizenship, feminist politics and female subjectivity* (pp. 48-68). London: Routledge.

Jamieson, K. (1996). *Packaging the presidency: A history and criticism of presidential campaign advertising.* New York: Oxford University Press.

Jones, N. (1995). *Soundbites and spin doctors: How politicians manipulate the media—and vice versa.* London: Indigo.

Jowett, G. S., & O'Donnell, V. (1992). *Propaganda and persuasion* (2nd ed.). Newbury Park, CA: Sage.

Just, M., Crigler, A., & Buhr, T. (1999). Voice, substance and cynicism in presidential campaign media. *Political Communication, 16*(1), 25-44.

Just, M. R., Crigler, A., Alger, D., Cook, T., Kern, M., & West, D. (1996). *Crosstalk: Citizens, candidates and the media in a presidential campaign.* Chicago: University of Chicago Press.

Kahn, K. F. (1993). Gender differences in campaign messages: The political advertisements of men and women candidates for U.S. Senate. *Political Research Quarterly, 46*(3), 481-503.

Kahn, K. F. (1994a). The distorted mirror: Press coverage of women candidates for statewide office. *Journal of Politics, 56*(1), 154-174.

Kahn, K. F. (1994b). Does gender make a difference? An experimental examination of sex stereotypes and press patterns in statewide campaigns. *American Journal of Political Science, 38*(1), 162-195.

Kahn, K. F. (1996). *The political consequences of being a woman: How stereotypes influence the conduct and consequences of political campaigns.* New York: Columbia University Press.

Kahn, K. F., & Goldenberg, E. N. (1991). Women candidates in the news: An examination of gender differences in U.S. Senate campaign coverage. *Public Opinion Quarterly, 55*, 180-199.

Kahn, K. F., & Goldenberg, E. N. (1997). The media: Obstacle or ally of feminists? In S. Iyengar & R. Reeves (Eds.), *Do the media govern? Politicians, voters and reporters in America* (pp. 156-164). Thousand Oaks, CA: Sage.

Kahn, K. F., & Gordon, A. (1997). How women campaign for the U.S. Senate. In P. Norris (Ed.), *Women, media and politics* (pp. 59-76). Oxford: Oxford University Press.

Kaid, L. L., & Holtz-Bacha, C. (1995). Political advertising across cultures: Comparing content, styles and effects. In L. L. Kaid & C. Holtz-Bacha (Eds.), *Political advertising in western democracies* (pp. 206-227). Thousand Oaks, CA: Sage.

Kaid, L. L., Myers, S. L., Pipps, V., & Hunter, J. (1984). Sex role perceptions and televised political advertising: Comparing male and female candidates. *Women and Politics, 4*(4), 41-53.

Karpf, A. (1999, August 7). Grillings and roastings. *Guardian.*

Kaufmann, K. M., & Petrocik, J. R. (1999). The changing politics of American men: Understanding the sources of the gender gap. *American Journal of Political Science, 43*(3), 864-887.

Kavanagh, D. (1995). *Election campaigining: The new marketing of politics.* Oxford: Blackwell.

Kendall, K. E. (1997). Presidential debates through media eyes. *American Behavioral Scientist, 40*(8), 1193-1207.

Kennamar, J. D. (1986). Gender differences in attitude strength, role of news media and cognition. *Journalism Quarterly, 63*(4), 782-788, 833.

Kennamar, J. D. (1987). How media use during campaigns affects the intent to vote. *Journalism Quarterly, 64*, 291-300.

Kern, M., & Just, M. (1997). A gender gap among viewers? In P. Norris (Ed.), *Women, media and politics* (pp. 99-112). Oxford: Oxford University Press.

Keswick, T., Pockley, R., & Guillaume, A. (1999). *Conservative women*. London: Centre for Policy Studies.

King, A. (1997). *New Labour triumphs: Britain at the polls*. Chatham, NJ: Chatham House.

King, F. (1993). Sensitive man—Bill Clinton's image as a sensitive male. *National Review, 45*(16), 72.

Kiousis, S. (2000, June). *Boomerang agenda-setting: Presidential media coverage and public confidence in the press*. Paper presented at the meeting of the International Communication Association, Acapulco, Mexico.

Kirkpatrick, J. (1974). *Political women*. New York: Basic Books.

Klein, E. (1984). *Gender politics*. Cambridge, MA: Harvard University Press.

Klein, J. (1992, September 7). Fighting the squish factor. *Newsweek*, p. 39.

Klotz, R. (1998). Virtual criticism: Negative advertising on the internet in the 1996 Senate races. *Political Communication, 15*(3), 347-365.

Labour Party. (1922). *Labour Party Report, 1922*. London: Labour Party.

Ladd, E. C. (1997) Media framing of the gender gap. In P. Norris (Ed.), *Women, media and politics* (pp. 113-128). Oxford: Oxford University Press.

Lake, C., DiVall, L., & Iyengar, S. (1997). Women as political candidates: Was 1992 the "Year of the Woman"? In S. Iyengar & R. Reeves (Eds.), *Do the media govern? Politicians, voters and reporters in America* (pp. 165-170). Thousand Oaks, CA: Sage.

Langdon, J. (1999, December 19). Tony's way with women. *Independent on Sunday*, p. 17.

Lasora, D. L. (1997). Media agenda setting and press performance: A social system approach for building theory. In M. McCombs, D. L. Shaw, & D. Weaver (Eds.), *Communication and democracy: Exploring the intellectual frontiers in agenda-setting theory* (pp. 155-167). Mahwah, NJ: Lawrence Erlbaum.

Lau, R. R., Sigelman, L., Heldman, C., & Babbitt, P. (1997, August). *The effects of negative political advertisments: A meta-analytic assessment*. Paper presented at the meeting of the American Political Science Association, Washington, DC.

Lazarsfeld, P., Berelson, B., & Gander, H. (1948). *The people's choice: How the voter makes up his mind in a presidential campaign*. New York: Columbia University Press.

LeDuc, L. (1990). Party strategies and the use of televised campaign debates. *European Journal of Political Research, 18*, 121-141.

Leeper, N. S. (1991). The impact of prejudice on female candidates: An experimental look at voter inference. *American Politics Quarterly, 19*, 248-261.

Lemert, J. B., Elliott, W. R., Rosenberg, W. L., & Bernstein, J. M. (1996). *The politics of disenchantment: Bush, Clinton, Perot and the press*. Cresskill, NJ: Hampton Press.

Levine, S., & Roberts, N. (1993). Agenda gap: Political perspectives and gender differences in New Zealand. *Political Science, 45*(1), 139-151.

Lewis, J. (1991). *The ideological octopus: An exploration of television and its audience*. New York: Routledge.

Liebes, T., & Peri, Y. (1998). Electronic journalism in segmented societies: Lessons from the 1996 Israeli elections. *Political Communication, 15*(1), 27-43.

Lindsay, B. (1999). Interest groups and the political process: Gender issues. In B. I. Newman (Ed.), *Handbook of political marketing* (pp. 643-670). Thousand Oaks, CA: Sage.

Lippman, W. (1922). *Public opinion.* London: Macmillan.

Liran-Alper, D. (1994, July). *Media representation of women in politics—Are they still "domineering dowagers and scheming concubines"?* Paper presented at the meeting of the International Association of Mass Communication Research, Seoul.

Liswood, L.A. (1995). *Women world leaders: Fifteen great politicians tell their stories.* London: Pandora.

Lovenduski, J. (1996). Sex, gender and British politics. In J. Lovenduski & P. Norris (Eds.), *Women in politics* (pp. 1-16). Oxford: Oxford University Press.

Malone, A., & Byrne, C. (1995, February 12). Constituencies defy Blair on women MPs. *Sunday Times*, p. 10.

Matland, R., & Taylor, M. (1997). Electoral systems effect on women's representation: Theoretical arguments and evidence from Costa Rica. *Comparative Political Studies, 39*(2), 200-215.

Matland, R. E., & Studlar, D. T. (1996). The contagion of women candidates in single-member district and proportional representation electoral systems: Canada and Norway. *The Journal of Politics, 58*(3), 707-733.

McAllister, I. (1992). *Political behaviour: Citizens, parties and elites in Australia.* Melbourne: Longman.

McCombs, M. E. (1981). The agenda-setting approach. In D. D. Nimmo & K. R. Sanders (Eds.), *The handbook of political communication* (pp. 121-140). Beverly Hills, CA: Sage Publications.

McCombs, M. E., & Shaw, D. (1972). The agenda-setting function of the mass media. *Public Opinion Quarterly, 36*, 176-187.

McDougall, L. (Director). (1998a). *Westminster women.* London: ITV.

McDougall, L. (1998b). *Westminster women.* London: Vintage.

McKibbon, R. (1974). *The evolution of the labour party 1910-1924.* Oxford: Oxford University Press.

McLeay, E. (1993). Women's parliamentary representation: A comparative perspective. *Political Science, 45*(1), 40-62.

McNair, B. (1996). *News and journalism in the UK: A textbook* (2nd ed.). London: Routledge.

McNair, B. (1995). *An introduction to political communication.* London: Routledge.

McTaggart, F. (2000). *Women in Parliament: Their contribution to Labour's first 1000 days.* London: Fabian Society.

Mies, M., & Shiva, V. (Eds.). (1993). *Ecofeminism.* London: Zed Books.

Millar, A. (1993). *Trust the women: Women in the federal parliament.* Canberra: Department of the Senate.

Miller, A. H., Wattenberg, M. P., & Malanchunk, O. (1986). Schematic assessments of presidential candidates. *American Political Science Review, 80*, 521-540.

Miller, M. M., Singletary, M. W., & Chen, S. L. (1988). The Roper question and television vs. newspapers as sources of news. *Journalism Quarterly, 65,* 12-19.

Miller, W. E., & Shanks, J. M. (1996). *The new American voter.* Cambridge, MA: Harvard University Press.

Morin, R. (1996, February 5-11). Tuned out, turned off. *The Washington Post National Weekly Edition,* pp. 6-8.

Mosco, V. (1996). *The political economy of communication: Rethinking and renewal.* London: Sage.

Mughan, T. (1996). Television can matter: Bias in the 1992 general election. In D.M. Farrell et al. (Eds.), *British elections and parties yearbook 1996* (pp. 128-142). London: Frank Cass.

Nadelson, R. (1996, January 26). Whos afraid of Tory woman? *Sunday Express Magazine,* p. 26.

Narayan, U. (1997). Towards a feminist vision of citizenship: Rethinking the implications of dignity, political participation and nationality. In M. L. Shanley & U. Narayan (Eds.), *Reconstructing political theory: Feminist perspectives* (pp. 48-67). Cambridge, UK: Polity Press.

Negrine, R. (1994). *Politics and the mass media in Britain* (2nd ed.). London: Routledge.

Negrine, R. (1996). *The communication of politics.* London: Sage.

Negrine, R. (1998). *Parliament and the media: A study of Britain, Germany and France.* London: Royal Institute of International Affairs/Cassell.

Nelson, C. (1995, May). The right to power. *Australian Women's Forum,* p. 13.

Nerone, J. C., & Barnhurst, K. G. (1995). Visual mapping and cultural authority: Design change in U.S. newspapers 1920-1940. *Journal of Communication, 45*(2), 9-53.

Neuman, W. R., Just, M. R., & Crigler, A. N. (1992). *Common knowledge: News and the construction of political meaning.* Chicago: University of Chicago Press.

Norris, P. (1996). Women politicians: Transforming Westminster? In J. Lovenduski & P. Norris (Eds.), *Women in politics* (pp. 91-104). Oxford: Oxford University Press.

Norris, P. (1997). Women leaders worldwide: A splash of color in the photo op. In P. Norris (Ed.), *Women, media and politics* (pp. 149-165). Oxford: Oxford University Press.

Norris, P., Curtice, J., Sanders, D., Scammell, M., & Semetko, H. A. (1999). *On message: Communicating the campaign.* London: Sage.

Norris, P., & Lovenduski, J. (1993). Gender and party politics in Britain. In J. Lovenduski & P. Norris (Eds.), *Gender and party politics* (pp. 35-59). London: Sage.

Okin, S. M. (1990). Thinking like a woman. In D. L. Rhode (Ed.), *Theoretical perspectives on sexual differences.* New Haven: Yale University Press.

Owen, D. (1997). Talk radio and evaluations of President Clinton. *Political Communication, 14,* 333-353.

Paolino, P. (1995). Group-salient issues and group representation: Support for women candidates in the 1992 Senate elections. *American Journal of Political Science, 39,* 294-313.

Pateman, C. (1989). *The disorder of women.* Cambridge, UK: Polity Press.

Pateman, C., & Gross, E. (Eds.). (1986). *Feminist challenges: Social and political theory.* London: Allen & Unwin.

Patterson, T. E. (1994). *Out of order.* New York: Knopf.

Patterson, T. E. (1996). Bad news, bad governance. *Annals of the American Academy of Political and Social Science, 456,* 97-108.

Peake, L. (1997, February). *Press coverage of women candidates for the U.K. Parliament.* Paper presented at the conference, European Consortium of Political Research Joint Session and Workshop, Bern.

Pelling, H. (1954). *The origins of the Labour Party.* London: Macmillan.

Pendakur, M. (1990). *Canadian dreams and American control: The political economy of the Canadian film industry.* Detroit: Wayne State University Press.

Perkins, A. (1999, April 29). So far, so what? *Guardian,* p. 6.

Perloff, R. M. (1998). *Political communication: Politics, press and public in America.* Mahwah, NJ: Lawrence Erlbaum Associates.

Petrocovik, J. R. (1996). Issue ownership in Presidential elections with a 1980 case study. *American Journal of Political Science, 40,* 825-850.

Pfau, M., Parrott, R., & Lindquist, B. (1992) An expectancy theory explanation of the effectiveness of political attack television spots: A case study. *Journal of Applied Communication Research, 20,* 263-253.

Phillips, A. (1993). *Democracy and difference,* Cambridge, UK: Polity Press.

Phillips, A. (1991). *Engendering democracy.* Cambridge, UK: Polity Press.

Phillips, A. (1992). Universal pretensions in political thought. In M. Barrett & A. Phillips (Eds.), *Destabilizing theory: Contemporary feminist debates* (pp. 10-30). Cambridge, UK: Polity Press.

Phoenix, A. (1987). Theories of gender and black families. In G. Weiner & M. Arnot (Eds.), *Gender under scrutiny: New inquiries in education* (pp. 50-61). London: Hutchinson.

Phoenix, A. (1994). Practising feminist research: The intersection of gender and race in the research process. In M. Maynard & J. Purvis (Eds.), *Researching women's lives from a feminist perspective* (pp. 49-71). London: Taylor & Francis.

Pinkleton, B. E., & Austin, E. W. (2000, June). *Exploring relationships among media use frequency, media importance, political disaffection and political efficacy.* Paper presented at the conference of the International Communication Association, Acapulco, Mexico.

Pinkleton, B. E., Austin, E. W., & Fortman, K. K. J. (1998). Relationships of media use and political disaffection to political efficacy and voting behavior. *Journal of Broadcasting and Electronic Media, 42*(1), 34-49.

Plutzer, E., & Zipp, J. (1996). Identity politics, partisanship and voting for women candidates. *Public Opinion Quarterly, 60,* 30-57.

Poole, B. (1993, Spetember 2-5). *Should women identify themselves as feminists when running for political office?* Paper presented at the meeting of the American Political Science Association, Washington, DC.

Poole, K. T., & Zeigler, L. H. (1985). *Women, public opinion and politics.* New York: Longman.

Popkin, S. L. (1991). *The reasoning voter; communication and persuasion in presidential campaigns.* Chicago: University of Chicago Press.

Popkin, S. L. (1997). Voter learning in the 1992 presidential campaign. In S. Iyengar & R. Reeves (Eds.), *Do the media govern? Politicians, voters and reporters in America* (pp. 171-180). Thousand Oaks, CA: Sage.

Pringle, R., & Watson, S. (1992). "Women's interests" and the post-structuralist state. In M. Barrett & A. Phillips (Eds.), *Destabilizing theory: Contemporary feminist debates* (pp. 53-73). Cambridge, UK: Polity Press.

Rees, L. (1992). *Selling politics*. London: BBC Books.

Reeves, R. (1997). Overview. In S. Iyengar & R. Reeves (Eds.), *Do the media govern? Politicians, voters and reporters in America* (pp. 1-8). Thousand Oaks, CA: Sage.

Reynolds, M. (1995). *The last bastion: Labor women working towards equality in the parliaments of Australia*. Sydney: Business and Professional Publishing.

Richards, S. (1996, July 12). Interview with Clare Short MP. *New Statesman*, p. 7.

Riddoch, L. (1999, December 13). Twinning peaks. *Guardian*, p. 10.

Robinson J. P., & Davis, D. K. (1990). Television news and the informed public: An information processing approach. *Journal of Communication, 40*(3), 106-119.

Robinson, G. J., & Saint-Jean, A. (1991). Women politicians and their media coverage: A generational analysis. In K. Megyery (Ed.), *Women in Canadian politics: Toward equity in representation* (Vol. 6, pp. 127-169). Royal Commission on Electoral Reform and Party Financing. Toronto: Buridurn Press.

Robinson, G.J., & Saint-Jean, A. (1997). *Women's participation in the Canadian news media: Progress since the 1970s*. Unpublished report. Montreal: McGill University.

Robinson, G.J., & Saint-Jean, A. (1996). From Flora to Kim: Thirty years of representations of Canadian women politicians. In H. Holmes & D. Taras (Eds.), *Seeing ourselves: Media power and policy in Canada* (pp. 23-36). Toronto: Harcourt Brace.

Romano, C. (1998). All is not fair in journalism—Fairness to people vs. fairness to the truth. *Media Studies Journal, 2*(2), 90-97.

Root, J. (1986). *Open the box: About television*. London: Channel 4 and Comedia Series, No. 34.

Rosenberg, S. W., Kahn, S., & Tran, T. (1991). Creating a political image: Shaping appearances and manipulating the vote. *Political Behavior, 13*, 345-367.

Rosenthal, C. S. (1995). The role of gender in descriptive representation. *Political Research Quarterly, 48*, 599-612.

Ross, K. (1994). Bambi, Thumper and the one in the dress: Press coverage of the Labour Party's leadership campaign—1994. *Everywoman, 110*, 12-13.

Ross, K. (1995a). Gender and party politics—How the press reported the Labour leadership campaign, 1994. *Media, Culture and Society, 17*(3), 499-509.

Ross, K. (1995b). Skirting the issue: Political women and the media. *Everywoman, 199*, 16-17.

Ross, K. (1995c). Women and the news agenda: Media-ted reality and Jane Public. *Discussion Papers in Mass Communications*. Leicester, UK: University of Leicester.

Ross, K. (1996). Political women, newspaper men: Analysing the intersections between gender, politics and press. In N. Dakovic, D. Derman, & K. Ross (Eds.), *Gender and media* (pp. 176-187). Ankara: Med-Campus.

Ross, K. (1997). Viewing (p)leasure, viewer pain: Black audiences and British television. *Leisure Studies, 16*(4), 233-248.

Ross, K. (1998a). Disability and the media: A suitable case for treatment? *Media and Communication, 65*(2), 14-20.

Ross, K. (1998b, July). *Sex, politics and the media: Selling women down the river.* Paper presented at the meeting of the International Association of Media and Communication Research, Glasgow.

Ross, K. (2000). In whose image? TV criticism and black minority viewers. In S. Cottle (Ed.), *Ethnic minorities and the media.* Buckingham: Open University Press.

Ross, K., & Sreberny, A. (2000). Women in the house: Media representations of British politicians. In A. Sreberny & L. van Zoonen (Eds.), *Gender, politics and communication* (pp. 79-100). Cresskill, NJ: Hampton Press.

Ross, K., & Sreberny-Mohammadi, A. (1997). Playing house—Gender, politics and the news media in Britain. *Media, Culture and Society, 19*(1), 101-109.

Salholz, E., Beachy, L., Miller, S., Annin, P., Barrett, T., & Foote, D. (1992, December 28). Did America get it? Women's gains in 92: A glass both half empty and half full. *Newsweek,* pp. 20-22.

Sancho-Aldridge, J. (1997). *Election '97.* London: Independent Television Commission.

Sanders, D., & Norris, P. (1997, September). *Does negative news matter? The effect of television news on party images in the 1997 British general election.* Paper presented at the Political Studies Association specialist conference on Elections, Public Opinion and Parties, Essex.

Sanders, M. (1993). Television: The face of the network news is male. In P. Creedon (Ed.), *Women in mass communication* (2nd ed., pp. 167-171). Newbury Park, CA: Sage.

Sapiro, V. (1998). Feminist studies and political science—And vice versa. In A. Phillips (Ed.), *Feminism and politics* (pp. 67-89). Oxford: Oxford University Press.

Sawer, M., & Simms, M. (1993). *A woman's place: Women and politics in Australia.* St. Leonards, New South Wales: Allen and Unwin.

Scammell, M. (1998). The wisdom of the war room: U.S. campaigning and Americanization. *Media, Culture and Society, 20*(2), 251-275.

Scammell, M. (1990). Political advertising and the broadcasting bill. *Political Quarterly, 61*(2), 200-213.

Scammell, M., & Semetko, H. A (1995). Political advertising on television. In L. L. Kaid, & C. Holtz-Bacha (Eds.), *Political advertising in western democracies* (pp. 19-43). Thousand Oaks, CA: Sage.

Schiller, H. (1989). *Culture inc.* New York: Oxford University Press.

Schumaker, P., & Burns, N. E. (1988). Gender cleavages and the resolution of local policy issues. *American Journal of Political Science, 32,* 1070-1095.

Schutz, A. (1998). Audience perceptions of politicians' self-presentational behaviors concerning their own abilities. *Journal of Social Psychology, 138*(2), 173-188.

Sedgemore, B. (1995). *The insiders guide to Parliament.* Cambridge, UK: Icon Books.

Segal, L. (2000, January 1). Feminist dreams, fragile realities. *Guardian,* p. 13.

Segal, L. (1999). *Why feminism?* Cambridge, UK: Polity.

Seltzer, R. A., Newman, J., & Leighton, M. V. (1997). *Sex as a political variable: Women as candidates and voters in U.S. elections.* Boulder, CO: Lynne Rienner Publishers.

Shaw, D. L., & Martin, S. E. (1992). The function of mass media agenda setting. *Journalism Quarterly, 69*(4), 902-920.

Short, C. (1996). Women and the Labour party. In J. Lovenduski & P. Norris (Eds.), *Women in politics* (pp. 19-27). Oxford: Oxford University Press.

Showalter, E. (1985). *The female malady: Women, madness and English culture 1830-1980.* New York: Penguin.

Sigelman, C. K., Thomas, D. B., Sigelman, L., & Ribich, F. D. (1986). Gender, physical attractiveness and electability: An experimental investigation of voter biases. *Journal of Applied Social Psychology, 16,* 229-248.

Simms, M. (1985). The 1984 Australian elections: Find the woman? *Politics, 20*(1), 105-112.

Sloman, A. (1999, December). Speech to the Electronic Democracy conference. Hansard Society/Voice of the Viewer and Listener, London.

Smeal, E. (1984). *Why and how women will elect the new President.* New York: Harper and Row.

Smith, T. W., & Selfa, L. A. (1992, September/October). When do women vote for women? *The Public Perspective,* pp. 30-31.

Smythe, D.W. (1957). *The structure and policy of electronic communications.* Urbana: University of Illinois Press.

Soothill, K., & Walby, S. (1991). *Sex crime in the news.* London: Routledge.

Spender, D. (1994, April 21). We'd like to give women pre-selection, but . . . *Courier Mail,* p. 8.

Squires, J. (1999). *Gender in political theory.* Cambridge, England: Polity Press.

Sreberny-Mohammadi, A., & Ross, K. (1996). Women MPs and the media: Representing the body politic. In J. Lovenduski & P. Norris (Eds.), *Women and politics* (pp. 105-117). Oxford: Oxford University Press.

Sreberny-Mohammadi, A. (1994). Women talking politics. In Broadcasting Standards Council (Ed.), *Perspectives on women in television.* Research Working Paper No. 9. London: Broadcasting Standards Council.

Steele, C. A., & Barnhurst, K. G. (1996). The journalism of opinion: Network news coverage of U.S. presidential campaigns 1968-1988. *Criticial Studies in Mass Communication, 13*(2), 187-209.

Steiner, L. (1998). Newsroom accounts of power at work. In C. Carter, G. Branston, & S. Allan (Eds.), *News, gender and power* (pp. 145-159). London and New York: Routledge.

Stephenson, M. A. (1998). *The glass trapdoor: Women, politics and the media during the 1997 general election.* London: Fawcett Society.

Strate, J. M., Ford, C. C., III, & Jankowski, T. B. (1994). Women's use of print media to follow politics. *Social Science Quarterly, 75*(1), 166-186.

Swanson, D., & Mancini, P. (Eds.). (1996). *Politics, media and democracy*. Westport, CT: Praeger.

Tavris, C. (1992). *The mismeasure of woman*. New York: Simon and Schuster.

Thomas, S. (1991). The impact of women on state legislative policies. *Journal of Politics, 53,* 958-976.

Thomas, S. (1994). *How women legislate*. New York: Oxford University Press.

Tinker, I. (Ed.). (1983). *Women in Washington: Advocates for public policy*. Beverly Hills, CA: Sage.

Tuchman, G. (1972). Objectivity as strategic ritual: An examination of newsmens notions of objectivity. *American Journal of Sociology, 77,* 660-679.

Tuchman, G., Daniels, A. K., & Benet, J. (Eds.). (1978). *Hearth and home: Images of women in mass media*. New York: Oxford University Press.

Tunstall, J. (1977). *The media are American*. London: Constable.

Vallance, E. (1979). *Women in the house: A study of women members of Parliament*. London: The Athlone Press.

Vallely, B. (1996). *What women want*. London: Virago and Women's Communication Centre.

van Zoonen, L. (1991). A tyranny of intimacy? Women, femininity and television news. In P. Dahlgren & C. Sparks (Eds.), *Communication and citizenship: Journalism and the public sphere in the new media age* (pp. 217-235). London: Routledge.

van Zoonen, L. (1994). *Feminist media studies*. London: Sage.

van Zoonen, L. (1998a). A day at the zoo: Political communication, pigs and popular culture. *Media, Culture and Society, 20*(2), 183-200.

van Zoonen, L. (1998b). A professional, unreliable, heroic marionette: Structure, agency and subjectivity in contemporary journalism. *European Journal of Cultural Studies, 1*(1), 123-143.

van Zoonen, L. (1998c). One of the girls? The changing gender of journalism. In C. Carter, G. Branston, & S. Allan (Eds.). *News, gender and power* (pp. 33-46). London and New York: Routledge.

Wahl-Jorgensen, K. (2000). Constructing masculinities in U.S. presidential campaigns. In A. Sreberny & L. van Zoonen (Eds.), *Gender, politics and communication* (pp. 53-78). Cresskill, NJ: Hampton Press.

Walkosz, B. J., & Kenski, H. C. (1995, April). *The year of the woman: How the national media portrayed women in the 1992 election year*. Paper presented at the meeting Console-ing Passions: Television, Video and Feminism, Tuscon, AZ.

Ware, V. (1992). *Beyond the pale: White women, racism and history*. London and New York: Verso.

Wasko, J. (1994). *Hollywood in the information age: Beyond the silver screen*. Cambridge, UK: Polity Press.

Watts, D. (1997). *Political communication today*. Manchester and New York: Manchester University Press.

Watts, G. (1999, July 2). Cases in need of evaluation. *Times Higher Education Supplement*, pp. 30-31.

Weaver, D.H. (1997). Women as journalists. In P. Norris (Ed.), *Women, media and politics* (pp. 21-40). New York: Oxford University Press.

Weaver, D. H., & Wilhoit, G. C. (1996). *The American journalist in the 1990s: U.S. news people at the end of an era.* Mahwah, NJ: Lawrence Erlbaum.

Welch, S., & Studlar, D. T. (1986). British public opinion toward women in politics: A comparative perspective. *Western Political Quarterly, 39,* 138-152.

West, D. (1993). *Air wars: Television advertising in election campaigns, 1952-1992.* Washington, DC: Congressional Quarterly.

West, D. M. (1991). Television and presidential popularity in America. *British Journal of Political Science, 21,* 199-214.

Wheeler, M. (1997). *Politics and the mass media.* Oxford: Blackwell.

White, A.B. (1994). Inequality in symbolism: Cultural barriers to female candidates in political advertising. *New Political Science, 28/29,* 53-70.

White, M. (2000, January 2). The trouble with Mo. *Guardian,* p. 2.

Whittaker, R. (1999). *Reading between the lines.* Belfast: Northern Ireland Women's European Platform.

Whitworth, S. (1994). Feminist theories: From women to gender and world politics. In P. R. Beckman & F. D'Amico (Eds.), *Women, gender and world politics: Perspectives, policies and prospects* (pp. 75-88). Westport, CT: Bergin and Garvey.

Wilcox, C. (1994). Why was 1992 the "Year of the Woman"? Explaining women's gains in 1992. In E. Cook, S. Thomas, & C. Wilcox (Eds.), *The year of the woman* (pp. 1-24). Boulder: Westview Press.

Williams, P.M. (1980). Interviewing politicians: The life of Hugh Gaitskell. *Political Quarterly, 51*(3), 303-316.

Winter, J. (1993). Gender and the political interview in an Australian context. *Journal of Pragmatics, 20,* 117-130.

Wirls D. (1986). Reinterpreting the gender gap. *Public Opinion Quarterly, 50,* 316-330.

Witt, L., Paget, K., & Matthews, G. (1994). *Running as a woman: Gender and power in American politics.* New York: Free Press.

Women in Journalism. (1996). *Women in the news: Does sex change the way a newspaper thinks?* London: Women in Journalism.

Women in Journalism. (1999). *Real women: The hidden sex.* London: Women in Journalism.

Woods, H. (1992, September 14). Are women becoming too nasty? *Los Angeles Times,* p. B5.

Wright, T. (1998). Inside the whale: The media from parliament. In J. Seaton (Ed.), *Politics and the media* (pp. 19-27). Oxford: Blackwell/The Political Quarterly.

Wykes, M. (1998). A family affair: The British press, sex and the Wests. In C. Carter, G. Branston, & S. Allan (Eds.), *News, gender and power* (pp. 233-247). London: Routledge.

Yishai, Y. (1997). The great losers: Women in the 1996 election. *Israeli Affairs, 4*(1), 187-208.

Young, I. M. (1989). Polity and group difference: A critique of the idea of universal citizenship. *Ethics,* 249-261.

Zhao, X., & Chaffee, S.H. (1995). Campaign advertisements versus television news as sources of political issue information. *Public Opinion Quarterly, 59,* 41-65.

Author Index

213

Subject Index